Duncan Forbes

A Grammar of the Persian Language

Salzwasser

Duncan Forbes

A Grammar of the Persian Language

1. Auflage | ISBN: 978-3-84604-976-1

Erscheinungsort: Frankfurt, Deutschland

Erscheinungsjahr: 2020

Salzwasser Verlag GmbH

A

GRAMMAR

OF THE

PERSIAN LANGUAGE.

TO WHICH IS ADDED,

A SELECTION OF EASY EXTRACTS FOR READING;

TOGETHER WITH

A VOCABULARY, AND TRANSLATIONS.

BY DUNCAN FORBES, A.M.,

MEMBER OF THE ROYAL ASIATIC SOCIETY OF GREAT BRITAIN AND IRELAND,
AND PROFESSOR OF ORIENTAL LANGUAGES AND LITERATURE
IN KING'S COLLEGE, LONDON.

لَیسَ لِلْاِنْسانِ اِلّا ما سعَي	من طریقِ سعَي مِي آرم بجا
ازغمِ و اندوه مانم برطرف	دامنِ مقصود اگر آرم بكف
من دران معذُور باشم و السّلام	ورنشُد از جهْدِ من كاري تمام

FOURTH EDITION.

LONDON.

WM. H. ALLEN & CO., 13, WATERLOO PLACE. S.W.

PUBLISHERS TO THE INDIA OFFICE.

1869.

PREFACE.

THE object of the following Work is to facilitate the acquisition of a language universally allowed to be the richest and most elegant of those spoken in Modern Asia. To the general scholar, the Persian recommends itself, from its vast stores of graceful and entertaining literature. To the traveller in the East, a knowledge of it is as essential as that of the French used to be in Europe. Lastly, to our British Youth, who annually resort to India, destined to become, in due time, the guardians of our Eastern Empire, an acquaintance with Persian is of the utmost importance. In the first place, it is the Court language of the Musalmān Princes, and that of the higher classes generally; and, in the second place, a knowledge of it is requisite for the proper attainment of the Hindūstānī, or popular language, which is spoken and understood, more or less, in every part of the country.

I have been long convinced, from experience, that a work like the present is a desideratum. A Grammar of any language, adapted for a beginner, ought to be brief and perspicuous, containing only the general and more useful principles of such language. It ought to be accompanied with Easy Extracts for practice, as well as a copious Vocabulary. At the same time, the shortest Grammar is too long for a beginner: therefore, those parts absolutely necessary for the first reading ought to be rendered more prominent, by the use of a larger type. Lastly, the work ought to be confined entirely to its legitimate purpose—the instructing of beginners; not deviating into ingenious metaphysical and etymological discussions, however interesting in their proper place: nor should it be over-crowded with superfluous paradigms of Verbs, &c., so as to swell up the volume to an undue extent.

If this criterion of a *good* elementary Grammar is sound, which I think few men of sense will dispute, then there is ample room for the present little work, however imperfect in execution, as the first attempt of the kind that has yet been made in this country, with regard to the Persian language.

Let it not be supposed, that because this book is small in bulk it must necessarily be superficial and imperfect; for, as *Sa'dī* says, نه هرچه بقامت مهتر بقیمت بهتر, which means, that "good gear may be contained in small parcels." In fact, I am convinced that the student will here find all the information of any consequence contained in larger volumes, and a great deal which they do not contain. I have endeavoured throughout the work to enlarge upon those parts of the subject which I have observed to be most needed by beginners. Such parts of the Grammar of the Persian language as agree with our own, or with that of European languages in general, I have passed over with the utmost brevity.

The only work on the subject to which I am under any obligation is the Persian Grammar of Dr. Lumsden, Calcutta, 1810, in two folio volumes. From this valuable work I have extracted many a pearl, though, it must be confessed, I was obliged often to dive through an enormous mass of water to procure it. Still, with all its metaphysics and verbosity, Dr. Lumsden's Grammar ought to be perused by every one who wishes to acquire a thorough knowledge of the Persian language. It is indeed a pity that the Work should not be reprinted in this country: it would form two octavo volumes; and, when printed in our elegant types, and on good paper, it would not look nearly so formidable and repulsive as it does in its present state.

The Selections for Reading, appended to the Grammar, consist of seventy-four tales and anecdotes, commencing with the shortest and easiest. In the first sixteen pages I have given the short vowels and the symbol *jazm* marked in full; and in the remainder the marks have been omitted, except in the case of an *iẓāfat*, or when there might arise an ambiguity from the omission. I have, throughout the Selections, employed a species of punctuation, which the reader will find very serviceable. The *dash* (—), denotes a half-stop, like our comma, or semicolon; the *star* (*), a full-stop; and the note of interrogation is the same as our own turned backwards. Of the propriety of employing some sort of punctuation in Oriental compositions there can be no doubt: the beginners will find difficulties enough to encounter, even when they know where the sentence begins and ends, which i really no unreasonable indulgence.

In the present Edition I have carried into effect the intention I expressed in the Preface of the Second Edition. 1st. A section on Arabic words, such as occur most frequently in Persian, confining myself chiefly to their mechanism, and the changes which they undergo; 2dly, A treatise on Prosody, which is greatly wanted, there being only two works in our language that treat of the subject, viz. Gladwin's and Professor Lee's, both of which are exceedingly meagre, inaccurate, and unintelligible. Without a knowledge of the various metres, much of the beauty of the Persian Poets is lost; and, besides, the metre frequently assists us in detecting errors of the copyists. At the same time, the Selections have been enriched by the addition of some specimens from the best Poets.

In conclusion, let me address myself to the student as to

what I consider the best plan for perusing this work. In the
first place, make yourself perfectly acquainted with the letters,
and their various sounds; after which, read and *remember* the
declension of the Substantives *mard* and *kitāb*, pages 32
and 33; and the Verb *rasīdan*, page 39. This done, read
over carefully the Fable, page 21, an analysis of which is
given in page 76; and, afterwards, read the Story, page 22,
ascertaining the meaning of every word from the Vocabulary.

The next step is, to study carefully all the paragraphs in
the Grammar printed in large type; after which, read and
translate, by the aid of the Vocabulary, the first ten or twelve
pages of the Selections. Being now able to read fluently,
peruse the Grammar from the very beginning till the end of
the Syntax. I do not mean that you should commit it *all* to
memory; but read it with such attention, that you may
afterwards be able to know where to look for any rule or
explanation of which you may feel the want. Preserve by
you an accurate translation of every story as you proceed in
the Selections; and, at the end of six weeks or two months,
endeavour to restore your translation back into Persian.
Proceed thus till you have finished the prose part of the book,
and you will then find yourself possessed of a very fair *elementary* knowledge of the language.

Finally, read attentively the Sections VI. and VII.; after
which, proceed to the Extracts from the Poets, carefully
examining the various metres, and scanning each line as you
go on. After this initiation, procure the latest edition of
Johnson's Persian Dictionary; and then I leave you to read
any Persian Author you may take a fancy to.

D. FORBES.

58, *Burton Crescent*, 1861.

TABLE OF CONTENTS.

PERSIAN GRAMMAR.

SECTION I.

ON THE LETTERS AND SYMBOLS USED IN WRITING.

1. THE Persians* have for many centuries adopted the Alphabet of the Arabs, consisting of *Twenty-eight* letters: to which they have added *four* other characters, to express sounds peculiar to their own language. These letters, then, *Thirty-two* in number, are all considered to be consonants, and are written and read from right to left; and, consequently, their books and manuscripts begin at what we should call the *end*. Several of the letters assume different forms, according to their position in the formation of a word or a combined group; as may be seen in the following Table, Column V. Thus, in a combination of three or more letters, the first of the group, on the right-hand side, will have the form marked *Initial;* the letter or letters between the first and last will have the form marked *Medial;* and the last, on the left, will have the *Final* form. Observe, also, that in this Table, Column I. contains the names of the letters in the Persian character; II. the same in Roman character; III. the detached form of the letters, which should be learned first; and IV. the corresponding English letters.

---

* The Alphabet here described is used, generally speaking, by all those nations who have adopted the religion of Muhammad; viz. along the North and East of Africa, in Turkey, Arabia, and Persia, and by the Musalmān portion of the people of India and Malacca.

B

THE PERSI-ARABIC ALPHABET.

I.	II. NAME.	III. DETACHED FORM.	IV. POWER.	V. COMBINED FORM.			VI. EXEMPLIFICATIONS.			
				Final.	Med.	Initial.	Final.	Final.	Medial.	Initial.
الف	*alif*	ا	*a, &c.*	ا	ا	ا	وا	تا	بار	اب
بي	*be*	ب	*b*	ـمب	بـ بـ بـ	بـ	باب	شَب	صَبر	بَر
پي	*pe*	پ	*p*	ـمپ	پـ پـ پـ	پـ	آپ	چپ	سپَر	پُر
تي	*te*	ت	*t*	ـمت	تـ تـ تـ	تـ	پوت	دَست	سَتَر	تَپ
ثي	*se*	ث	*s̤*	ـمث	ثـ ثـ ثـ	ثـ	روث	خُبث	بَثَر	ثور
جيم	*jim*	ج	*j*	ـج	جـ جـ	جـ	كاج	گَنج	شَجَر	جَبر
چي	*che*	چ	*ch*	ـچ	چـ چـ	چـ	كوچ	هيچ	بَچّه	چَپ
حي	*he*	ح	*ḥ*	ـح	حـ حـ	حـ	روح	صُبح	بَحر	حَر
خي	*khe*	خ	*kh*	ـخ	خـ خـ	خـ	شاخ	يَخ	تُخم	خَر
دال	*dāl*	د	*d*	ـد	ـد د	د	صاد	صَد	فدا	دُر
ذال	*ẕāl*	ذ	*z*	ـذ	ـذ ذ	ذ	باذ	كاغَذ	نَذر	ذَم
ري	*re*	ر	*r*	ـر ـر	ر ر	ر	مار	مَر	مَرد	رَم
زي	*ze*	ز	*z*	ـز	ـز ز	ز	باز	گَز	بَزم	زَر
ژي	*zhe*	ژ	*zh*	ـژ	ـژ ژ	ژ	كاژ	پاپَژ	غَرب	ژَرف
سين	*sīn*	س	*s*	ـس	ـسـ سـ	سـ	باس	بَس	فَسق	سَر
شين	*shīn*	ش	*sh*	ـش	ـشـ شـ	شـ	پاش	پَش	نَشُد	شُد
صاد	*ṣād*	ص	*ṣ*	ـص	ـصـ صـ	صـ	ناص	نَص	قَصد	صَد

I.	II.	III.	IV.	V.			VI.			
NAME.		DETACHED FORM.	POWER.	COMBINED FORM.			EXEMPLIFICATIONS.			
				Final.	Med.	Initial.	Final.		Medial.	Initial.
ضاد	*ẓād*	ض	*ẓ*	ض	ـض	ض	بُعُوُض	بَعَض	خِضَر	ضِدّ
طوٌي	*ṭo,e*	ط	*ṭ*	ط	ـط	ط	خُطُوط	خَطّ	بَطَن	طَي
ظوٌي	*ẓo,e*	ظ	*ẓ*	ظ	ـظ	ظ	حِفاظ	حِفَظ	نَظَر	ظَفَر
عَين	*'aïn*	ع	*'a,* &c.	ع	ـﻊ	ﻋ	صِناع	صَنَع	بُعْد	عَسَل
غَين	*ghaïn*	غ	*gh*	غ	ـغ	غ	باغ	تِيغ	بَغِي	غُسَل
في	*fe*	ف	*f*	ـف	ـﻓ	ﻓ	كاف	كَف	سَفَر	في
قاف	*ḳāf*	ق	*ḳ*	ق	ـﻗ	ﻗ	باق	بَق	سَقَر	قَدّ
كاف	*kāf*	ك	*k*	ـك	ـﻜ	ﻛ	خاك	يَك	بِكُن	كُن
گاف	*gāf*	گ	*g*	ـگ	ـگ	گ	راگ	رَنگ	جِگَر	گَز
لام	*lām*	ل	*l*	ـل	ـلـ	ل	سال	گُل	عِلْم	لَب
مِيم	*mīm*	م	*m*	ـم	ـمـ	ﻣ	تَمام	سِتَم	چَمَن	مَن
نُون	*nūn*	ن	*n*	ـن	ـنـ	نـ	نُون	صَحْن	چَنْد	نَم
واو	*wāw*	و	*w,* &c.	و	و	و	رو	بُو	پُور	وَجَد
هي	*he*	ه	*h*	ـه	ـهـ	ه	ماه	نَه	بَها	هُنَر
يي	*ye*	ي	*y,* &c.	ي	ـيـ	يـ	جائي	بِي	حِيد	يَد

2. Perhaps the best mode of learning the Alphabet, is, First, to write out several times the detached or full forms of the letters in Column III. Secondly, to observe what changes (if any) these

undergo, when combined in the formation of words, as exhibited in Column V. Thirdly, to endeavour to transfer, into their corresponding English letters, the words given as exemplifications in Column VI. This last process to be performed twice; viz. let the learner, in the first place, transfer the words, letter for letter, without minding the short vowel marks and other symbols. This done, let him carefully read the Grammar up to § 21, and then, for the *second time*, transfer all the words in Column VI., with all the appropriate vowels, &c.

a. The learner will observe, that the letters ا, د, ذ, ر, ز, ژ, and و do not alter in shape, whether Initial, Medial, or Final. Another peculiarity which they have, is, that they never unite with the letter following, to the left. The letters ط and ظ, in like manner, do not alter, but they always unite with the letter following on the left hand.

PRONUNCIATION OF THE LETTERS.

3. In the foregoing Table, most of the letters are sufficiently represented by the corresponding English characters given in the parallel Column, No. IV. Suffice it for us here, then, to offer a few brief observations on such letters as differ from our own in sound, or such as require two of our characters to represent them :

ت *t.* The sound of this letter is softer and more dental than that of the English *t :* it corresponds with the *t* of the Gaelic dialects, or that of the Italians in the word *sotto.* It is identical with the Sanskrit त, not the ट.

ث *s̱,* is sounded by the Arabs like our *th* hard, in the words *thick, thin ;* but by the Persians and Indians it is pronounced like our *s* in the words *sick, sin.*

 چ *ch*, has the sound of our *ch* in *church*.

ح *h*, is a very strong aspirate, somewhat like our *h* in the word *haul*, but uttered by compressing the lower muscles of the throat.

خ *kh*, has a sound like the *ch* in the word *loch*, as pronounced by the Scotch and Irish; or the final *ch*, in the German words *schach* and *buch*.

د *d*, is more dental than the English *d*: the former is the Sanskrit त, the latter is nearer the ड. The *d* of the Celtic dialects, and of the Italian and Spanish, corresponds with the Persian د

ذ *z*, is sounded by the Arabs like our *th* soft, in the words *thy* and *thine;* but in Persia and India it is generally pronounced like our *z* in *zeal*.

ر *r*, is to be sounded more distinctly than we do in English, such as the French have it in the word *pardon*.

ژ *zh*, is pronounced like the *j* of the French, in the word *jour*, or our *z* in the word *azure*, or our *s* in *pleasure*.

ش *sh*, is uniformly sounded as in our words *shun* and *shine*. In a few instances it may happen that we shall have occasion to employ *sh* and *zh* to represent, in the Roman character, the letters س and ه, or ز and ه respectively, when following each other without an intervening vowel, as in the words أَسْهَل *as,hal*, "more or most easy," and أَزهار *az,hār*, ' plants." In such rare instances, the mark ـ inserted (as in the preceding words) before the *h* will serve as a sufficient distinction.

ص *s*, has a stronger or more hissing sound than our *s*. In Persia and India, however, there is little or no distinction between it and س.

ض *z*, is pronounced by the Arabs like a hard *d* or *dt*, but in Persia and India it is sounded like *z*.

ط *t*, and ظ *z*. These letters are sounded, in Persian, like ت and ز, or very nearly so. The anomalous letter ع will be noticed hereafter.

غ *gh*, has a sound somewhat like *g* in the German word *sagen*. About the banks of the Tweed, the natives sound what they fancy to be the letter *r*, very like the Eastern غ.

ق *k*, bears some resemblance to our *c* hard, in the words *calm, cup*; with this difference, that the ق is uttered from the lower muscles of the throat.

ک *k*. This letter is sounded like our *k* in *king*, or *kalendar*. It was of old written ك, in which case the mark ء served to distinguish it from ل. In course of time, however, it came to be written ک; consequently the mark ء was no longer required, though our type-founders still superfluously retain it. As an Initial and Medial it assumes, in Arabic manuscripts, the forms ﻛ and ﻜ respectively; which are also met with in our best founts.

گ *g*, is sounded like our hard *g* (only), as in *go, give*; but never like our *j*, as in the words *gem, gentle*. As it is a modification of ک, it of course may assume all the forms of that letter, with the additional line at the top.

ل *l*. This letter is sounded like our own *l* in *law*. When the letter *alif* is combined with it, the two assume the form لا or لا *lā*.

ن *n*, at the beginning of a word or syllable, is sounded like our *n*; but at the end of a word or syllable, if preceded by a long vowel, it has a soft nasal sound, like that of the French in such words as *mon, garçon*, where the effect of the *n* is to render the preceding vowel nasal, while its own sound is scarcely perceptible. When followed by the labials ب *b*, پ *p*, or ف *f*, it assumes the sound of *m*, as in the word گنبد pronounced *gumbad*, not *gunbad*.

ه *h*, is an aspirate, like our *h* in *hand, heart*; but at the end of a word, if preceded by the short vowel *a* (Fatḥa, § 4), the ه has no sensible sound, as in دانه *dāna*, "a grain"; in which case it is called هاي مختفي *hā,e - mukhtafī*, i. e. the *obscure* or *imperceptible h*. In a few words, where the *fatḥa* is a substitute for the long vowel *alif*, the final *h* is fully sounded, as in شه *shah* (for شاه *shāh*), "a king," or مه *mah* (for ماه *māh*), "a month." It is also sounded in the word ده *dah*, "ten," and all its compounds (v. § 54). It is imperceptible in the words که and چه, with their compounds, whether they be pronouns or conjunctions. Should we have occasion to write in English characters a Persian word ending in the imperceptible *h*, the *h* will be omitted in writing, as in نامه *nāma* (not *nāmah*), "a letter."

a. At the end of words derived from Arabic roots, this letter is frequently marked with two dots, thus, ة; and sounded like the letter

ت *t.* In such words, when introduced into their language, the Persians generally convert the ة into ت; but sometimes they leave the ة un-altered; and frequently they omit the two dots, in which case the letter becomes imperceptible in sound.

b. Much more might have been said in describing the sounds of several of the letters; but we question much whether the learner would be greatly benefited by a more detailed description. It is difficult, if not impossible, to give, in writing, a correct idea of the mere sound ot a letter, unless we have one that corresponds with it in our own language. When this is not the case, we can only have recourse to such languages as happen to possess the requisite sound. It is possible, however, that the student *may be* as ignorant of these languages as of Persian. It clearly follows, then, as a general rule, that the correct sounds, of such letters as differ from our own, must be learned *by the ear*—we may say, by a *good ear*; and, consequently, a long description is needless. This remark applies in particular to the letters ت ح خ د ص ض غ ق, and the nasal *nūn.*

OF THE PRIMITIVE VOWELS.

4. The Primitive Vowels in Arabic and Persian are three, which are expressed by the following simple notation. The first is called فتحة *fatḥa,* and is written thus, ◌َ over the consonant to which it belongs. Its sound is that of a short *a,* such as we have in the word *calamus,* which is of Eastern origin, and of which the first two syllables or root, *calam* or *ḳalam,* are thus written, قَلَم. In such Oriental words as we may have occasion to write in Roman characters, the *a,* unmarked, is understood always to represent the vowel *fatḥa,* and to have no other sound than that of *a* in *calamus* or *calendar.*

5. The second is called كِسْرَة *kasra,* and is thus ◌ِ written

under the consonant to which it belongs. Its sound is generally that of our short *i* in the words *sip* and *fin*, which in Persian would be written سپ and فن. In the course of this work, the letter *i* unaccented is understood to have the sound of *i* in *sip* and *fin*, in all Oriental words written in the Roman character.

6. The third is called ضمّه *zamma*, which is thus ‑ʼ written over its consonant. Its sound is like that of our short *u* in the words *pull* and *push*, which in Persian would be written پل and پش: we have its sound also in the words *foot* and *hood*, which would be written فت and هد. In all Oriental words in the Roman character, it is understood to have the sound of *u* in *pull* and *push;* but never that of our *u* in such words as *use* and *perfume*, or such as *sun* and *fun.* In Persian, the three short vowels are also called زبر *zabar*, زیر *zer*, and پیش *pesh*, respectively.

OF THE CONSONANTS ا, و, ع, AND ی.

7. At the beginning of a word or syllable, the letter ا, like any other consonant, depends for its sound on the accompanying vowel: of itself, it is a very weak aspirate, like our *h* in the words *herb, honour,* and *hour.* It is still more closely identified with the *spiritus lenis* of the Greek, in such words as ἀπὸ, ἐπὶ, ὀρθός. In fact, when we utter the syllables *ab, ib,* and *ub,* there is a slight movement of the muscles of the throat at the commencement of utterance; and the spot where that movement takes place, the Oriental grammarians con-

sider to be the مَخْرَج *makhraj*, i. e. "the place of utterance" of the consonant ا, as in اَ *ă*, اِ *ĭ*, and اُ *ŭ*, just the same as the lips form the *makhraj* of *b*, in the syllables بَ *bă*, بِ *bĭ*, and بُ *bŭ*. Finally, the ا may be considered as the *spiritus lenis*, or weak aspirate of the letter ه.

8. The consonant ع has the same relation to the strong aspirate ح that ا has to ه; that is, the ع, like the ا, is a *spiritus lenis*, or weak aspirate; but the *makhraj*, or place of utterance of ع, is in the lower muscles of the throat. With this distinction, its sound, as in the case of the letter ا, depends on the accompanying vowel, as عَب *'ab*, عِب *'ib*, عُب *'ub*, which, in the mouth of an Arab, are very different sounds from اَب *ab*, اِب *ib*, and اُب *ub*. At the same time, it is impossible to explain in writing the true sound of this letter, as it is not to be found in any European language, so far as we know. The student who has not the advantage of a competent teacher may treat the Initial ع as he does the ا until he has the opportunity of learning its true sound by the ear.

9. Of the consonants و and ي very little description is necessary. The letter و has generally the sound of our *w* in *we, went*. The modern Persians, particularly those bordering on Turkey, pronounce the و like our *v*, as in the words شَوَم *shavam*, or, more nearly, *shĕvĕm*, and شَوِي *shĕvī*, which in Eastern Persia and India are pronounced *shawam* and *shawī*. The sound of the consonant ي is exactly like our own *y* in *you, yet*, or the German *j* in *jener*.

a. In our own language we have a similar rule, viz. the letters *w* (و) and *y* (ى) are what *we* call consonants at the beginning of a word or syllable; in all other situations they are vowels, or letters of prolongation.

OF THE SYMBOL *JAZM* ـْ.

10. When a consonant is accompanied by one of the three primitive vowels, it is said to be مُتَحَرِّك *mutaḥarrik,* that is, *moving,* or *moveable,* by that vowel. Oriental grammarians consider a syllable as a *step* or *move* in the formation of a word or sentence. In Persian and Arabic, the first letter of a word is always accompanied, or moveable, by a vowel. With regard to the following letters there is no certain rule. When, in the middle or end of a word, a consonant is not accompanied by a vowel, it is said to be ساكِن *sākin,* "*resting*" or "*inert.*" Thus, in the word مَرْدُم *mardum,* the *mīm* is *moveable* by *fatḥa;* the *re* is *inert,* * having no vowel; the *dāl* is moveable by *ẓamma;* and, finally, the *mīm* is *inert.* The symbol ـْ, called جَزْم *jazm,* which signifies *amputation,* is placed over a consonant to shew when it is *inert,*

---

* I should have apologized for making use of this novel term here, were it not for its being more appropriate than that which is usually employed. In most Persian and Arabic Grammars, a letter not followed by a vowel is called *quiescent:* now, I object to the latter term, as it is apt to mislead the beginner, it being already applied in English Grammar in the sense of *not sounded.* For instance, the letter *g* is *quiescent* in the word *phlegm;* we cannot, however, say that *m* is *quiescent* in the same word, though we may say that it is *inert.* The student will be pleased to bear in mind, then, that a letter is said to be *inert* when it is not followed by a vowel.

as in the word *mardum*, where the ر (*r*) and final م (*m*) are *inert*. As a general rule, the last letter of a Persian word is always *inert*; hence it is not necessary to mark the last letter of a word with the *jazm*.

OF THE SYMBOL *TASHDĪD* ـّ.

11. When a letter is doubled, the mark ـّ, called *tashdīd*, which signifies *corroboration*, is placed over it. Thus, in the word شِدّت *shid-dat*, where the first syllable ends with د (*d*) and the next begins with د (*d*), without a vowel intervening, instead of the usual mode شِدْدَت, the two *dāls* are united into one, and the mark ـّ indicates this union.

OF LONG VOWELS, OR LETTERS OF PROLONGATION.

12. The letters ا، و، and ي, when *inert*, serve to prolong the preceding vowel, as follows. When ا *inert* is preceded by a letter moveable by *fatha*, the *fatha* and *alif* together form a long sound like our *a* in *war*, or *au* in *haul*, which in Persian might be written وَار and حَال. Now it so happens, that the ا *inert* is always preceded by *fatha*: hence, as a general and practical rule, *alif* not beginning a word or syllable forms a long sound like our *a* in *war*, or *au* in *haul*.

a. On a similar principle, we may consider the unaspirated *h* as a letter of prolongation in the German words *wahr* and *zahl*. We may also consider the second *a* as *inert* in the words *aachen* and *waal*.

13. When the letter و *inert* is preceded by a consonant moveable by the vowel *zamma*, the *zamma* and و together form a sound like our *oo* in *food*; which in Persian might be

written فُوْد, or, which is the same thing, like our *u* in *rule*, which the Persians would write رُوْل. The same combination forms also another sound, like our *o* in *mole*, which they would write مُوْل, or, perhaps still nearer, like our *oa* in *boat*, which they would write بُوْت.—In the Arabic language, the latter sound of و, viz. that of *o* in *mole*, is unknown; hence grammarians call it *Majhūl*, or *'Ajamī*, i.e. the Unknown or Persian و; whereas the former sound, that of the *u* in *rule*, is called *Ma'rūf*, the Known or Familiar و. If the letter و be preceded by a consonant moveable by *fatḥa*, the *fatḥa* and و united will form a diphthong, nearly like our *ou* in *sound*, or *ow* in *town*, but more exactly like the *au* in the German word *kaum*, which in Persian or Arabic might be written قَوْم. If the و be preceded by the vowel *kasra*, no union takes place, and the و preserves its natural sound as a consonant, as in the word سِوَا *siwā*.

a. In English, the *w* is a letter of prolongation in many words, as *draw*, *crow*, &c.; it also contributes to the formation of a diphthong, as in *town*, *gown*, &c.

b. When the letter و is preceded by خ moveable by *fatḥa* and followed by ا, the sound of و is scarcely perceptible; as in the word خَواهَم, pronounced *khāham*, not *khawāham*. This rule, however, applies only to words purely Persian; never to those borrowed from the Arabic language, which are very numerous. In writing such words in the Roman character, the و will be represented by *w*, which the student will bear in mind is not to be sounded.

c. In like manner, when و preceded by خ moveable by *fatḥa*, and sometimes by *ẓamma* or *kasra*, is followed by any of the letters پ, d, ر ز, س ش, ن, ة, or ي, the و occasionally loses its usual sound, as in the word خَوْد, pron. *khăd*, not *khaud* or *khawad*; so in خُود, pron. *khŭd*, not *khūd*; also in خویش, pron. *khĕsh*, not *khiwesh*. This rule also applies only to words purely Persian; and, as it is by no means general, the student must ascertain the pronunciation in such cases from a Dictionary of standard authority; such as Professor Johnson's last edition of Richardson's Persian Dictionary. In the few words of this description which we may have occasion to write in the Roman character, the *w* will be altogether omitted, and the vowel marked with a dot underneath, as in خود *khud*.

14. When the letter ی *inert* is preceded by a consonant moveable by *kasra*, the *kasra* and the ی unite, and form a long vowel, like our *ee* in *feel*, which in Persian might be written فِیل; or, which is the same thing, like our *i* in *machine*, which in Persian would be written مشین. The same combination may also form a sound like our *ea* in *bear*, which would be similarly written بِیر, or like the French *ê* in the words *tête* and *fête*; or the German *e* followed by *h* in the words *sehr*, *gelehrt*. In the Arabic language, the latter sound of ی is unknown: hence, when the ی forms the sound of *ea* in *bear*, &c., it is called *Yā,e Majhūl*, or *Yā,e 'Ajamī*, that is, the *Yā* Unknown (in the Arabic language), or Persian ی; whilst the former sound—that of *ee* in *feel*, or *i* in *machine*—is called *Yā,e Ma'rūf*, the Known or Familiar ی. When the letter ی *inert*, is preceded by a consonant moveable by *fatha*, the *fatha* and the ی unite, and form a diphthong, like *ai* in the German word *Kaiser*, which in Arabic and Persian is written قیصر. This sound is really that of our own *i* in *wise*, *size*, which we are pleased to call a vowel, but which is really a diphthong. When the ی is preceded by *zamma*, no union takes place, and the ی retains its usual sound as a consonant, as in the word مُیَسَّر *muyassar*.

a. In English, the letter *y* is a letter of prolongation in the words *say* and *key*; it also contributes to the formation of a diphthong in the word *buy*, which in Persian might be written بِی.

b. Sometimes the letter ی at the end of a word, when preceded by the long vowels *ā*, *ō*, or *ū*, has scarcely any perceptible sound; thus, پای *pā*, "foot," رُوی *rū*, "face:" hence the words are frequently written without the ی, as پا and رُو.

15. It appears, then, from what we have stated, that the Persian language has ten vocal sounds ; viz. 1st, Three short or *primitive* vowels, as in the syllables بَد *băd*, بِد *bĭd*, بُد *bŭd* (pronounced *boŏd*). 2dly, Three corresponding long vowels, formed by introducing the homogeneous letters of prolongation immediately after the preceding short vowels, as in بَاد *bād*, بِید *bīd*, بُود *būd*. 3dly, Two diphthongs, as in بَیْد *baid*, the *ai* pronounced like our *i* in *abide* ; and بَوْد *baud*, the *au* pronounced like our *ou* in *loud*. 4thly, The two long vowels, peculiarly Persian, or *Majhūl*, as بِیل *bĕl*, pronounced like the English word *bail*, and رُوز *rôz*, pronounced very nearly like the English word *rose*.

a. It may be proper to notice here, that the people of Persia, of the present day, are said to have discarded the *majhūl* sounds *e* and *o* altogether from their language; so that, instead of *bel* and *roz*, they now sound the words *bĭl* and *rūz*. Vide § 56½.

b. It must be observed, that there are very few Persian works, manuscript or printed, in which all the vowels are marked as we have just described. The primitive short vowels are almost always omitted, as well as the marks ‒ *jazm* and ‒ *tashdĭd*; nor is the omission of any consequence to the natives, nor to those who know the language. To the young beginner, however, in this country, it is essential to commence with books having the vowels carefully marked ; otherwise, he will contract a vicious mode of pronunciation, which he will find it difficult afterwards to unlearn. At the same time, it is no easy matter in printing to insert all the vowel-points, &c. in a proper and accurate manner. In the present work, a medium will be observed, which, without over-crowding the text with marks, will suffice to enable the learner to read without any error, provided he will attend to the following

RULES FOR READING.

16. In the first place,—the last letter of every word (as already mentioned, § 10) is *inert:* hence the mark ـْ *jazm* is in that case dispensed with: when there is an exception to this rule, as in the formation of the genitive case (§ 28), the last letter will be marked with the requisite vowel. Secondly, the short vowel *fatha* ـَ is of more frequent occurrence than the other two: hence it is omitted in the printing; and the learner is to supply it for every consonant in a word, except the last, provided he see no other vowel, nor the mark *jazm* accompanying any of the consonants aforesaid. Thirdly, the letters ا, و, and ي, not initial, are generally *inert;* hence, they are not in such cases marked with the *jazm:* whenever و and ي, not initial, are moveable consonants, they are marked with the requisite vowels. Fourthly, To distinguish between the *majhūl* and *ma'rūf* sounds of و and ي, the following rule is observed. When و and ي follow a consonant, un-marked by a short vowel or *jazm*, they are understood to have the *majhūl* sound, or that of *o* and *e* respectively, as in مور *mor*, "an ant," and شير *sher*, "a lion." If, on the other hand, the consonant preceding و have the vowel ـُ, and that preceding ي the vowel ـِ, they have the *ma'rūf* sound, or that of *u* in *rule* and *i* in *machine*

respectively, as in the words سُود *sūd*, "gain," and شِير *shīr*, "milk." If the preceding consonant be marked with *jazm*, و and ي are consonants, and sounded as at the beginning of a word or syllable (§ 9). Finally, The vowel *fatḥa* is written before the letters و and ي when they form diphthongs, as in قَوم *ḳaum*, "a tribe," and سَيِر *sair* (pronounced like the English word *sire*), "a walk."

VOWELS, MEDIAL AND FINAL.

17. According to this method, the ten vocal sounds will be uniformly represented as follows, both in the Persian text, and in such Persian words as we may have occasion to write in Roman characters. 1st, Three short vowels, بِر *bar*, بِن *bin*, سُر *sur*. 2dly, Three corresponding long, بار *bār*, بِين *bīn*, سُور *sūr*. 3dly, Two diphthongs, سَيِر *saīr*, قَوم *ḳaum*. 4thly, The two sounds called *Majhūl*, not used in Arabic, بيِل *bēl*, روز *rōz*.

INITIAL VOWELS.

18. The letters ا and ع, beginning a word or syllable, form, according to our notions, an initial vowel; although the Orientals deny the possibility of such a thing: thus—

اد ايد ;أَود آيد ;أُود ايد (for ااد) آد ;أُد اد اد

ad id ud; ād   īd   ūd; aid aud; ēd ōd

OF THE SYMBOL *MADDA*.

19. Instead of writing two *alifs* at the beginning of a word, as in أَاد *ād*, it is usual (except in Dictionaries) to

write one *alif* with the other curved over it; thus, آد. This symbol ‿ is called مَدَّه *madda*, "extension," and denotes that the *alif* is sounded long, like our *a* in *water*.

20. The letter ع *'ain*, like the ا *alif*, at the beginning of a word, depends for its sound on the accompanying vowel. It differs from the *alif*, inasmuch as it is uttered from the lower muscles of the throat; thus,

عَود عَيد ;عُوِد عِيد عاد ;عُد عِد عَد

'ad 'id 'ud; 'ād 'īd 'ūd; 'aid 'aud

a. The learner may view the ا and ع in any of the three following lights. 1st, He may consider them of the same value as the *spiritus lenis* (') in such Greek words as ἀν, ἐν, &c. 2dly, He may consider them as equivalent to the letter *h* in the English words *hour*, *herb*, *honour*, &c. Lastly, he may consider them as mere blocks, whereupon to place the vowels requisite to the formation of the syllable. Practically speaking, then, ا and ع *when initial*, and و and ي *when not initial*, require the beginner's strictest attention, as they all contribute in such cases to the formation of several sounds.

b. It further appears, that when, in Persian, a word or syllable begins with what we consider to be a vowel, such words or syllables must have the letter ا or ع to start with. Throughout this work, when we have occasion to write such words in the Roman character, the corresponding place of the ع will be indicated by an apostrophe or *spiritus lenis*; thus, عسل *'asal,* عابد *'ābid,* بَعْد *ba'd,* to distinguish the same from اسل *asal,* آبِد *ābid,* بد *bad,* or باد *bād.*

21. When one syllable of a word ends with a vowel, and, according to our ideas of orthography, the following syllable begins with a vowel, that is, virtually, with an ا in Persian, the mark ٔ (sometimes ئ) *hamza* is used instead of the ا; thus, پاٴي *pā,e,* instead of پااي; فائده *fa,ida,* instead of فاأده.

a. The sound of the mark *hamza,* according to the Arabian Grammarians, differs in some degree from the letter ‏ا‎, being somewhat akin to the letter ‏ع‎, which its shape ‏ء‎ would seem to warrant; but in Persian this distinction is overlooked. According to the strict rule, the *hamza* ought to be used whenever a syllable beginning with a vowel is added to a root, in the way of inflexion or derivation, as ‏دِيدِيُم‎ *didem,* "*we saw,*" from ‏دِيد‎; ‏بَدِّي‎ *bad-ī,* "*badness,*" from ‏بَد‎ *bad;* but this rule is seldom or never observed. Practically speaking, then, in Persian the *hamza* in the middle of a word is nearly of the same import as our hyphen in such words as *re-open,* which in the Persian character might be written ‏رِيئُوپِن‎. At the end of words terminating with the imperceptible *h* ‏ه‎, or ‏ي‎, the *hamza* has the sound of *e* or *i,* long or short, as will be observed hereafter.

b. In such Persian words as we may have occasion to write in the Roman character, the *hamza* will be represented by the small mark (,) between the vowels, as in the word *fā,ida.*

22. As words and phrases from the Arabic language enter very freely into Persian composition, we cannot well omit the following remarks. Arabic nouns have frequently the definite article ‏ال‎ (*the*) of that language prefixed to them; and if the noun happens to begin with any of the fourteen letters ‏ت‏, ‏ث‏, ‏د‏, ‏ذ‏, ‏ر‏, ‏ز‏, ‏س‏, ‏ش‏, ‏ص‏, ‏ض‏, ‏ط‏, ‏ظ‏, ‏ل‎, or ‏ن‎, the ‏ل‎ of the article assumes the sound of the initial letter of the noun, which is then marked with *tashdīd;* thus, ‏النُّور‎ *the light,* pronounced *an-nūru,* not *al-nūru.* But in these instances, although the ‏ل‎ has lost its own sound, it must always be written in its own form. Sometimes when the noun begins with ‏ل‎, the ‏ل‎ of the article is omitted, and the initial *lām* of the noun marked by *tashdīd,* as ‏الَّيلَة‎ *al-lailatu,* "the night," instead of ‏الْلَّيلَة‎.

a. The fourteen letters, ت &c., above mentioned, are, by the Arabian Grammarians, called *solar* or *sunny* letters, because, forsooth, the word شمس *shams*, "the sun," happens to begin with one of them. The other letters of the Arabic alphabet are called *lunar*, because, we presume, the word قمر *ḳamar*, "the moon," begins with one of the number, or simply because they are *not solar*. Of course, the captious critic might find a thousand equally valid reasons for calling them by any other distinctive terms, such as *gold* and *silver*, *black* and *blue*, &c.; but we merely state the fact as we find it.

b. In general, the Arabic nouns of the above description, when introduced into the Persian language, are in a state of construction with another substantive which precedes them; like our Latin terms "*jus gentium*," "*vis inertiæ*," &c. In such cases, the last letter of the first or governing word is generally moveable by the vowel *ẓamma*, which serves for the enunciation of the ‌ا following; and, at the same time, the ا is marked with the symbol ‌ـ‎, called وصله *waṣla* (conjunction), to denote such union, as in the following words:

امير المومنين *Amīru-l-mūminīn*, "Commander of the Faithful;"

اقبال الدوله *Iḳbālu-d-daula*, "The dignity of the state."

c Arabic nouns occasionally occur in Persian having their final letters marked with the symbol called *tanwīn*, which signifies the using of the letter ن, or *nūnation*. The *tanwīn*, which in Arabic grammar serves to mark the inflexions of a noun, is formed by doubling the vowel-point of the last letter, which indicates at once its presence and its sound; thus, باب *bābun*, باب *bābin*, بابا *bāban*. The last form requires the letter ا, which does not, however, prolong the sound of the final syllable. The ا is not required when the noun ends with a *hamza* or the letter ة, as شي *shai-an*, حكمة *ḥikmatan*; or when the word ends in ی *ya*, surmounted by ا (in which case the ا only is pronounced), as هدی *hudan*. In words ending in ی, surmounted by ا, without the *tanwīn* or *nūnation*, the *alif* is sounded like the *alif* of prolongation, as تعالی *ta'ālā*, عقبی *'uḳbā*, &c. The *n* of the *nūnation* will be represented in the Roman character by *n*, and the final ی by *ạ* or *ā*.

d. The eight letters, ث, ج, ص, ض, ط, ظ, ع, and ق, are peculiar to the Arabic language: hence, as a general rule, a word containing any one of these letters may be considered as borrowed from the Arabic: and should it include the long vowels و or ي, they cannot have the *majhūl* sound, except it be the ي (*e*) of *unity* (of which more hereafter) added at the end. The four letters پ, چ, ژ, and گ, are not used in the Arabic language: hence, a word in which any one of them occurs may be considered as purely Persian or Turkí. The remaining twenty letters are common to both languages.

EXERCISES IN READING.

23. A careful perusal of the two following stories will fully exemplify all that we have already detailed on the subject of reading. An analysis of the first will be found in § 60, and a literal translation is appended to the second.

a. Before commencing, however, the learner had better reconsider all that has gone before, and be sure that he thoroughly recollects the meaning of the following symbols : ◌ِ, ◌ٰ, ◌ُ, ◌ٔ, ◌ْ, ◌ٌ, آ and اٗ, as well as the different sounds which ا, ع و, and ي contribute to form.

STORY I.

حِکایتِ دِهْقان وخَر

دِهْقانِي خَرِي داشت * از سببِ بِي خَرْجِي خَررا برائِي
چرِيدن بَه باغِي سرِ مِي داد * مَرْدُمانِ باغ خَررا مِي زدنْد ـ
و از زراعت بَه در مِي کَرْدنْد * روزِي دِهْقان پوسْتِ
شِيررا بر خَر بسْت ـ و گُفْت وَقْتِ شب برائِي چرِيدن
تُو برآءِي و آواز مکُن * همْچُنان هر شب باپوسْتِ شِير

آن خر به باغ مِي‌رفت ٭ هر كه به شب مِي‌ديد ـ يقين

مِي‌دانِست كه اين شير اسْتِ ٭ شبِي باغْبان اورا دِيد ـ

و از تَرس بر بالاىِ درخْتِي رفْت ٭ در اثْناىِ آن خرِي

دِيگر كه در آن نزْدِيكِي بُود آواز كرْد ـ و خرِ دهْقان نِيز به

اواز در آمد ـ و بانْگِ زدن مِثْلِ خرانِ گرِفْت ٭ باغْبان

اورا شناخْت ـ و دانِسْت كه اين كِيسْت ٭ از درخْت

فرود آمد و آن خررا بِسيار لت به زد ٭ از اينْجا خِرَدْمنْدان

گُفْته انْد ـ كه خرانرا خاموشِي بِه ٭

a. A translation and analysis of the preceding anecdote will be found
in § 60, a., at the beginning of the Syntax. The student's object at
present is to endeavour to write out the whole in the Roman character.
He may then compare his performance with the transcript given in
§ 60, a.

b. We may here observe, that in the following story, the preposition به
ba, "to," "at," "in," "by," which, in the preceding story, we
have written separate, is frequently joined to its substantive; and the
same may be said of the prefix مِي of the verb; as also of the negative
particle نه na, "not," which it seems optional to write separately or
unite with the verb. When به and نه are joined to the following
word, the weak ه is suppressed; thus, we may write به شب or بشب
"by night." Lastly, the termination را, rā, the sign of the Dative and
Accusative, may be joined to the last letter of a word, or written separately; thus, باغْبانرا or باغْبان را bāghbān-rā, "to the gardener."

STORY II.

مرْدِي براىِ دِيدنِ شخْصِي به خانهٔ او به وقْتِ

چاشْتِ دو پهْر آمد ٭ آن شخْص در خانهٔ خوُد از راهِ
غرفه میدید که این مرْد می‌آید ٭ به نوَکران خوُد گفْت
ـ همائگـاه بپرْسد کـه صاحبِ خانه کُجاسْت ؟ شُمه
بگوئید کـه همین زمان بخانهٔ کسی مهْمان رفْته اند ٭
همان‌گاه او آمده پرُسید که صاحب خانه کُجاسْت ؟ گفْتنْد
همین ساعت بیروُن رفْته انْد ٭ گفْت عجب احْمق اسْت
که در این وقْتِ گرْما از خانهٔ خوُد رفْته اسْت ٭ صاحبِ
خانه سر از دریِچه بر آورْده گفْت احْمق توُئِي که این وقْت
میگرْدِي ـ من در خانهٔ خوُد خوُش نِشسْته ام ٭

TRANSLATION.

A man went, for the purpose of seeing a certain person, to his house,
at the time of the midday meal. That person, in his own house, saw
this man coming. He said to his servants, "When he asks where the
master of the house is, you will say that he is now gone to dine with
some one." In the mean while, the man having arrived, asked, "Where
is the master of the house?" They said, "He is just this moment
gone out." The man said, "A rare fool he is, to have gone out of his
house at such a sultry hour." The master of the house, putting his head
out of the window, said, "You are a fool, to wander about at this time.
I am comfortably reposing in my own house."

24. We may here mention, that the twenty-eight letters
of the Arabic language are also used (chiefly in recording
the dates of historical events) for the purpose of Numerical
computation. The Numerical order of the Letters, however,
in this case, differs from that given in the Alphabet; being,

in fact, the identical arrangement of the Hebrew, so far as
the latter extends, viz. to the letter ت, 400.   The following
is the order of the Numerical Alphabet, with the corresponding number placed above each letter ; the whole being
grouped into eight unmeaning words, to serve as a *memoria
technica*—

ابجد هوز حُطّي كلمن سعْفص قُرشت ثُخذ ضظغ

where ا denotes one, ب two, ج three, د four, &c.

a. In reckoning by the preceding system, the four letters peculiarly
Persian (21), viz. پ, چ, ژ, and گ, have the same value as their
cognate Arabic letters, of which they are modifications, that is, of
ب, ج, ز, and ك, respectively.   The mode of recording any event is,
to form a brief sentence, such, that the numerical values of all the letters,
when added together, amount to the year (of the Hijra) in which the
event took place.   Thus, the death of Ahlī of Shīrāz, who may be
considered as the last of the Classic Poets of Persia, happened in
A.H. 942.   This date is recorded in the sentence بادشاه شعرا بود اهلي,
i.e. "Ahlī was the king of poets;" which at once records an event,
and pays a high tribute to the merits of the deceased.   The following
date, on the death of the renowned Hyder 'Ali of Maisūr, A.H. 1196
(A.D. 1782), is equally elegant, and much more poetic.   The reader
will bear in mind that *Bālāghāt* is the scene of one of Hyder's most
celebrated victories ; hence the appropriateness of the following well-
chosen expression :

جان بالا گهات برفُت

"The spirit of Bālāghāt is gone."

b. Sometimes the title of a book is so cunningly contrived as to
express the date of its completion.   Thus, several letters, written on
various occasions by Abul Fazl, surnamed 'Allāmī, when secretary to
the Emperor Akbar, were afterwards collected into one volume by
Abdu-s-samad, the secretary's nephew, and the work was entitled

مُكاتبات علامي *Mukātabāti 'Allāmī*, "The Letters of 'Allāmī," which at the same time gives the date of their publication, A.H. 1015, (A.D. 1606.)

c. A letter marked with *tashdīd*, though double, is to be reckoned only once, as in the word *'allāmī*, where the *lām*, though double, counts only 30. The Latin writers of the middle ages sometimes amused themselves with learned trifles of this description, although they had only seven numerical letters to work with, viz. I, V, X, L, C, D, and M. This kind of verse they called *carmen eteostichon* or *chronostichon*, out of which the following effusion on the restoration of Charles II., 1660, will serve as a specimen—" *Cedant arma oleæ, pax regna serenat et agros;*"—where C, D, M, L, and X, amount to the date required, viz. M DC LX.

24½. In Arabia and Persia, the art of printing is as yet very little used: hence their books, as was once the case in Europe, are written in a variety of different hands. Of these, the most common are, 1st, the *Naskhī* نسخي, of which the type employed in the two Stories, § 23, is a very good imitation. Most Arabic Manuscripts, and particularly those of the Ḳur̤ān, are in this hand; and from its compact form, it is generally used in Europe for printing books in the Arabic, Persian, Turkish, and Hindūstānī languages. 2dly, The *Ta'līḳ* تعليق, a beautiful hand, used chiefly by the Persians in disseminating copies of their more esteemed authors. In India, the Ta'līḳ has been extensively employed for printing, both in Persian and Hindūstānī; and within the last thirty years, a few Persian works, in the same type, have issued from the Pāshā of Egypt's press at Būlaḳ. 3dly, The *Shikasta* شكسته, or *broken* hand, which is used in correspondence. It is quite irregular, and unadapted for printing; but not inelegant in appearance, when properly written.

a. For a more ample account of this subject, see "Essai de Caligraphie Orientale," in the Appendix to Herbin's "Développements des Principes de la Langue Arabe," 4to. Paris, 1803; Ouseley's "Persian Miscellanies," 4to. London, 1799; Stewart's "Persian Letters," 4to. London, 1825; and, lastly, "Oriental Penmanship," 4to. London, 1849, Messrs. Allen and Co., 7 Leadenhall Street. We may state, however, in conclusion, that the grand secret of reading all sorts of manuscripts, good, bad, and indifferent, consists in possessing a thorough knowledge of the language.

═══

SECTION II.

ON SUBSTANTIVES, ADJECTIVES, AND PRONOUNS.

25. The Grammarians of Arabia and Persia reckon only Three Parts of Speech—the Noun اِسْم *Ism*, the Verb فِعْل *Fi'l*, and the Particle حَرْف *Ḥarf.* Under the term Noun, they include Substantives, Adjectives, Pronouns, Participles, and Infinitives: their Verb agrees in its nature with ours; and their Particle includes Adverbs, Prepositions, Conjunctions, and Interjections.

a. In the present work we shall, in preference, adhere to that division of the Parts of Speech which is followed in the Latin Grammar, with which the student is supposed to be already acquainted.

OF GENDER.

26. In the Persian language, the Gender of Nouns agrees exactly with that of the same Part of Speech in English; males being masculine, females feminine, and all other words neuter, or, more strictly speaking, of no gender.

a. Animals have either different names to express male and female; as, پِسر *pisar*, "a son;" دُختَر *dukhtar*, "a daughter:" or the terms نر *nar* (male), and ماده *māda* (female), added or prefixed, serve the same purpose; as, شیرِنر *sher-i-nar*, "a lion," شیرِماده *sher-i-māda*, "a lioness;" so, نرگاو *nar-gāw*, "a bull," ماده‌گاو *māda-gāw*, "a cow."

b. Many Arabic Nouns form the feminine gender by adding the imperceptible ه to the masculine; as, ملك *malik*, "a king;" ملکه *malika*, "a queen."

FORMATION OF THE PLURAL NUMBER.

27. All names applicable to human beings, and, in general, all names of animals, particularly those of the larger description, form the plural by adding the termination ان *ān* to the singular; thus, مرّد *mard*, "a man," pl. مرّدان *mardān*, "men;" زن *zan*, "a woman," زنان *zanān*, "women;" اسپ *asp*, "a horse," اسپان *aspān*, "horses." All names of lifeless things, and of the more minute description of animated beings, form the plural by adding ها *hā* to the singular; thus, در *dar*, "a door," pl. درها *darhā*, "doors;" روز *roz*, "a day," روزها *rozhā*, "days;" مور *mor*, "an ant," مورها *morhā*, "ants." This general rule, however, is subject to some exceptions.

a. All names applicable to persons, and epithets descriptive of human beings, make the plural in ان; thus, بادشاه *bādshāh*, "a king," بادشاهان *bādshāhān*, "kings;" کنیزک *kanīzak*, "a damsel," کنیزکان "damsels;" دل فریب *dil-fireb*, "an allurer of hearts," pl. دل فریبان *dil-firebān*. Names of animals not rational, form the plural, generally, by adding ان, but often by ها; as, اسپ *asp*, "a horse," pl. اسپان *aspān*; شتر *shutur*, "a camel," pl. شتران *shuturān*, or شترها *shuturhā*, "camels." Names of inanimate objects add ها generally, sometimes ان—; as, قلم *ḳalam,* "a pen," pl. قلمها *ḳalamhā,* "pens;" درخت *dirakhht,* "a tree," pl. درختها *dirakhhtā,* "trees," and frequently درختان *di-rakhhtān.*

b. When nouns ending in the obscure *h* ه (§ 3) have occasion to add ان—, the ه is converted into گ; as, فرشته *firishta,* "an angel," pl. فرشتگان *firishtagān,* "angels:" and sometimes the ه is retained, and the گان added as a separate termination; as, مُرده "dead," pl. مُردهگان. When such nouns have occasion to add ها, the final ه of the singular disappears; as, نامه *nāma,* "a book or letter," pl. نامها *nāmahā.* When nouns ending in ا (*ā*) or و (*ū* or *ō*) have occasion to add ان—, the letter ي (*y*) is inserted, to avoid a hiatus; as, دانا *dānā,* "a sage," pl. دانایان *dānāyān;* so, پري رُو *parī-rū,* "fairy-faced," pl. پري رُویان *parī-rūyān,* "the fairy-faced ones:" and sometimes, though rarely, the letter ي is omitted after و; as, بازو "the arm," pl. بازوان *bāzuwān.*

c. In some modern Persian works, written in India, names applicable to females, or to things without life, frequently form their plural by adding ات—, and sometimes یات—, to the singular; thus, نوازش "a favour," pl. نوازشات "favours;" نقل "an anecdote," نقلیات "anecdotes." When the singular ends in the imperceptible ه *h,* the plural is sometimes formed by adding جات *jāt,* the ه being suppressed; as, نامه "a letter," نامجات; so, قلعه "a fort," قلعجات.

d. There are several other modes of forming the plural adopted in the Persian language from the Arabic; thus, the word عیب "vice," "blemish," may have the regular Persian plural عیبها, as well as the irregular Arabic forms عیوب and عوائب. In like manner قلعه may have the regular Persian plural قلعها, or the Arabic plural قلاع, or, lastly, the more barbarous plural قلعجات. The word نائب "a deputy," or "viceroy," may have the regular Persian plural نائبان, or the Arabic forms نوب and نواب. The latter form is said to be the origin of our word *Nabob,* used in the plural form as a mark of respect, unless we consider it to be a substantive singular of the form

فَعَّال, or " Noun of excess," as the Arabs call it. In India, the word is uniformly pronounced *Nauwāb* (not *nūwāb*) denoting " governor," or " viceroy."

e. According to Mirzā Ibrāhīm, it would appear that, in the spoken language of the present day, there is a tendency to form *all plurals* by adding ها to the singular.　In the Mirzā's Grammar, page 29, he states, that " If a foreigner, speaking good Persian, adheres uniformly to the use of ها in forming the plural, he will be much nearer the mark."　It must be remembered, however, that this novel rule of the Mirzā's does not apply to the written language, even of the present day.　The Mirzā, indeed, tries to prove too much, when he states, in page 26, " In one instance (but, I believe, the only one in all his writings) he (Sa'dī) has indeed been compelled,* as it were, to form the plural of an inanimate thing, viz. درختان *dirakhtān*, " trees," (pl. of *dirakht*), by adding آن to the singular; a transgression of which none but himself (though only for once) could venture to be guilty, and for which nothing but the splendid composition in which it occurs could have secured him against the censure of the learned."　Now all this sounds to us very strange, when in no fewer than five different passages of Sa'dī's Gulistān alone, we find درختان " trees," used as the plural of درخت, in all editions, manuscript or print.　Of these five passages, four occur in the Preface, and the fifth in Book II. Tale 32; and, moreover, three of the passages alluded to are in plain prose, where the author is under no compulsion on the score of metre!

28. Persian Nouns undergo no change in termination corresponding to the various Cases of the Greek and Latin. The word *Case*, however, is here retained in the Oriental sense of the term, حالت *ḥālat*, i. e. state or situation, as it forms the simplest means for explaining how the various relations of Substantives are expressed in this language.

---

* It is a pity the Mirzā did not explain to us the nature of the *compulsion* here alluded to. This grossly inaccurate assertion of his with respect to Sa'dī, throws a shade of suspicion over the rest of his performance.

29. The *Genitive* or *Possessive Case* is formed by the juxta-position of two Substantives; where the *regimen*, or thing possessed comes always first, having its final letter sounded with the vowel *kasra* (*i*)—called كسرهٔ اِضافت *Kasra-i Izāfat*, "The *kasra* of relationship;"—thus, پسرِ ملك *pisar-i-malik*, "The son of the king (*filius regis*);" so كتابِ پسرِ ملك *kitāb-i pisar-i malik*, "The book of the son of the king (*liber filii regis*)." If the governing word ends in the long vowels ‍ا (*ā*) or و (*ū* or *ō*), instead of these letters being followed by the *kasra* (or short *i*), as above, the letter ي (*majhūl*) with the mark *hamza*, or the *hamza* alone, with the *kasra* (expressed or understood) is used; as, پائِي مُرد or پاءِ مرد *pā,e mard*, "The foot of the man;" so, رُوئِي پسر or رُوءِ پسر *rū,e pisar*, "The face of the boy." If the governing word ends with the obsure ه (*h*), or the long vowel ي (*ī* or *e*), the mark *hamza*, with the vowel *kasra* (expressed or understood) is used; as, خانهٔ مُرد *khāna,e mard*, "The house of the man;" ماهئ دَريا *māhī,e daryā*, "The fish of the sea." In practice, however, when the ي is employed, the *hamza* is generally suppressed; as, پاي مرد and رُوي پسر.

a. In English we form the Possessive Case in two ways; thus, "The king's son," or "The son of the king:" the latter mode agrees exactly with that of the Persian; and the vowel *kasra* &c. (*i* &c.), added to the governing word in Persian, corresponds to the particle *of* in English. Hence, in turning English into Persian, should a complex string of words related to each other in the genitive case occur, the student has, in the first place, to resolve the same in his mind into that form of the genitive case which is made by the particle *of* in English; then convert the same into Persian in the very same order, inserting the proper marks of the *iẓāfat*. Thus, to assume an extreme case, we shall suppose the student has to express in Persian, "The colour of the king of Irān's horse's head." Let him, in the first place, endeavour to express the plain meaning of the phrase in English, by the aid of the particle *of* alone; thus, "The colour of the head of the horse of the king of Irān:" then the Persian will easily follow ; as, رنگِ سرِ اسپِ پادشاهِ ایران *rang-i sar-i asp-i padshāh-i Irān;* the order being the same.

b. The words صاحب *ṣāḥib,* denoting "possessed of," and سر *sar,* denoting "source," when united with another word, generally omit the *kasra;* as, صاحبِ دل *ṣāḥib-dil,* "a sage" (homme d'esprit); so سر مایه *sar māya,* "the source of wealth," or "capital in trade." The rule does not hold, however, when these words are used in a specific or restricted sense; as, صاحبِ خانه "the master of the house ;" سرِ تو "thy head."

30. *Dative Case.*—The syllable را is added to a Noun when it stands in that relation to a Verb which corresponds with the Dative Case of the Latin; as, مردرا کتاب دادم *mardrā kitāb dādam* (viro librum dedi), "I gave the book to the man." Sometimes the Dative is formed, as in our own language, by prefixing to the Noun the particle به *ba,* "to" or "for:" this holds in particular when, at the same time, the Verb governs an Accusative requiring the termination را *rā* (§ 73, *a.*) ; as, لعلرا به زن داد *la'l-rā ba zan dād,* "He gave the ruby to the woman."

31. *Accusative Case.*—The Accusative Case in Persian is generally the same as the Nominative, and can only be known as such from its *situation* in the sentence ; thus, مردي دیدم *marde dīdam,* "I saw a man." In some instances it is necessary to add the termination را *rā,* to distinguish the Accusative, as will be more fully shewn in the

Syntax; as, اسپرا دیدم asp-rā dīdam, "I saw the horse." Vide § 72, a.

32. *Vocative Case.*—The Vocative is formed, as in English, by placing some Interjection before the Nominative; as, اي مرد Ai mard! "O man!" In poetry, and also in prose compositions denoting prayer and supplication, the Vocative is frequently formed by adding ا ā to the Nominative; as, بلبلا bulbulā! "O nightingale!" دوستا dostā! "O friend!"

33. *The Ablative Case.*—The Ablative is formed, as in English, by prefixing the Prepositions از az, "from" or "by," در dar, "in," &c., to the Nominative; as, از مرد az mard, "from the man;" در خانه dar khāna, "in the house." The Cases of the Plural Number are formed exactly in the same way, the plural terminations being superadded.

34. To conform with the mode of European Grammars, we shall add two examples of the Declension of a Persian Noun.

مرد Mard, "Man."

SINGULAR.		PLURAL.	
Nom.	مرد mard; VIR.	مردان mardān; VIRI.
Gen.	مرد ‎—‎*i-mard; VIRI.	مردان ‎—‎ i-mardān; VIRORUM.
Dat.	مرد را mard-rā; VIRO.	مردان را mardān-rā; VIRIS.
Acc.	{ مرد mard; / مرد را mard-rā; } VIRUM.	{ مردان mardān; / مردان را mardān-rā; } VIROS.
Voc.	اي مرد ai mard; VIR.	اي مردان ai mardān; VIRI.
Abl.	از مرد az mard; VIRO.	از مردان az mardān; VIRIS.

---

* The symbol ‎—‎ before the Genitive Case, merely indicates the place of the governing word, the last letter of which must have the vowel ‎—‎ (ه or ي) affixed, as explained in § 29.

کِتاب *Kitāb*, " A Book."

	SINGULAR.		PLURAL.
Nom.	کتاب *kitāb*, a book, the book.	کتابها *kitābhā*, books.
Gen.	ـِکتاب *i-kitāb*, of a book.	ـِکتابها *i-kitābhā*, of books.
Dat.	کتابرا *kitāb-rā*, to a book.	کتابهارا *kitābhā-rā*, to books.

Acc. { کتاب *kitāb*,   کتابرا *kitāb-rā*, } the book.   { کتابها *kitābhā*,   کتابهارا *kitābhā-rā*, } books.

| Voc. | أي کتاب *ai kitāb*, O book! | أي کتابها *ai kitābhā*, O books! |
| Abl. | از کتاب *az kitāb*, from a book. | از کتابها *az kitābhā*, from books. |

a. In like manner may be declined every Substantive in the Persian language. The only questions are, in the first place, whether ـِ, ي, or ﻩ, will be used as the sign of the *izāfat* or Genitive Case; which is easily solved by the rule laid down in § 29, the choice depending on the last syllable of the preceding or governing word; and, secondly, whether ان or ﻫ is to be added in the plural, which is decided by a careful perusal of § 27.

35. In Persian, there is no word corresponding exactly to our Definite Article *the;* so that common names, as مرد *mard*, may signify "man," or "the man," according to circumstances, which the context will generally indicate. A Common Substantive in the Singular Number, however, is restricted to unity, by adding the letter ي *e* (*majhūl*) to it; as, مردي *mard-e*, "one man," or " a certain man."

a. The same letter, ي, added to Nouns (plural as well as singular), followed by the particle که, indicating a relative clause of a sentence, seems to have the effect of our *definite article;* thus, کساني که بقوّت از من بيش اند " The (or Those) persons who in power are my superiors."—Anwāri Suhaili, Book III. Likewise, in the following passage from the Gulistān of Sa'dī. Book I. :

اَبْلَهِي كو روزِ روشن شمْعِ كافُورِي نِهد "The fool who in bright day *ets up (burns) a camphor candle." Sometimes the ي *majhūl* added to a Noun gives it a sense of excess or universality; as in Hafiz, عِشق آفتي اسْت "Love is one (excessive) calamity:" so, عالمي "The whole world:" خلْقي "The whole nation *or* people." Words ending in the obscure ه add a *hamza*, instead of the ي (*majhūl*); as, خانهٔ *khana-e*, "one house;" where the *hamza* has the same sound as the ي which it represents.

<h2 align="center">OF ADJECTIVES.</h2>

36. Persian Adjectives are indeclinable; and in construction, they follow the Substantives which they qualify; at the same time, the last letter of the Substantive must have the *kasra* ِ (or ي, or و) superadded, as in the formation of the Genitive Case (§ 29): thus, مَرْدِ نيك *mard-i nek*, "a good man;" عُمْرِ دراز *'umr-i darāz*, "a long life;" رُوِي خُوب *rū-e khūb*, "a fair face;" بنْدهٔ وفادار *banda,e-wafādār*, "a faithful slave."

<h2 align="center">DEGREES OF COMPARISON.</h2>

37. The only variation which Persian Adjectives undergo is that of Comparison, in which respect they very much resemble the same part of speech in English. The Comparative Degree is formed regularly, by adding to the Positive the syllable تر *tar*; and the Superlative, by adding تریِن *tarīn*: thus, خُوب *khūb*, "fair," خُوبْتر *khūb-tar*, "fairer," خُوبْتریِن *khūb-tarīn*, "fairest."

a. The terminations تر and تریِن may be joined to the Adjective, or written separately, at pleasure: thus, in the above example, we might write خوبتر and خوبترین.

b. In a few instances we meet with the termination ترین of the Superlative contracted into ین *īn*, as برین *barīn*, for برترین *bartarīn*, "highest" or "uppermost;" so, بهین, for بهترین.

c. Arabic Adjectives, if triliteral (vide Arabic Grammar), form the Comparative and Superlative Degrees by prefixing the letter ا *alif* to the *triliteral* root; thus, حسن *ḥasan*, "beautiful," comp. and superl. احسن *aḥsan*, "more beautiful," or "most beautiful." Generally speaking, however, Arabic Adjectives, occurring in Persian, form their degrees of comparison in the Persian manner; as, فضل "excellent," فضلتر "more excellent," فضلترین "most excellent:" but sometimes the comparison is effected as in Arabic; thus, افضل "more *or* most excellent;" and occasionally we meet with both forms united, as افضلتر. When any Adjective is used as a Substantive, it forms the plural in accordance with the Nouns Substantive represented; as, نیکان "the good," خوبان "the fair," &c.; دادها "things given."

<h2 style="text-align:center">PRONOUNS.</h2>

38. The Personal Pronouns, من *man*, "I;" تو *tū*, "thou;" او *o*, "he, she, *or* it," are declined as under:—

FIRST PERSON.

	SINGULAR.	PLURAL.
Nom.	من *man*, "I."	ما *mā*, "we."
Gen.	ِ من *i-man*, "of me," "my."	ِ ما *i-mā*, "of us," "our."
Dat. Acc.	مرا *marā*, "to me," "me."	مارا *mārā*, "to us," "us."

SECOND PERSON.

	SINGULAR.		PLURAL.
Nom.	تُو *tū*, "thou."	شُما *shumā*, "you."
Gen.	تُو ‍ـِ *i-tū*, "of thee," "thy."	شُما ‍ـِ *i-shumā*, "of you," "your."
Dat. Acc.	تُرا *turā*, "to thee," "thee."	شُمارا *humārā*, "to you," "you."

THIRD PERSON.

Nom.	او *o*, "he, she, *or* it."	ایشان *eshān*, "they."
Gen.	او ‍ـِ *i-o*, "of him," "his," &c.	ایشان ‍ـِ *i-eshān*, "of them," "their."
Dat. Acc.	اورا *orā*, "to him," "him," &c.	ایشانرا *eshānrā*, "to them," "them."

a. The third person has, in the singular, the form وَي *wai*, and sometimes اوی *o,e*; and, in the plural, اوشان *oshān*, and شان *shān*. When the third person represents a lifeless thing, the demonstratives آن and اِین (v. § 40), with their plurals آنها and اینها, are generally used instead of او, وَي, or ایشان, as will be more fully explained in the Syntax.

b. The inflection of the Personal Pronouns differs in no respect from that of Nouns. They all form the Genitive Case, like the Substantives, by placing the governing word, with the sign of the *izāfat* before the Nominatives (sing. or plur.) of the Pronouns; as, پدرِمن *padar-i man*, "my father;" اسپِ تُو *asp-i tū*, "thy horse;" کتابِ او *kitābi o*, "his *or* her book;" قیمتِ آن *kimat-i ān*, "its price;" خانۂ ما *khāna-e mā*, "our house," &c. The Dative and Accusative are formed by adding را. In the first person singular, the form مرا is evidently a contraction of منرا, as تُرا is of تُورا in the second person singular. The second person forms the Vocative by prefixing an Interjection; as, اَي تُو *ai tū*, "O thou!" The first and third persons cannot, in their nature, have a Vocative, without virtually becoming the second person. They all form the Ablative by prefixing the simple Prepositions از, در, با, &c. to the Nominative; as, از من *az man*, "from me;" با تُو *bā tū*, "with thee;" بر او *bar ō*, "on him;" در آن *dar ān*, "in it."

39. Besides the regular inflections of the Personal Pronouns, there are certain contracted forms or affixes, which, when joined to Nouns or Verbs, may denote the Genitive, Dative, or Accusative Case. These are, ـَم *am*, for the first pers. sing.; ـَت *at*, for the second; and ـَش *ash*, for the third; as, دِلَم *dil-am*, "my heart;" سرت *sar-at*, "thy head;" دستش *dast-ash*, "his hand:" but the explanation of these, as well as of the Reciprocal Pronoun خُود *khud*, or خویش *khwesh* (§ 13, *b*), "self," or "selves," belongs more properly to the section on Syntax.

40. The Demonstrative or Adjective Pronouns are, اِین *īn*, "this" or "these," and آن *ān*, "that" or "those." As Adjectives, they are indeclinable, and applicable to all Genders and Numbers; thus, اِین مَرد *īn mard*, "this man;" اِین مَردان *īn mardān*, "these men;" آن کِتاب *ān kitāb*, "that book;" آن کِتابها *ān kitābhā*, "those books." When used as the representatives of Nouns, they form the plural in the same manner as the Noun for which they stand; thus, اِینان *īnān*, "these" or "they," if applicable to persons; and اِینها *inhā*, "these" or "they," when referring to inanimate things; and in like manner آنان and آنها "those" or "they."

40. The Interrogative Pronouns are کِه *ki* (Dative and Accusative, کِرا *kirā*), "who?" "whom?" and چِه *chi*

(Dative and Accusative, چرا *chirā*), "what?" "which?" They are applicable to both numbers; the former generally relating to persons, and the latter to things. To these may be added, كُدَام *kudām*, "Which of two?" or "Which out of any number?" چند *chand*, "how many?" also, "some" or "several," which are equally applicable to persons and inanimate things. When كه and چه are added to the word هر *har* or هرآن *har-ān*, they correspond to our *who-*, *what-*, or *which-soever*; as, هركه *harki*, or هرآنكه *harānki*, "whosoever," &c. Finally, كه and چه are sometimes used as substitutes for the Relative Pronouns, of which more hereafter, in the Syntax.

a. The Persian language, like the Arabic, generally dispenses with, or rather does not possess, a Relative Pronoun exactly similar to the *qui, quæ, quod* of the Latin. For instance, "The man whom I saw," *Vir quem vidi*, would be expressed in Persian thus, آن مرد كه ديدمش *ān mard ki ora dīdam*; or, آن مرد كه اورا ديدم *ān mard ki dīdamash*; literally, "The man that I saw him." In these expressions it will be seen that the particle كه is not a Relative Pronoun, but a Conjunction. This remark, which may be considered premature, is sufficient to shew that the explanation of this peculiarity belongs more properly to the Syntax.

b. The Indefinite Pronouns require no particular notice. As Adjectives they are all indeclinable; thus, هر *har*, "every;" يك or يكي *yak* or *yake*, "one," "some one;" كس or كسي *kas* or *kase*, "somebody;" "a certain one;" هريك "every one;" هركس "every person;" چند *chand*, "some," "several," "a few;" تني چند *tane chand*, "sundry individuals."

SECTION III.

ON THE VERB.

42. The Persian Verb is extremely regular in its structure, there being only *one form* or *conjugation*, applicable to every Verb in the language. All the Tenses are formed either from the Root or from the Infinitive, as will be seen in the following example of the Verb رسیدن *rasīdan,* "to arrive." The root of this Verb is رس *ras* (which is also the 2d pers. sing. of the Imperative); from which the following *four* Tenses, the Noun of Agency, and the Present Participle are formed :

TENSES OF THE ROOT.

1st.—THE AORIST, *I may* or *can arrive ;* formed by adding the terminations *am, ī, ad ; em, ed, and ;* to the root.

PERS.	SINGULAR.	PLURAL.
1.	رسم RAS-*am,* "I may arrive."	رسیم RAS-*em,* "We may arrive."
2.	رسي RAS-*i,* "Thou mayest arrive."	رسید RAS-*ed,* "You may arrive."
3.	رسد RAS-*ad,* "He may arrive."	رسند RAS-*and,* "They may arrive."

2d.—THE PRESENT TENSE, *I am arriving,* or *I arrive ;* formed by merely prefixing the Particle مي *mī* (sometimes همي *hamī*) to the Aorist; as,

	SINGULAR.	PLURAL.
1.	مي رسم *mī-*RAS-*am,* "I am arriving."	مي رسیم *mī-*RAS-*em,* "We are arriving."
2.	مي رسي *mī-*RAS-*ī,* "Thou art arriving."	مي رسید *mī-*RAS-*ed,* "You are arriving."
3.	مي رسد *mī-*RAS-*ad,* "He is arriving."	مي رسند *mī-*RAS-*and,* "They are arriving."

3d.—The Simple Future, *I shall*, or *will*, or *may arrive*; formed by prefixing the Particle بـﻪ or بـ *bi* to the Aorist.

PERS.	SINGULAR.		PLURAL.
1.	برسم *bi-RAS-am*, "I shall arrive."		برسيم *bi-RAS-em*, "We shall arrive."
2.	برسي *bi-RAS-i*, "Thou wilt arrive."		برسيد *bi-RAS-ed*, "You will arrive."
3.	برسد *bi-RAS-ad*, "He will arrive."		برسند *bi-RAS-and*, "They will arrive."

a. This Tense seems to differ very little from the Aorist, which, in its nature, frequently denotes futurity. The student, therefore, may consider it as a Simple Future, or as a modification of the Aorist; the latter being the opinion of all the Native Grammarians that we have had an opportunity of consulting.

4th.—The Imperative, *Let me arrive*. The same as the Aorist, except in the 2d pers. sing., which consists of the mere root, without any termination.

1.	رسم RAS-*am*, "Let me arrive."	رسيم RAS-*em*, "Let us arrive."
2.	رس RAS, "Arrive thou."	رسيد RAS-*ed*, "Arrive you."
3.	رسد RAS-*ad*, "Let him arrive."	رسند RAS-*and*, "Let them arrive."

a. The second persons (singular and plural) of the Imperative have frequently the Particle بـ or بـﻪ *bi*, prefixed to them; thus, برس or بـﻪرس *bi-ras*, "arrive thou;" so, in the plural, برسيد or بـﻪرسيد "arrive ye." When the first letter of the Imperative, or of the simple Future, has *zamma* for its vowel, the Particle بـ *bi* may optionally become بـ *bu*; thus, the 2d pers. sing. كن "do," or "make," may be written بكن or بكن.

b. The 3d pers. sing. of the Imperative may be rendered Precative or Benedictive, by lengthening the vowel *fatha* of its final syllable; thus, رسد, "Let him arrive:" رساد, "O that he may arrive!" "God grant he may arrive!"

c. From the root are also formed the Noun of Agency, by adding the termination ‿ـنده *anda*, as, رسنده *rasanda,* "the arriver;" and also the Present Participle, by adding ان, as, رسان *rasān,* "arriving." Finally, the root furnishes, if required, the Causal Verb, by adding ‿ـانیدن *ānīdan,* or ‿ـاندن *āndan,* which then becomes a Causal Infinitive; as, رسانیدن *rasānīdan,* or رساندن *rasāndan,* "to cause to arrive," "to send."

The following Tenses are all formed, directly or indirectly, from the Infinitive, deprived of its final syllable ‿ـن *an,* which then serves as a *secondary root* or *basis.* To this new basis the foregoing terminations are added in all the persons of the Preterite and its formatives, with the exception of the third person singular, to which no termination is added.

5th.—PRETERITE, or INDEFINITE PAST, *I arrived.*

PERS.	SINGULAR.	PLURAL.
1.	رسیدم RASĪD-*am,* "I arrived."	رسیدیم RASĪD-*em,* "We arrived."
2.	رسیدی RASĪD-*ī,* "Thou arrivedst."	رسیدید RASĪD-*ed,* "You arrived."
3.	رسید RASĪD, "He arrived."	رسیدند RASĪD-*and,* "They arrived."

6th.—IMPERFECT, *I was arriving;* formed by prefixing the Particle می *mī* (sometimes همی *hamī*) to the Preterite.

1.	می رسیدم *mī* RASĪD-*am,* "I was arriving."	می رسیدیم *mī* RASĪD-*em,* "We were arriving."
2.	می رسیدی *mī* RASĪD-*ī,* "Thou wast arriving."	می رسیدید *mī* RASĪD-*ed,* "You were arriving."
3.	می رسید *mī* RASĪD, "He was arriving."	می رسیدند *mī* RASĪD-*and,* "They were arriving."

7th.—The Past Potential, or Habitual, *I might arrive,* or *I used to arrive*; formed by adding ي *e* (*yae, majhūl*) to all the persons of the Preterite, except the 2d pers. sing., which is unchanged.

PERS.	SINGULAR.		PLURAL.
1.	رسیدمی RASĪD-*ame,* "I might arrive."		رسیدیمی RASĪD-*eme,* "We might arrive."
2.	رسیدی RASĪD-*ī,* "Thou mightest arrive."		رسیدیدی RASĪD-*ede,* "You might arrive."
3.	رسیدی RASĪD-*e,* "He might arrive."		رسیدندی RASĪD-*ande,* "They might arrive."

8th.—Compound Future, *I will arrive*; formed by adding the Infinitive, generally deprived of its final syllable ـن, to the Aorist (خواهم, &c.) of the Verb خواستن *khwāstan,* which signifies *to intend* or *wish.*

1.	خواهم رسید *khwāham* RASĪD, "I shall *or* will arrive."		خواهیم رسید *khwāhem* RASĪD, "We shall *or* will arrive."
2.	خواهی رسید *khwāhī* RASĪD, "Thou shalt *or* wilt arrive."		خواهید رسید *khwāhed* RASĪD, "You shall *or* will arrive."
3.	خواهد رسید *khwāhad* RASĪD, "He shall *or* will arrive."		خواهند رسید *khwāhand* RASĪD, "They shall *or* will arrive."

The three following Tenses are compounded of the Preterite Participle, and Auxiliaries. This Participle is regularly formed by changing the final ن *n* of the Infinitive into the obscure ه *h*; as from رسیدن *rasīdan,* "to arrive," comes رسیده *rasīda,* "arrived" or "having arrived." The final ه *h* of the Participle, not being sounded, is of course omitted in the Roman character.

9th.—The PERFECT TENSE, *I have arrived.*

PERS.	SINGULAR.	PLURAL.

1. رسیده ام RASĪDA-*am*, "I have arrived." — رسیده ایم RASĪDA-*em*, "We have arrived."

2. رسیده ای or رسیدهه RASĪDA-*ī*, "Thou hast arrived." — رسیده اید RASĪDA-*ed*, "You have arrived."

3. رسیده است RASIDA-*ast*, "He has arrived." — رسیده اند RASĪDA-*and*, "They have arrived."

10th.—PLUPERFECT TENSE, *I had arrived.*

1. رسیده بودم RASĪDA *būdam*, "I had arrived." — رسیده بودیم RASĪDA *būdem*, "We had arrived."

2. رسیده بودی RASĪDA *būdī*, "Thou hadst arrived." — رسیده بودید RASĪDA *būded*, "You had arrived."

3. رسیده بود RASĪDA *būd*, "He had arrived." — رسیده بودند RASĪDA *būdand*, "They had arrived."

11th.—FUTURE PERFECT, *I shall have arrived.*

1. رسیده باشم RASĪDA *bāsham*, "I shall have arrived." — رسیده باشیم RASĪDA *bāshem*, "We shall have arrived."

2. رسیده باشی RASĪDA *bāshī*, "Thou shall have arrived." — رسیده باشید RASĪDA *bāshed*, "You shall have arrived."

3. رسیده باشد RASĪDA *bāshad*, "He shall have arrived." — رسیده باشند RASĪDA *bāshand*, "They shall have arrived."

a. There are a few other compound Tenses, or rather modes of expression, besides those given in the paradigm of رسیدن, which will be treated of in the Syntax. Vide § 75.

43. In the same manner may be conjugated every Verb in the Persian language. Hence it would be, on our

part, downright waste of time and space to swell our little work (as is the case in some Grammars we could name) with repeated examples of the same thing. If the student will carefully keep in view the following general principles, he will meet with no difficulty on this subject:—

1st, Every Infinitive ends in دن *dan* or تن *tan*; and the Imperative or Root is found by the rules which we are about to give. 2dly, The Aorist is formed by adding to the *root* the terminations *am, ī, ad; em, ed, and.* 3dly, By dropping the final ن of the Infinitive, we have the 3d pers. sing. of the Preterite, or what we may consider as the *secondary basis* of the Verb; and, by adding the terminations above given, the rest of the Preterite is invariably formed. 4thly, The Perfect Participle is formed by changing the final ن of the Infinitive into ه imperceptible; and thence may be formed the Compound Tenses. It is evident, therefore, that if the Infinitive and Imperative be known, the remaining parts of the Verb are easily formed.

44. Infinitives in دن are preceded by the long vowels ا *ā*, ي *ī*, و *ū*, (and a few by the *fatḥa* ﹷ *a*), or by the consonants ر *r* or ن *n*. Those in تن *tan*, are preceded by the stronger consonants خ *kh*, س *s*, ش *sh*, or ف *f*; hence the following rules for ascertaining the root:—

I. Infinitives in ادن *ādan* and یدن *īdan* (and the few that have a *fatḥa* before the *dan*) reject these terminations for the root; as, فرستادن *firistādan*, " to send," root فرست *firist.* "send thou;" so پرسیدن *pursīdan*, " to ask,"

root پُرس *purs,* "ask thou;" آژدن آ *āzhadan,* "to sew,"
آژ آ *āzh.*

Exceptions.—دادن *dādan,* "to give," root دہ—چیدن *chīdan,* "to collect," چین—دیدن *dīdan,* "to see," بین *bīn*—آمدن *āmadan,* "to come," آ or آي *ā* or *āy*—زدن *zadan,* "to strike," زن *zan* آمادن—ستان *sitān* سِتادن *sitādan,* or سِتدن *sitadan,* "to seize," آمادن *āmādan,* "to prepare," makes آما or آماي *āmā* or *āmāy*—زادن *zādan,* "to bring forth" (young), also "to be born," زا or زاي *zā* or *zāy*—گادن *gādan,* "to embrace," گا or گاي *gā* or *gāy*—گشادن (or گشادن) *kushādan,* "to open," کشا *kushā* &c.—آفریدن *āfrīdan,* "to create," آفرین—شنیدن *shunīdan,* "to hear," شنو *shunu*—گزیدن *guzīdan,* "to choose," گزین.

II. Infinitives in ودن *ūdan,* reject that termination and substitute ا *ā,* or اُي *ā,e,* for the root; thus سِتودن *sitūdan,* "to praise," سِتا or سِتاُي *sitā* or *sitā,e.*

Exceptions.—بودن (for شودن) "to be," باش or بو *bāsh* or *bu;* and شدن "to be" or "to become," شو. تنودن "to draw," makes تنو—درودن "to reap," درو—زنودن "to neigh," "to howl," زنو—شنودن "to hear," شنو—غنودن "to slumber," غنو.

III. Infinitives in دن preceded by ر *r* or ن *n,* reject the termination دن for the root, as پرورْدن *parwardan,* "to cherish," پرور *parwar*—کندن *kandan,* "to dig," کن *kan.*

Exceptions.—بردن "to bring," "to relate," آوردن or آر *āwar* or *ār*—بردن "to bear," بر *bar*—کردن "to do," "to make," کن *kan*—مردن "to die," سپردن "to vex," makes افشردن "to press," آزار—آزردن "to vex," میر—

شُمار— "to entrust" or "consign," شُمردن—سِپار "to reckon," كَند.—"to rot," كندن—فْرُكَنْد "to dig" (a canal), فْرُكَنْدن

IV. Infinitives in تن *tan*, preceded by خ *kh*, reject تن, and change خ into ز for the root; as, اندَاخْتَن *andākhtan*, "to throw," انداز *andāz*.

Exceptions.—فروخْتَن—شِناس "to know," شِناخْتَن "to sell," آخْتَن "to draw" (a sword), makes آخ—"to break," "to split," گُسِل—گُسِيخْتَن; and دوخْتَن—دوش "to milk," سُخْتَن—"to weigh," سَنْج.

V. Infinitives in تن, preceded by س *s*, reject both the تن and س for the root; as, زِيسْتَن *zīstan*, "to live," زِي *zī*. or جُو—جُسْتَن "to seek," بَند—بِتْسْن "to bind," خواسْتَن "to wish," خِيز—"to rise," to "go away," جوی—خاسْتَن "to leap," خواه—پِيوسْتَن "to mix," "to join," makes پِيوند—جَسْتَن جِه—رُسْتَن "to grow," رُه—رُسْتَن "to escape," رِيسْتَن—رُوي "to spin," شكسْتَن—شِكَن "to break," شُسْتَن—شوی "to wash," گُسِل—گُسِسْتَن—"to break" or "split," كاهِ—"to diminish," كاسْتَن نِشِسْتَن—نِشان "to cause to sit," "to place," نِشاسْتَن "to sit down," نِشِين

VI. Infinitives in تن, preceded by ش *sh*, reject تن, and change ش into ر; as, داشْتَن *dāshtan*, "to have," دار *dār*.

Exceptions.—نَوِيس—نوِشْتَن "to write," گُرد—گَشْتَن "to become," آغاشْتَن—هِشْن or هِل "to quit," هِشْتَن—افراشْتَن "to exalt," آغوش—آغوشْتَن "to embrace," آغاش—كُشْتَن—كار "to sow a field," رِيس—رِشْتَن "to spin," كُشْتَن—افراز كُش.—"to slay,"

VII. Infinitives in تن, preceded by ف *f,* generally reject تن, and change ف into ب *b,* as, تافتن. "to shine," "twist," &c. تاب; but in some verbs the ف remains unchanged in the root, as, بافتن "to weave," باف.

Exceptions.—خفتن "to sleep," makes خسپ — رفتن "to go," گو " to say," گفتن — گیر "to take," "to seize," گرفتن — رو سفت "to bore," سفتن — پذیر "to accept," پذیرفتن — گوی or شنو " to expand as a flower," شنفتن—شکف " to hear," شکفتن — کاو "to dig," کافتن. Sometimes the short vowel preceding the termination of the Infinitive is lengthened in the root; as, رفتن " to sweep," روب.

45. Let the student carefully commit to memory the preceding rules, together with their exceptions; after which he will have no difficulty in conjugating every Persian Verb in existence. Let it be remembered, at the same time, that there is not, strictly speaking, any *Irregular Verb* in this language. For instance, the verbs دیدن بین, " to see," and کردن کن, " to do," are no more irregular than the corresponding Latin Verbs, *video, vidi, visum;* and *facio, feci, factum;* for in both languages the various tenses &c. are formed from their respective sources or principal parts, according to general rules. It may be observed, also, that most of the roots given as exceptions to the preceding rules have regular Infinitives in *īdan* still in use; in fact, we ought in strictness to consider the Infinitives as anomalous, and the roots regular. Thus, هشتن " to quit," "dismiss," has for its root هل or هش, which really come from the

regular Infinitives هِلیدن and هِشِیدن, still in use; whilst هِشتَن itself is a very natural contraction of هِشِیدن into هِشدن, and ultimately هِشتَن.

a. As a specimen of an anomalous Verb (if we may so call it), we here subjoin the verb زدن *zadan,* "to strike," root زن *zan,* which, to save room, we shall give in the Roman character.[*]

1st.—TENSES OF THE ROOT.

	SINGULAR.			PLURAL.		
Aorist	zan-am	-ī	-ad	-em	-ed	-and
Present	mī-zan-am	-ī	-ad	-em	-ed	-and
Simple Future,	bi-zan-am	-ī	-ad	-em	-ed	-and
Imperative . .	zan-am	zan	zan-ad	-em	-ed	-and

Agent and Participle Active, { zananda, "the striker," zanān, "striking."

2d.—TENSES OF THE INFINITIVE.

Preterite	zadam	zadī	zad	zad-em	-ed	-and
Imperfect .	mī-zadam	—	—	—	—	—
Past Potential .	zadam-e	zadī	zad-e	zad-em-e	-ed-e	-and-e
Comp. Future .	khwāham zad,	khwāhī zad,	khwāhad zad, &c.			
Pret. Participle,	zada, "stricken," "struck," or "having struck."					
Perfect	zada-am	-ī	-ast	-em	-ed	-and
Pluperfect . . .	zada-būdam	būdī	būd	būd-em	-ed	-and
Future Perfect .	zada-bāsh-am	-ī	-ad	-em	-ed	-and

---

[*] It will be a useful exercise for the student to write out this Verb at full length in the Persian character; to which he may add, *dīdan,* "to see," root *bīn; dādan,* "to give;" *būdan,* "to be;" *kardan,* "to do;" and *guftan,* "to speak;" all of which have, with their respective roots, already occurred in § 44.

b. To this we may add another useful Verb of frequent occurrence, شدن *shudan*, "to be," "to go," "to become," root شو *shav.*

Aorist	*shav-am*	-*ī*	-*ad*	-*em*	-*ed*	-*and*
Present	*mī-shav-am*	—	—	—	—	—
Simple Future .	*bi-shav-am*	—	—	—	—	—
Imperative . . .	*shav-am*	*shav*	*shad-ad*	—	—	—
Agent and Part.	*shav-anda* and *shav-ān,* "being," or "becoming."
Preterite	*shud-am*	*shud-ī*	*shud,* &c.
Imperfect . . .	*mī-shud-am,* &c.
Past Potential .	*shudam-e*	*shud-ī*	*shud-e,* &c.
Comp. Future .	*khwāham shud, khwāhī shud,* &c.
Pret. Participle,	*shuda,* "been," or "become."
Perfect	*shuda-am, shuda-ī, shuda-ast,* &c.
Pluperfect. . .	*shuda-būdam, shuda-būdī, shuda-būd,* &c.
Future Perfect,	*shuda-bāsham, shuda-bāshī, shuda-bāshad,* &c.

PASSIVE VOICE.

46. The Passive Voice is regularly formed by prefixing the Preterite Participle to the various Tenses of the Verb شدن, which we have just exemplified. Thus, the Passive of the verb زدن is formed as follows:

PRESENT.

SINGULAR.	PLURAL.
زده شوم "I may be struck."	زده شويم "We may be struck."
زده شوي "Thou mayest be struck."	زده شويد "You may be struck."
زده شود "He may be struck."	زده شوند "They may be struck."

PRETERITE.

SINGULAR.	PLURAL.
زده شدم "I was struck."	زده شديم "We were struck."
زده شدي "Thou wast struck."	زده شديد "You were struck."
زده شد "He was struck."	زده شدند "They were struck."

It would be superfluous to add more of the Passive Voice, in the formation of which the Persian very much resembles our own language.

50 ON THE VERB.

46½. It may be proper here to observe, that, according
to the authority of Dr. Lumsden, the sound of the letter
ي in the terminations يم— and يد— (1st and 2d persons
plur.) of all the Tenses of Persian Verbs, is what is called
majhūl; that is, having the sound of *ea* in *bear* (vide § 15, *a*).
The final ي added to the Preterite in forming the Potential, or Continuative Past Time, is *majhūl* in the 1st and 3d
persons singular, and in the three persons plural. In all the
Tenses, the final ي (or *hamza* when substituted), in the 2d
pers. sing., is *ma'rūf*.

a. Mīrzā Ibrāhīm tells us, in his Persian Grammar, that the term
majhūl, or "unknown," was first applied to the long vowels *e* and *o*
by the Indian Grammarians! This is too ridiculous to require refutation. The term was applied by the Arabs, as we know from
Surūrī's Analysis of Sa'dī's Gulistān.

b. I have in the present work, as a general rule, distinguished the
ma'rūf from the *majhūl* sounds, for the following reasons:—1st, The
distinction is strictly observed in India to this day, both in speaking
and reading the Persian language; and also in such Persian words
as are introduced into Hindūstānī, which may amount to one quarter
of the vocables of the latter tongue. 2dly, In conformity with the
opinion of Dr. Lumsden, who thus speaks decisively on the subject,
Pers. Gram. vol. i. p. 72: "I shall take this opportunity of inserting
an observation, which I omitted in its proper place; namely, that the
unlearned part of the inhabitants of Īrān (Persia) often deny the
existence, in the Persian language, of the sound represented by *wāo*
and *yā, majhūl*, which they invariably pronounce like *wāo* and *yā,
ma'rūf*. The distinction, however, is recognised in every Lexicon, and
will not be controverted by a well-educated Persian. It ought therefore to be carefully retained by those who are desirous of acquiring
an accurate and classical pronunciation." 3dly, We have the authority of analogy on our side for the use of the *majhūl* sounds in a great
many words, such as سوگ *sog*, " grief," Sanskrit, *shoka;* دوش *dosh*,
" the shoulder," Sansk. *dosa;* میغ *megh*, "a cloud," Sansk. *megha;*

ميش *mesh*, "a sheep," Sansk. *mesha*, &c. Lastly, without this distinction a great many words will be confounded with one another; thus, *sher*, "a lion," and *shīr*, "milk," Sansk. *kshīra*, will be pronounced alike; so, *bādshāhe*, "a certain king," will be confounded with *bādshāhī*, "sovereignty," or, as an Adjective, "royal:" the expression *rased*, "you may arrive," will be the same as *rasīd*, "he arrived." We would therefore, in conclusion, advise the student, if destined for India, to be careful in observing the distinction between the و and ي *majhūl* and *ma'rūf*. If he merely studies the language as an amateur, for the sake of perusing its numerous literary works, he may follow his own inclination; and, if he is likely to visit Persia, then let the *majhūl* sounds be discarded altogether, should he find reason to believe that such is really the custom of the country.

CAUSAL VERBS.

47. These are formed, as already stated, by adding the termination انيدن‌ـ *ānīdan*, or, contracted, اندن‌ـ *āndan*, to the root of the Primitive Verb; thus, جستن *jastan*, "to leap," root جه *jah*; from which comes جهانيدن *jah-ānīdan*, or جهاندن *jahāndan*, "to cause to leap." All Causal Verbs form their roots according to Rules I. and III.

48. The verbal terminations of the Perfect Tense (§ 42), are frequently affixed to Substantives, Adjectives, and Participles, to denote simple affirmation or assertion. In such cases, the initial *alif* of the auxiliary is omitted, and the vowel which it forms becomes united with the last consonant of the word preceding; thus,

SINGULAR.	PLURAL.
من شاگردم "I am a scholar."	ما شاگردانيم "We are scholars."
تو چاكري "Thou art a servant."	شما چاكرانيد "You are servants."
او عاقلست "He is sensible."	ايشان دزدانند "They are thieves."

a. If the preceding word ends in the weak ه, the ا is retained in the verbal terminations; as, تُو دِيوانَه اِي "I am a slave;" بِنْدَه اَم "Thou art mad;" فِرِشْتَه اَسْت "He (she *or* it) is an angel." or تُو دِيوانَه "If the preceding word ends in the vowels ا or و, the letter ي is inserted, to avoid a hiatus between these and the verbal terminations; as, بِينايِم "I am seeing;" دانائِي "Thou art wise;" خوبرووَسْت and (contracted) خوبرويِسْت "He *or* she is fair-faced."

b. Somewhat akin to the preceding auxiliary is another fragment of a Verb, denoting "to be," "to exist," used under the form of a Preterite, but with the sense of a Present Tense; as,

SINGULAR.		PLURAL.	
هَسْتَم	"I am *or* exist."	هَسْتِيم	"We are *or* exist."
هَسْتِي	"Thou art *or* existest."	هَسْتِيد	"You are *or* exist."
هَسْت	"He is *or* exists."	هَسْتَنْد	"They are *or* exist."

c. It is highly probable that there was a simpler form of this Verb once in use, a form which pervades almost all the languages of the Indo-European family, viz.—

اَسْتَم	"I am *or* exist."	اَسْتِيم	"We are."
اَسْتِي	"Thou art."	اَسْتِيد	"You are."
اَسْت	"He, &c., is."	اَسْتَنْد	"They are."

By adding this last form of the auxiliary to the secondary basis of any Verb, there results a variation of the Preter-Perfect Tense, chiefly used by Poets; thus, شُنِيدَسْتَم "I have heard;" دِيدَسْتِي "Thou hast seen;" پُرسِيدَسْت "He has asked." This form of the Preter-Perfect is frequently used in poetry, simply because it may happen to suit the Poet's metre. It does not seem to differ in signification from the ordinary form given in § 42.

OF NEGATIVE AND PROHIBITIVE VERBS.

49. A Verb is rendered negative by prefixing the Particle نَه (or نِ) *na,* "not;" as نَه رِسِيد or نَرِسِيد "He did not

arrive." With the Imperative, the Particle مه (or مـ) *ma* is employed in like manner, to express prohibition; as, مه پُرس or مپُرس "Ask not;" so, مباد or مبادا "Let it not be," frequently used in the sense of "God forbid!"

a. When the Particles بِ, نَ, or مـ are prefixed to a Verb beginning with ا, not marked by the symbol *madda* — (§ 19), the letter ي is inserted, to prevent a hiatus; the ا is then omitted, and its vowel transferred to the inserted ي; thus, انداخت *andākht*, "He threw;" نینداخت *nayandākht*, "He did not throw:" Aorist, أفتم *uftam*, "I may fall;" Future, بیفتم *biyuftam*, "I shall fall;" انگار "consider;" مینگار "consider not." If the Verb begins with آ, the ا remains, but the *madda* — is rejected; thus, آرد "He may bring;" بیارد "He will bring;" آر "Bring thou;" میار "Do not bring;" but this, in reality, is in strict conformity with the general rule; for آ is equivalent to اَر: hence, in prefixing the particles along with the letter ي, the first ا is rejected, as we stated at the outset. Finally, the negative نَ, in the older Poets, frequently unites with the following آ, without the intervention of the ي; as, نامد, for نیامد, "He came not."

b. On a similar principle the initial ا is omitted in the Pronouns او "he, she, *or* it," این "this," and آن (properly اَن) "that," when they are closely connected with the preceding word; as, برین "on this," instead of براین; so, دران "in that," for درآن. I have reason to believe that this principle is of a very extensive application; but the discussion to which it would lead would be here out of place.

b. The old substantive Verb استم is rendered negative by substituting نی for the initial *alif*—

SINGULAR.		PLURAL.	
نیستم	"I am not."	نیستیم	"We are not."
نیستی	"Thou art not."	نیستید	"You are not."
نیست	"He, &c., is not."	نیستند	"They are not."

c. To denote simple negation, the verbal terminations of the Perfect are subjoined to the Particle نَ, in the following manner—

نِيَم "I am not."	نَّيِم "We are not."
نِهٖ or دِي "Thou art not."	نَّيِد "You are not."
نِيسْت "He, &c., is not."	نِيِند "They are not."

SECTION IV.

ON THE INDECLINABLE PARTS OF SPEECH.—CARDINAL NUMBERS.—DERIVATION AND COMPOSITION OF WORDS.

ADVERBS.

50. The Persian language offers no peculiarity on the score of Adverbs, except its extreme simplicity: hence it would be superfluous to occupy our pages with a dry list of words, which more properly belong to the Vocabulary. We may briefly mention, that, in this language, Adverbs are formed, or rather adopted, as follows:

a. 1st, *Substantives* with or without a Preposition; as, گاهِي "once," or "any time;" نام "by name;" شب و روز "night and day;" به خُوبِي "perfectly;" در نِهان "secretly." 2dly, Adjectives without undergoing any change; as, خُوب "well;" سَخْت "severely," &c. In fact, all Adjectives may be used adverbially, if necessary, as is frequently the case in German, and sometimes in English; thus, "the eagle soars high;" "the fish swims deep." 3dly, Adjective or Interrogative Pronouns with Substantives; as, اِيْنجا "here," آنْجا "there;" كُجا "where?" كُدام طرف "whither?" چِگُونه "how?" &c. These again may be preceded by a Preposition; as, از اِيْنجا "hence;" در آنْجا "there." Lastly, there are some Arabic Nouns in the Accusative

Case used adverbially in Persian; as, حالاً "presently;" قصْداً "purposely."

b. The following is a useful list of Adverbs, in addition to those already mentioned:

1st, *Of Place.*—از آنجا "thence;" اینسُو "hither;" آنسُو "thither; از کُجا "whence; اندرون ,دُرُون, "within;" بیرُون ,بِرُون "without," هر کُجا کِه, "under, beneath;" بالا "over, upon, above;" فرو ,فرود, "wheresoever;" هیچ جا "somewhere;" هیچ جا نه "nowhere."

2nd, *Of Time.*—شام گاه "in the evening;" سَحرگاه ,بامْداد, "in the morning;" پیش "before;" دِي "yesterday;" فَرْدا "to-morrow;" همْاندم "instantly;" آنگاه "then;" اکنُون "now;" پس "after;" بعْد از آن "afterward;" هنوز "yet;" هرگِز نه "never;" هرگِز "ever;" همیشه "always."

3rd, *Of Number.*—باري ,یکْبار, "once;" دیگربار "another time;" سِهبار "thrice," &c.; and so through دوبار "twice;" باز "again;" all the numbers, adding the termination بار *bār*, "time;" چنْد بار "so often;" چنْدان بار "sometimes;" گاهي or گاهگاه "many times;" کم بار "often;" بارها "many times," بِسیار بار "very often;" نیز "also." "seldom;"

4th, *Of Interrogation.*—کو "where?" چِرا "why?" چُون "how?" کي "how? or when?" چنْد "how many?"

PREPOSITIONS.

51. The simple Prepositions in this language are very few, probably not more than seven or eight in number. These are, از (in poetry frequently contracted into زِ) "from," "by;" با "with" (in company with); بر and ابر "on," "upon;" به or بِ "in," "by," "to;" بي "without" (deprived of); تا "up to," "as far as;" جُز "except," "besides;" در "in." In their application they are placed before the simple or nominative forms both of Nouns and Pronouns; as,

در شهر "in the city ;" بر من "on me ;" با تُو "with thee ;"
جُز ایشان " except them."

a. The rest of the Prepositions are, strictly speaking, Substantives or Adjectives, having one of the simple Particles above mentioned expressed or understood. Such of them as are Substantives require the *iẓāfat*, or sign of the Genitive Case, between them and the Noun which they govern ; as, زیر زمین " under the ground ;" بالاٸي درخَّت " above the tree" (*i.e.* on the top of the tree); به نزدیك شهر " near the city," literally, " to, or in the vicinity of the city." Some of them may be viewed as Adjectives denoting comparison ; as, پیش از من (for پیشتر از من) "before me ;" پس از آن " after that." All these compound Prepositions may of course be used adverbially when occasion requires, as is the case in English ; thus, بیرُون رفَت " he went out ;" پیش آمد " he came forward ;" پس ماند " he remained behind."

b. LIST OF USEFUL PREPOSITIONS.—بجاي *bajāe*, " instead of ;" برابر *barābar*, " opposite," or " equal to ;" براي *barāe*, " on account of ;" بعد از *ba'd az*, " after ;" بغَیر *baghair*, " except ;" در میان *dar mīyān*, " between ;" سواي *siwā,e*, " except," " besides ;" سوي *sū,e*, " towards ;" بیرُون *berūn*, " without ;" اندرُون *andarūn*, " within ;" زبر *zabar*, " above ;" زیر *zer*, " beneath."

CONJUNCTIONS.

52. Primitive Conjunctions, like the simple Prepositions, are not numerous. The following are of frequent occurrence :—اگر گر " if ;" بلكه " but," " on the contrary ;" تا " whilst," " until ;" چُون, چُو " when," " as ;" كه, چه " that," " for," " as ;" لیكن or امّا " but ;" نیز " also ;" وَ " and" (pronounced *wa*, and sometimes *o*); هم " even," " also ;" یا " or," " either."

a. The rule for pronouncing the *wāw-i-'aṭf,* or conjunctive و *wāw* seems to be nearly as follows:—When it connects sentences, or clauses of a sentence, it is pronounced *wa*; thus, آمد و رفت *āmad wa raft*, "he came, and he went." Again, when it merely unites words in the formation of a phrase, it is sounded *o*; as, آمد و رفت *āmad-o-raft*, "coming and going," "a thoroughfare;" شب و روز *shab-o-roz*, "night and day," "perpetually."

b. There are also, as might be expected, many compound expressions employed in this language as Conjunctions; as, حال آن که "whereas," "inasmuch as;" پیش ازانکه "before that" (*antequam*); so, بعد ازانکه "after that" (*posteaquam*); هر چند که or هر چند "notwithstanding;" گرچه or اگرچه "although;" بنابرین "therefore."

INTERJECTIONS.

53. In Persian, as in other languages, Interjections consist partly of adventitious sounds denoting the passions and emotions of the speaker; as, آه "ah!" اَی "O!" &c. ; and partly of Substantives expressive of pain or pleasure, used elliptically, or in the Vocative Case; as, افسوس "Alas!" دریغا or دریغ "Oh, misery!" To say more about this part of speech (if it may be correct to call it so) would be uselessly encroaching on the department of the Vocabulary or Dictionary.

NUMERALS.

54. In the following Table we shall give the leading Cardinal Numbers, together with the corresponding Arabian and European figures. It is needless to say that the whole system is extremely simple, and very similar to what we have in English.

CARDINAL NUMBERS.

یك	١	1	بیسْتُ و دُو	٢٢	22
دُو	٢	2	سی	٣٠	30
سه	٣	3	چهِل	۴٠	40
چهار	۴	4	پنجاه	۵٠	50
پنج	۵	5	شصت	٦٠	60
شش	٦	6	هفتاد	٧٠	70
هفت	٧	7	هشتاد	٨٠	80
هشت	٨	8	نُود	٩٠	90
نه	٩	9	صد	١٠٠	100
ده	١٠	10	صد و یك	١٠١	101
یازده	١١	11	دُوصد	٢٠٠	200
دوازده	١٢	12	سِصد	٣٠٠	300
سیزده	١٣	13	چهارصد	۴٠٠	400
چهارده	١۴	14	پانصد	۵٠٠	500
پانزده	١۵	15	ششصد	٦٠٠	600
شانزده	١٦	16	هفتصد	٧٠٠	700
هفده	١٧	17	هشتصد	٨٠٠	800
هشده	١٨	18	نهصد	٩٠٠	900
نوزده	١٩	19	هزار	١٠٠٠	1000
بیست	٢٠	20	ده هزار	١٠٠٠٠	10,000
بیسْتُ و یك	٢١	21	لك	١٠٠٠٠٠	100,000

a. The formation of the Ordinal Numbers will be treated of under the head of Derivative Adjectives. All the other numbers occurring between the *tens* are formed simply by adding the smaller number to the *decade*, by means of the Conjunction و *o*; thus, شصّت و شش "sixty and six," and so for all others.

b. The above figures or numeric cyphers, now used by the Arabs and Persians, are read like ours, from left to right; thus, the year of our æra 1861 is ١٨٦١; so the corresponding year of the Hijra 1278 is ١٢٧٨. It is generally admitted, even by the Arabs themselves, that the decimal scale of notation was invented in India, and thence brought to Arabia. By the Arabs it was introduced into Europe through Spain or Sicily; and hence the system goes under the name of the Arabian Notation. At first sight it would appear to be at variance with the Arabian mode of reading (from right to left); but this is not really the case, as the Arabs do read the numbers from right to left. Thus, instead of saying, "In the year of the Hijra (١٢٧٨) One thousand two hundred and seventy-eight," the Arabs say, "In the year of the Hijra, Eight and seventy and two hundred and one thousand," or "Eight and seventy and two hundred after the thousand."

c. The Musalmāns reckon by lunar time in all their transactions, commencing from the day of the *Hijra*, or "Flight," viz. that on which Muḥammad departed or fled from Mecca to Medina; which, according to the best accounts, took place on Friday, the 16th of July (18th, new style), A.D. 622. Their year consists of 12 lunations, amounting to 354 days and 9 hours, very nearly: hence their New-year's Day will happen every year about eleven days earlier that in the preceding year. It follows, then, that there must be some difficulty in finding the exact day of the Christian æra which corresponds to any given day and year of the Hijra.

d. The following rule will suffice for finding the number of solar or Christian years elapsed *since* any given Musalmān date :—"Subtract the given year of the Hijra from the current year of the same, and from the remainder deduct *three per cent.;* then you will have the number of solar or Christian years elapsed." Thus, suppose we see a manuscript written A. H. 681, and wish to know its real age in Christian years, we subtract, in the first place, the number 681 from the current year of the Hijra, say 1256, and there remains 575: from this last we deduct three per cent., or 17, and there remains 558, which at that period is the real·age of the manuscript in solar years.

e. If the object, however, be to find the precise Christian date corre_ sponding to any given year of the Hijra, apply the following rule :—

From the given number of Musalmān years, deduct *three per cent.*, and to the remainder add the number 621·54: the sum is the period of the Christian æra at which the given current Musalmān year ends. For example, we mentioned that the death of the poet Ahlī happened A. H. 942: from this number deduct three per cent., or 28·26, and the remainder is 913·74. To this last add 621·54, and the sum = 1535·28, which shews that the Musalmān year 942 ended in the spring of 1536. This very simple rule is founded on the fact that 100 lunar years are very nearly equal to 97 solar years, there being only about eight days of excess in the former period; hence to the result found, as just stated, it will be requisite to add 8 days, as a correction, for every century elapsed of the Hijra. A more accurate proportion would be 101 lunar to 98 solar years, but this would lead to a less convenient rule for practical use.

f. When great accuracy is required, and when the year, month, and day of the Muhammadan æra are given, the precise period of the Christian æra may be found as follows :—*Rule.* Express the Musalmān date in years and decimals of a year; multiply by ·970225: to the product add 621·54, and the sum will be the *precise* period of the Christian æra. This rule is exact to a day, and if in the Musalmān date the day of the week be given, as is often the case, the *very day* is easily determined.

55. The Muhammadan or lunar months are made to consist of 30 and 29 days alternately; but in a period of thirty years, it is found necessary to intercalate the last month eleven times, so as to be reckoned 30 days instead of 29. The months retain their Arabic names in all Muhammadan countries, and they are the following :—

NAME.	DAYS.	NAME.	DAYS.	NAME.	DAYS.
مُحَرّم	30	جمادِيُّ آلاول	30	رمضان	30
صفر	29	جمادِيُ آلثاني	29	شَوّال	29
رِبيعُ آلاول	30	رجب	30	ذِي القَعْده	30
رِبيعُ آلثاني	29	شعبان	29	ذِي آلحِجه	29

a. The following are the names of the days of the week, both Persian and Arabian.

	PERSIAN.		ARABIAN.	
Sunday.	يكشنبه	*yak-shamba.*	يَوْمُ ٱلاحد	*yaumu-l-ahd.*
Monday.	دو شنبه	*dū-shamba.*	يوم ٱلاثنين	*yaumu-l-asnain.*
Tuesday.	سه شنبه	*si-shamba.*	يوم ٱلثلاثاء	*yaumu-l-salāsa.*
Wednesday.	چهار شنبه	*chahār shamba.*	يوم ٱلاربعا	*yaumu-l-arba'ā.*
Thursday.	پنجشنبه	*panj-shamba.*	يوم لخميس	*yaumu-l-khamis.*
Friday.	آدينه	*ādīna.*	يوم الجمعه	*yaumu-l-jum'a.*
Saturday.	شنبه	*shamba.*	يوم السبت	*yaumu-l-sabat.*

DERIVATION OF WORDS.

56. In Persian, the derivation of one word from another is effected by means of certain terminations, in a mannei similar to that which prevails in most of the European languages. The words so derived are chiefly Substantives and Adjectives, together with a few Verbs and Adverbs, all of which we shall notice in their order.

1st.——OF SUBSTANTIVES.

a. Substantives denoting an agent or performer are derived from other Substantives or Adjectives, by adding the terminations بان or وان, كار, گار or گر; as, from در "a door," درْبان or درْوان " a door-keeper;" from بد "evil," بدكار " evil-doer;" so, from خِدمت "service," خِدمتگار "a servant or attendant;" from زر "gold," زرگر " a gold-smith, or worker in gold." In modern Persian, the terminations حِي and چِي (from the Turkish) are sometimes met with; as, from بندُوق "a musket," بندُوقچِي " a musketeer." After a soft letter, the termination جِي is added; as, بُوستانجي "a gardener," from بُوستان "a garden or orchard."

b. Names relating to the place of any thing are formed by adding لاخ; as, شِيرِستان "a place abounding with lions," from شِير "a lion;" and شَن, زار, دان, بار, ستان, ستان "a candlestick," from شَمع "a candle or lamp;" گُلشَن, or گُلزار, "a rose-bed," from گُل "a rose or flower;" so, from سَنگ "a stone," سَنگلاخ "a place abounding with stones." A few are formed by adding سار and بار; as, كُوهسار "a hilly country;" رُودبار "the channel of a stream," from كُوه and رُود.

c. Diminutives are formed by adding ك for names of animals; زَه (sometimes يزَه) for inanimate beings; and چه, or يچه, applicable to any Nouns; thus, مَردك "a little man," from مَرد "a man;" دانزَه "a small grain," from دانه "a grain;" دَريچه "a little door or window," from دَر "a door." By adding the ه imperceptible to the diminutive in *ak*, it denotes littleness in a disparaging sense; as, مَردكه "a sneaking or contemptible mannikin."

d. An Abstract Noun may be formed from any Adjective, simple or compound, by the addition of ي *ma'rūf*; as, نِيكِي "goodness," from نِيك "good;" جهانداري "the possessing of the world," "royalty," from جهاندار "world-possessing," an epithet applied to monarchs. By adding ي to Appellative Nouns an Abstract will be formed, denoting the state or profession indicated by the Noun; as, بادشاهِي "sovereignty," from بادشاه "a king;" سوداگري "traffic;" from سوداگر "a merchant." If the primitive word should end in the weak ه, the ه is suppressed, and the letter گ inserted before adding the termination ي; as, آزُرده "sad," آزُردگي "sadness;" so, بَنده "slave," بَندگي "slavery." A few Abstracts are formed by adding ا; as, گَرما "heat," from گَرم "hot."

e. Verbal Nouns are formed by changing the final syllable ن‍ـَ *an* of the Infinitive into ‍ـَار; as, دیدن "to see," دیدار "seeing," "a sight." This termination occasionally gives the word the sense of *agent*; as, خریدار "a purchaser," فروختار "a seller." The Infinitive itself is frequently used as a general Verbal Noun, like our words in *ing*; as, آمدنِ رستم "the coming of Rustam." In a few phrases the final ن‍ـ of the Infinitive is rejected; as, آمد و شُد "coming and going;" so, خرید و فروخت "buying and selling," "traffic." Another useful class of Verbal Nouns, denoting fitness, is formed from the Infinitive by adding ی‍ـ *ma'rūf*; as, کردنی "duty," "that which is fit or necessary to be done;" so, خوردنی "any thing eatable:" these may, of course, be also viewed as Adjectives, according to the context.

f. Another class of Verbal Nouns is formed from the root by adding ی‍ـ or ش‍ـ; as, گوی "speaking," "conversation," from گو, the root of گفتن "to speak;" so, آفرینش "creation," from آفرین, the root of آفریدن "to create." The Noun denoting the Agent of a Verb is formed (as already stated, page 41) by adding the termination ‍ـَنده to the root; as, آفریننده "the Creator:" and if the root ends with the long vowels *ā* or *ō*, the letter ی is inserted between it and the termination; as, گوینده "the speaker."

g. Sometimes the root itself is used as a Verbal Noun; thus, رنج "grief," from رنجیدن "to grieve," or "be grieved;" so, سوز "ardour," or "burning," from سوختن "to burn." A few Nouns may be formed from the root by adding ‍ـَاک, ‍ـَان (peculiar to Verbs in ‍ـُودن) or ه imperceptible; thus, سوزاک "inflammation," from سوز, the root of سوختن; فرمان "a command," from فرمودن; لرزه "trembling," from لرزیدن "to tremble."

2nd.—OF ADJECTIVES.

h. Adjectives denoting possession, &c. are formed by adding to Nouns the terminations ﻳﻦ‎ or ﻭﺭ‎, and ﺳﺎﺭ, ﻧﺎﻙ, ﻣﻨﺪ, ﮔﻴﻦ, ﻭﺍﺭ, ﻭﺭ‎ ﺍ‎, as, from the root ﺩﺍﻥ‎ "know," ﺩﺍﻧﺎ‎ "learned;" ﺷﺮﻣﺴﺎﺭ‎ "bashful," from ﺷﺮﻡ‎ "shame;" ﻏﻤﮕﻴﻦ‎ "sorrowful," from ﻏﻢ‎ "sorrow;" ﺩﻭﻟﺘﻤﻨﺪ‎ "wealthy;" ﻫﻮﻟﻨﺎﻙ‎ "frightful;" ﺍﻣﻴﺪﻭﺍﺭ‎ "hopeful," from ﺍﻣﻴﺪ‎ "hope;" ﺟﺎﻧﻮﺭ‎ "possessed of life," "an animal," from ﺟﺎﻥ‎ "life," "soul;" ﺭﻧﺠﻮﺭ‎ "sorrowful," from ﺭﻧﺞ‎ "sorrow;" ﺯﺭﻳﻦ‎ "golden," or "made of gold," from ﺯﺭ‎ "gold."

i. The terminations ﺁﺳﺎ, ﺩﻳﺲ‎ or ﺩﺱ, ﺳﺎ, ﺳﺎﺭ‎, and ﻭﺵ‎, added to Nouns, form Adjectives denoting similitude; ﻓﺎﻡ‎ (rarely ﭘﺎﻡ‎ and ﻭﺍﻡ‎) and ﮔﻮﻥ‎ denote resemblance in colour; as, ﻣﺸﻚ‌ﺁﺳﺎ‎ "like musk;" ﻣﻬﻮﺵ‎ "like the sun;" ﺧﺎﻛﺴﺎﺭ‎ "like dust," "humble;" ﺧﻮﺭﺩﻳﺲ‎ "like the moon;" ﻟﻌﻞ‌ﻓﺎﻡ‎ "ruby-coloured;" ﻻﻟﻪﮔﻮﻥ‎ "of the colour of the tulip."

k. A large class of Adjectives, which may be termed gentile, patronymic, or relative, is formed from Substantives, by adding the termination ﻱ‎; thus, from ﺍﻳﺮﺍﻥ‎ "Persia," ﺍﻳﺮﺍﻧﻲ‎ "Persian;" from ﻫﻨﺪ‎ "India," ﻫﻨﺪﻱ‎ "Indian;" from the city ﺷﻴﺮﺍﺯ‎ comes ﺷﻴﺮﺍﺯﻱ‎ "of, or belonging to Shīrāz;" so, from the Substantives ﺷﻬﺮ‎ "a city," ﺟﻨﮕﻞ‎ "a forest," ﺑﺤﺮ‎ "the sea," are formed the Adjectives ﺷﻬﺮﻱ, ﺑﺤﺮﻱ, ﺟﻨﮕﻠﻲ‎. This termination is of extensive use in the formation of both Substantives and Adjectives.

l. The terminations ﺍﻧﻪ‎ and (sometimes) ﻭﺍﺭ‎ added to Nouns, form Adjectives, denoting general or natural resemblance: hence *fitness* or *worthiness*, of the original Noun; as, ﻣﺮﺩﺍﻧﻪ‎ "manful," "worthy of a man;" ﺩﻳﻮﺍﻧﻪ‎ "demoniac," "worthy of a (ﺩﻳﻮ‎) demon;" ﺷﺎﻫﻮﺍﺭ‎ "princely, or fit for a prince." We have mentioned already (§ 50, *a.*) that Adjectives are, when needed, used Adverbially; hence derivatives of this form are often employed as Adverbs.

m. By adding the termination ﻡ‎ to the cardinal numbers, we form the corresponding ordinal; thus, ﻫﻔﺘﻢ‎ "the seventh," from ﻫﻔﺖ‎

"seven." When more words than one are required to express the ordinal number, the ــُم is added to the last only; as, بیست و هفتُم "the twenty-seventh." The word expressing the first of the ordinals, نخستین, is an exception: the Arabic word اوّل is also frequently used; as, بابِ اوّل "Book or Section the First;" but these words are not used, except for the *first* only. In the case of a number expressed by two or more numerals, of which the last is unity, the ordinal is formed by adding ــُم to the یك; as, بیست و یکُم "the twenty-first." The ordinals *second* and *third* may be سوم, دوم or سیم, دویم; the rest follow the rule.

n. A numeral followed by a Substantive, particularly those expressive of time, and a few others, will form a Compound Adjective denoting the same, by adding the ه imperceptible; thus, یك روز "one day," یك روزه "of one day's duration;" so, یکساله "one year old," مردِ سیساله "a man aged thirty years." In like manner, from دو دل "two hearts," comes the Adjective دودله or دُدله, "two-hearted," *i.e.* "wavering, or fickle."

<h3 align="center">3d.—OF VERBS.</h3>

o. The principal Derivative Verbs in Persian are those called Causal, already mentioned (§ 47). A few Verbs are derived from Arabic roots, by adding ـیدن; as, طلبیدن "to seek," or "send for;" فهمیدن "to understand;" from the Arabic roots طلب "seeking," and فهم "perception or understanding."

<h3 align="center">4th.—OF ADVERBS.</h3>

p. We have already stated that Adverbs in Persian have nothing peculiar in their formation, most Adjectives being used as Adverbs when occasion requires. This remark applies particularly to Adjectives in ـانه and وار, which, when they denote manner, as is often the case, may be considered as Adverbs; as, پیاده‌وار "in the manner of a pedestrian," or "pawn at chess;" عاقلانه "wisely;" دلیرانه "bravely."

K

COMPOUND WORDS.

57. The Persian language abounds with compound words, consisting principally of Substantives and Adjectives, in the formation of which it bears a considerable resemblance to the English and German. We might even say, that, in this respect, it equals or surpasses the Sanskrit and Greek; with this difference, however, that in Persian, the members of the compound are generally written separate, and being void of inflexions, they are not so conspicuous to the sight as they are in the ancient and classical languages of India and Ionia. We shall here endeavour to describe the mode of forming the more useful compounds of the language, in the same order as in the preceding paragraph on Derivative Words.

SUBSTANTIVES.

a. A numerous class of Compound Substantives is formed by the mere juxta-position of any two Nouns, in the reverse order of the Genitive Case, the sign of the *iẓāfat* being rejected; as, خانه باورچي "cook-house, or kitchen," from باورچي "cook," and خانه "a house." This is, in fact, equivalent to خانهٔ باورچي "the house of the cook," with the order of the words reversed; so, رزمگاه "the battle-field," from رزم "contest," and گاه "a place:" in like manner, جهان پناه "the asylum of the world, an epithet applied to an Eastern monarch, equivalent to our words "Her or His Majesty," from جهان "the world," and پناه "refuge;" so, روز نامه "a day-book," خرد نامه "the book of wisdom," &c. Compounds of this kind are extremely common in English and German; witness such words as London Bridge, Custom House, Thames Tunnel, and thousands besides.

b. There is a class of Verbal Nouns, not very numerous, consisting, 1st, of two contracted Infinitives, connected with the conjunction و; as, گفت و شنود "conversation," literally, "speaking and hearing;"

آمد و رفت "coming and going," "intercourse." 2ndly, A contracted Infinitive, with the corresponding root; as, جست و جو "searching;" گفت و گو "conversation." The conjunction و in such cases is occasionally omitted; as, گفت گو, آمد شد, the same as آمد و شد, &c.

c. There are a few compounds similar to the preceding, consisting of two Substantives, sometimes of the same, and sometimes of different signification; as, مرز و کشور or مرز و بوم "an empire or kingdom," literally, "boundary and region;" so, آب و هوا "climate," literally, "water and air;" نشو و نما "rearing or bringing up (a plant or animal)." In these, also, the conjunction و may be omitted; as, نشو نما, مرز بوم, &c.

d. An Infinitive or Verbal Noun, preceded by the Particle نا, is rendered negative; as, نا شنودن the "non-hearing." The difference between the use of the نا and نه is simply this, that نا corresponds with our prefixes *un, in,* or *non;* and نه with our *no* or *not:* in other words, نا *nā* is used only in composition, and نه *na* as the negative of a Verb.

e. A few Substantives are compounded of a numeral and another Substantive; as, چارپائي "a quadruped;" سه پهر "the afternoon," being the third *pahr* or watch of the day; so the days of the week, يك شنبه "Sunday," دو شنبه "Monday," سه شنبه "Tuesday," &c.

ADJECTIVES, OR EPITHETS.

f. In these the Persian language is particularly rich, every writer using them more or less, according to his own pleasure. A very numerous class of Epithets is formed by the union of two Substantives; as, لاله رُخ "having cheeks like the tulip;" پري رُوي "having the face of a fairy;" سنگ دل "having a heart like stone;" شكر لب "having lips (sweet) as sugar." It would be needless to extend the list; we may merely observe that the idea conveyed by compounds of this sort is, that the person to whom the epithet is applicable is possessed of the object expressed in the second member of the compound, in a degree equal to, or resembling, the first. In English we have many instances, in the more familiar style, of this kind of compound; as, " iron-hearted," " bull-headed," " lynx-eyed," &c.

g. Another numerous class, similar to the preceding, is formed by prefixing an Adjective to a Substantive; as, خُوب رُوئی " having a fair face;" پاک رأی " of pure intention;" تنگ دل " distressed in heart;" زرِین قلم " of a golden pen," an epithet applied to Mullā Muḥammad Ḥusain Kashmīrī,[*] the finest writer of the Ta'līḵ hand at the munificent Court of Akbar, and in all probability the finest that ever lived. The idea conveyed by these compounds is, that the person to whom they apply possesses the object expressed in the second member of the compound, in the state or manner indicated by the first. We have many such compounds in English, used in familiar conversation, and newspaper style, such as " clear-sighted," " long-headed," " sharp-witted," " hard-hearted," &c.

h. Perhaps the most numerous class of the Epithets is that composed of Verbal Roots joined to Substantives or Adjectives; as, عالم گیر " world-subduing ;" فتنه انگیز " strife-exciting;" جان آسا " giving rest to the soul ;" دل ستان " ravishing the heart ;" سبک رو " moving lightly." Most Grammarians consider the Verbal Roots in such compounds as contractions of the Present Participle in ان— or ا—. We do, indeed, sometimes find the real Participle in use ; as, دل آوران " intrepid," literally, " heart-bearing," (German, *herzhaft*); so, سرو روان " moving or waving like a cypress;" but the occurrence of such phrases is very rare, compared with those ending in the verbal root. The Greek language has numerous compounds of the same kind, in substance similar to the Persian, such as ἐργολάβος " one who undertakes a work,"

---

[*] It is impossible to imagine any thing more beautiful of its kind than the penmanship of Mullā Ḥussain. I happen to possess a manuscript of the Bustān of Sa'dī, written by him ; and assuredly the perusal of a page thereof makes one view all other *fine* manuscripts as downright deformity. It is but fair to observe, that *several* penmen have either received or assumed the epithet of *Zarīn-Ḵalam*; but there is but *one*, Mullā Ḥusain, worthy of the designation.

and ἱπποτρόφος "one who rears horses," where we have the Noun and Verbal Root in the simple state, or crude form, with the termination ος superadded; so that the agreement between the Greek and Persian compound is complete, it being borne in mind that the latter language has no termination to add. Hence there is no solid reason for calling the Verbal Roots, in Persian compounds, *Participles;* while, on the contrary, the use of the term is objectionable, as it misleads the student. Compound Epithets of a similar kind are frequently used by our best English Poets; such as, "the night-tripping fairy;" the cloud-compelling Jove;" "the temple-haunting martlet:" but though we use the Present Participle in such compounds, it by no means follows that other languages should do the same.

i. Another class of Epithets is compounded of a Substantive and a Past Participle; as, جهان‌دِیدَه "experienced," "one who has seen the world;" جنگ‌آزموده "one who has been tried in battle," *i e.* "trained to war;" so, غم‌خورده "one who has felt sorrow;" دام‌نهاده "one who has laid a snare;" مِحنَت‌کشِیده "one who has endured affliction."

k. There is an extensive class of Adjectives formed by prefixing the Particles با "with, or possessed of;" and بي "without, or deprived of," to Substantives; as, بامال "rich," "possessed of wealth;" بارامِش "cheerful, or joyous," an epithet applied to the planet Venus; so, بي‌دِل "heartless, or disconsolate;" بي‌انصاف "unjust;" بي‌نِیاز "without need," "He who is above all assistance," an epithet applied to the Almighty.

l. The Particles کم and هم, prefixed to Nouns and Verbal Roots, form a considerable class of Epithets. کم literally denotes "little;" but in composition it seems almost to convey the idea of "nothing, or negation;" as, کم‌زور "of little strength;" کم‌خِرد "of little sense," "stupid;" کم‌خُور "eating little," "abstemious;" کم‌یاب "improcurable." The Particle هم denotes "equality, or association," and, like the preceding, is compounded with Nouns or Verbal Roots. Its effect is the same as the Greek ἅμα, or the Latin *con;* as, هم‌راه "a fellow-traveller, or one who goes on the same road," the same as ακολουθος (from ἀμα and κελευθος); so, هم عمر "of the same age," "coeval;" هم نشين "intimate," "sitting together;" هم باز "a playfellow." We may add, in conclusion, that almost all the compounds, of the species described in paragraphs *f, g, h, i, k,* and *l,* may occur either as Substantives or Adjectives; hence they may be appropriately classed under the term Epithets or Compound Epithets

m. The Particle نا, prefixed to an Adjective, simple or compound, renders it negative; as, ناپاك "impure," from پاك "pure;" so, from پاك راي "of pure or sincere intention," comes ناپاك راي "of wicked intention." It is also prefixed to Verbal Roots and Participles; as, نادان "ignorant," ناسِتُوده "not commended," "disreputable." Sometimes it is prefixed to Substantives; as, ناكام "not according to one's desire," perhaps elliptically for نا بكام; for we meet with ناكار and نابكار "worthless," still in use.

VERBS.

n. Persian Verbs, like those of the Sanskrit, Greek, &c., may be compounded with a Preposition; as, در آمدن "to come in;" برخاستن "to rise up." Adverbs may also be prefixed in like manner; as, فرو نِشَستن "to sit down;" بالا پريدن "to soar upwards;" but in such phrases there is hardly any peculiarity deserving the name of a compound.

o. The Verbs نمودن, and فرمودن, ساختن, كردن are frequently used with Substantives or Adjectives, in the general sense of "making;" as, حكم كردن "to make an order," "to command;" خشنود ساختن "to make content," "to satisfy;" الْتَفات نمودن "to pay attention," "to notice;" مطالعه فرمودن "to peruse (a letter)." The Verbs داشتن and زدن are occasionally used in the same sense; s, طلب داشتن "to make search;" راي زدن "to express an opinion." The Verbs خوردن and ديدن are used in the sense of "to suffer," "to experience;" as, غم خوردن "to grieve;" محنت ديدن "to suffer affliction." In this general acceptation, the Verb ديدن

" to see " occasionally applies to some of the other senses ; as, بُوٰئي دِيدن " to smell," literally, " to see or experience fragrance."

58. A knowledge of the Persian compounds will be absolutely necessary, in order to peruse with advantage the finest productions of the language. The Poets in general make frequent use of such terms; and several grave Historians indulge freely in the practice. In the version of Pilpay's Fables, entitled, The Anwārī Suhailī, by Ḥusain Vā'iz, there are at least as many compounds as sentences; and the same may be said of the Tales of 'Ināyat Ullāh, called, The Bahār i Dānish : but the perfection of the system will be found in the commencement of a Persian epistle, where it is a point of etiquette to employ a great number of fine-sounding words, that mean nothing. The *business* part of the Letter is generally disposed of in a few words, or at most lines, at the conclusion.

SECTION V.

ON SYNTAX.

ANALYSIS OF SENTENCES.

59. In the preceding Sections we have treated of the letters, syllables, and words of the Persian language. We now come to the most important part of the subject—the construction of sentences, or, in other words, the rules for speaking and writing the language correctly. We have

hitherto taken for granted that the student is acquainted with the ordinary terms of Grammar, and is able to distinguish the various parts of speech (common to all languages) from one another. It is probable, however, that he may not have turned his attention to the analysis of sentences, which ought to form a preliminary step to the Syntax of every foreign tongue. On this account, we request his attention to the following general, or rather universal principles of language, an acquaintance with which will enable him to comprehend more fully some of the rules which we are about to state.

a. A simple sentence consists of three parts; viz. a Nominative, or Agent; a Verb; and an Attribute, or Complement; as, " Fire is hot ;" " Fire consumes wood." In the first sentence, *fire* is the Nominative, or subject of affirmation; *hot* is the Attribute, or that which is affirmed of the subject, *fire*; and the Verb *is* serves to express the affirmation. Again, in the sentence " Fire consumes wood," *fire* is the Nominative, or Agent, *consumes* is the Verb, and *wood* is the *object*. It appears, then, that the shortest sentence must consist of three words, expressed or understood; and it will be found that the longest is always reducible to three distinct parts, which may be considered as so many compound words. For example: " The scorching fire of the thunder-cloud utterly consumes the tall and verdant trees of the forest." In this sentence, the words *fire*, *consumes*, and *trees*, are qualified or restricted by particula circumstances: still, the complex term, " The scorching fire of the thunder-cloud" is the Nominative; " utterly destroys" is the Verb; and " the tall and verdant trees of the forest" is the object. The Sanskrit language, the most philosophic of human tongues, or, as the Brāhmans not unreasonably say, " the language of the gods," would easily and elegantly express the above sentence in three words. " The scorching fire of the thunder-cloud" might be thrown into one compound word in the Nominative Case; the Verb " utterly consumes" would be expressed by a Preposition in composition with the Verb *to consume*; and " the tall and verdant trees of the forest" might be formed into one compound word in the Accusative Case plural.

b. Although every simple sentence is reducible to three distinct parts, yet it is not easy to find a general term that will accurately apply to any of these parts except the Verb. When the sentence is expressed by the Verb " to be," the three parts may be called the *Nominative,* the *Verb,* and *Attribute;* as, " James is diligent." When the sentence is expressed by any other Neuter *Verb,* the parts may be called *Nominative, Verb,* and *Complement;* as, "James went from England to India." Lastly, when the sentence has an Active Verb, the parts are *Agent, Verb,* and *Object;* as, " James purchased a horse." Perhaps the terms least liable to objection will be *Nominative, Verb,* and *Complement;* yet even these would be found inadmissible when applied to the Hindūstānī, the Marhattī, and several other dialects of that class. In Persian, however, the latter terms are not inapplicable: we shall therefore employ them in this sense in the next paragraph, when treating of the arrangement of words.

c. A compound sentence, or period, consists of two or more simple sentences connected by a Conjunction, expressed or understood; as, " Knowledge fills the mind with entertaining views, and administers to it a perpetual series of gratifications: it gives ease to solitude; fills a public station with suitable abilities; and, when it is mixed with complacency, it adds lustre to such as are possessed of it." It will be a useful exercise for the student to analyse, by himself, the above compound sentence, which consists of five simple sentences, in all of which, *knowledge,* or its substitute *it,* is the Nominative. The last two clauses make but one simple sentence, for they amount merely to this: " Knowledge, mixed with complacency, adds lustre to such as are possessed of it."

d. It may happen that the Nominative to the Verb is a short sentence; as, " What he says is of no consequence." So the Complement may also be a sentence; as, " I know not what he thinks." These sentences are equivalent to, " His speech, or speaking, is of no consequence;" and, " I know not his thoughts." It may also happen that the Nominative, or the Complement, or both, may be qualified with a relative clause, which is equivalent to an Adjective. When such relative sentences or clauses occur, they must not be confounded with a compound sentence. Thus, "God, who is Eternal and Invisible, created the world, which is perishable and visible," may at first sight appear a compound sentence; which is not the case, for it is equivalent to, "The Eternal and Invisible God created the perishable and visible world."

ARRANGEMENT OF WORDS.

60. As a preliminary step to our remarks on Persian Syntax, we may briefly notice the manner in which the words of that language are usually arranged in the formation of a sentence. In prose compositions the following rule generally holds; viz. In a simple sentence, the Nominative is put first; then the Object, or Complement; and, lastly, the Verb. Thus, in the sentence, "The Mughal purchased the parrot," the collocation of the words in Persian will be "The Mughal—the parrot—purchased," or مغل طُوطِي را خَرِید *Mughal ṭūtī-rā kharīd*. Here *the Mughal* is the Nominative, beginning the sentence; طُوطِي را *the parrot*, is the Complement, or Object, in the Accusative Case, governed by the Verb خَرِید *purchased*, which comes last. So in the sentence, "Tīmūr arrived in India," تِیمُور به هِندُوسّتان رِسِید *Tīmūr ba Hindūstān rasīd*. *Tīmūr* is the Nominative, *arrived* is the Verb, which is placed at the end of the sentence, and *in India* is its Complement. It may happen that the subject, or the object of the sentence, or both, may be restricted by, or in combination with, words or phrases denoting various circumstances of time, place, motive, &c., and the Verb qualified by an Adverb: still the above arrangement holds good; the

Nominative, with all its restricting circumstances, coming first; then the Complement; and, lastly, the Verb, with its qualifying word immediately before it. Words and phrases denoting time, manner, &c., when they apply to the whole sentence, and not to any particular part of it, are placed first; as, روزي در شهري درويشي بر دُوكانِ بقّالي رفت *roze, dar shahre, darweshe bar dukāni bakkāle raft*, "One day, in a certain city, a darwesh went to the shop of a certain trader." When the Complement of a Verb is a complete sentence it is put last, as in English; thus, آن مرد گفت مرا احمق مي پنداري *ān mard guft, marā ahmak mī-pindārī?* "That man said, 'Do you consider me a fool?'" So in the sentence, پادشاهي درخواب ديد كه تمام دندانهاي او افتاده اند *pādshāhe dar khwāb dīd ki tamāmi dandānhā,e o uftāda and*, "A certain king saw in a dream that the whole of his teeth had dropped out," where the phrase "the whole of his teeth had dropped out" is the Complement to the Verb "saw," or "saw in a dream." When the Object is qualified by a relative sentence, the Object is placed before the Verb, and the qualifying phrase after it, as in the beginning of the Gulistān of Sa'dī: پادشاهي را شُنيدم كِه بكُشتنِ اسيري اِشارت كرد *pādshāhe rā shunīdam ki ba kushtani asīre ishārat kard*, "I have heard of a king who issued the order (made the signal) for the executing of a certain captive." So in the sentence, يكي را از مُلوكِ عجم حِكايت كُنند كِه دستِ

تطاوُل بمالِ رعیّت دراز کَرد yake rā az mulūki 'Ajam ḥikāyat kunand ki dasti taṭāwul ba mālī ra'īyat darāz kard, "They relate of one of the kings of Persia, that he extended the hand of usurpation over the property of the people;" where the relative phrase comes last.

a. In further illustration of the preceding general rule, together with its occasional exceptions, let us analyze the story given as an exercise in reading (§ 23), viz. that of the Villager and his Ass—*hikāyati dihkān o khar*; and to make the matter less difficult at this stage of the student's progress, we shall still employ the Roman character. First sentence : *Dihkāne khare dāsht*—"A villager had an ass." This sentence is exactly like the first quoted above, only *the object* (*khare*) has not the sign *rā* attached to it, which, as we shall see hereafter, is not always necessary, nor even admissible, to distinguish the Accusative Case. Second sentence : *Az sababi be-kharjī, khar-rā barā,e charīdan ba-bāghe sar mī-dād*—"For the sake of economy (non-expenditure), (he) gave its head (*i.e.* its liberty) to the ass, for the purpose of grazing in a certain garden." In this sentence the subject, the Verb, and the object are complex, or accompanied by circumstances. The Nominative is, "the villager," qualified by the phrase "from motives of economy;" the Verb is, *mī-dād*, "gave, or used to give," qualified by the word *sar* "head;" and the object, or Complement, is, "to the ass, for the purpose of grazing in a certain garden." Third sentence : *Mardumāni bāgh khar rā mī-zadand ; wa az zarā'at ba dar mī-kardand*—"The people of the garden used to beat the ass; and (they) used to drive him out from the cultivated ground." This is a compound sentence, consisting of two distinct assertions, connected by the Conjunction *wa* "and." The Nominative of both sentences is, "The people of the garden;" the Object is, "the ass;" and in the last sentence, the Verb *mī-kardand* is qualified by the words, "out from the cultivated ground." Fourth sentence : *Roze dihkān posti sher rā bar khar bast ; wa guft, wakti shab barā,e charīdan tū bar ā,ī, wa āwāz makun*—"One day the villager fastened the skin of a lion upon the ass ; and said (to the brute), At the time of night, you go forth for the purpose of grazing, and do not make a noise." Here, again, we have a compound sentence made up of two propositions, as in the preceding. We may observe that the words "one day," being applicable to the whole sentence, and not to any particular member of it, are placed first of all. The Nominative is, "the villager;" the Verb, "fastened;" and, "the skin of the lion upon the ass" is the Complement. In the second part of this compound sentence, the Nominative is still "the villager;" the Verb is *guft* "said;" and the rest of the sentence is the Complement to that Verb. This, as we have stated, is an exception to the general rule; viz. when the Complement to a Verb is a complete sentence, simple or compound, such Complement follows the Verb. Fifth sentence: *Hamchunān har shab bā posti sher ān khar ba-bāgh mī-raft*—"Thus, every night, with the lion's skin, the ass used to go into the garden." This sentence requires little remark. The Nominative is *ān khar* "that ass," accompanied with circumstances; viz. "in that manner, with the lion's skin." *Har shab*, "every night," qualifies the whole sentence. Sixth sentence: *Harki ba shab mīdīd, yakīn mī-dānist ki īn sher ast*—"Whoever saw (him) by night thought for certain that this is a lion." A compound sentence; the Nominative of the first part of which is "whoever;" the Verb is "saw," qualified by the words, "by night;" and "him" is the Object. In the second part the Nominative "he" is understood; the Verb is "thought," qualified by the Adverb "for certain;" and the Complement (following the Verb, as in the fourth sentence) is, "that this is a lion." Seventh sentence: *Shabe bāghbān orā dīd, wa az tars bar bālāe darakhte raft*—"One night the gardener saw him; and from fear he went upon the top of a tree." Here the word *shabe*, "one night," qualifies the whole compound sentence, and comes first of all. In the second clause, *bāghbān* (understood) is the Nominative, with the accompanying circumstance, *az tars*, "from fear." Eighth sentence: *Dar asnāe ān, khare dīgar ki dar ān nazdīkī būd, ānvāz hard; wa khari dihkān nīz ba āwāz dar āmad; wa bāng zadan misli kharān girift*—"In the midst of this (mean while), another ass, which was in that vicinity, made a noise; and the ass of the villager also into braying came; and began to raise a cry in the manner of asses." This is a compound sentence, consisting of three simple sentences; in the first of which is placed *Dar asnāe ān*, which qualifies the whole sentence. *Khare dīgar ki dar ān nazdīkī būd* is the Nominative of the first sentence, qualified by a relative clause, which the Sanskrit would have expressed by a Compound Adjective.   Ninth sentence : *Bāghbān orā shinākht wa dānist ki īn kīst*—" The gardener recognised him, and knew who this was."   A compound sentence: the Complement to the Verb *dānist*, in the last clause, is *ki īn kīst*, which is placed after the Verb.   Tenth sentence : *Az darakht farod āmad, wa ān khar rā bisyār lat bi-zad*— " From the tree he came down, and very much did beat that ass with a stick."   Eleventh sentence : *Az īnjā khiradmandān gufta and ki, "kharān rā khāmoshī bih "*—" On this subject the wise have said, ' That for the asses silence is best.' "   It is needless to add any remark on the last two sentences, which present no peculiarity that we have not already noticed.

b. The preceding story in the native character (§ 23) will afford the student an easy example for his first lesson in translating.   He ought, at the same time, to ascertain the exact meaning of each word, from the Vocabulary, and be able to parse the whole of them, by a reference to the preceding portion of the Grammar.   In like manner let him analyse and translate Story II., after which he may proceed to the Selections at the end of the work.   When he has read, and carefully analysed, from fifteen to twenty pages of the Selections, he may then with advantage peruse the rules of Syntax which follow.

CONSTRUCTION OF SUBSTANTIVES, ADJECTIVES, AND PREPOSITIONS.

61. As the Adjectives in Persian are all indeclinable, the learner is freed from all anxiety on the score of concord : he has merely to remember, that, as a general rule, Adjectives follow the Substantiyes which they qualify, and the Substantive in such circumstances takes the mark of the *izāfat*, as in the formation of the Genitive Case, explained in § 29; thus, وزِيرِ ناصِح "the sincere minister;" خُوب رُوي " a beautiful face ;" طُرّهٴ مُشْكبُوُّي " a ringlet with the fragrance of musk."

a. In poetry it is not uncommon to place the Adjective first, exactly as in English; thus, Firdausī has " هُشيوار دستُور بر دستِ شاه an intelligent counsellor by the hand of the king;" where the Adjective هشيوار precedes the Substantive دستُور.   When the Adjective thus precedes the Substantive (which sort of construction is, in Persian, called "the inverted epithet"), the mark of the *iẓāfat* is not used.

b. We have already explained (§ 57, *f.* &c.) the nature of Compound Adjectives: we may further observe here, that any Noun with a Particle prefixed to it may become an expressive Epithet; as, مَرْدِ باـمال "a man possessed of wealth."   Many Epithets consist of three or more words; as, مُلْك بجنگ گرفته " "a country taken in war;" so بنداه حلقه بگوش " "a slave with a ring in his ear."   So in the Bustān of Sa'dī we have حكيم سُخن بر زبان آفرين " "The Allwise, who endows the tongue with speech;" where the Substantive حكيم has the rest of the line for its Epithet.   In fact, there is no limit to the extent to which the composition of Epithets may be carried in this language; and it is necessary that, in every instance, the student should be able to distinguish them, that he may add the mark of the *iẓāfat* to the preceding Noun, which they serve to qualify.

c. Numeral Adjectives precede the Substantives to which they belong; and what is altogether at variance with our notions of concord, the Substantive is generally put in the singular number; as, صد سال "a hundred years," instead of صد سالها; so, ده دَرويش " "ten darweshes," instead of دَرويشان; in which expressions the numeral word prefixed is sufficient to indicate the plurality of the Noun, without adding the usual termination.   In fact, we frequently hear in our own language, among the common people, such phrases as "five pound," "ten mile:" and the expressions, "a hundred horse," "three hundred cannon," &c. are allowed to be good historical English.

d. Sometimes a phrase from the Arabic, constructed according to the grammatical rules of that languages, may be introduced as an Epithet to a Persian Substantive; thus, درويشِ مُستجابُالدَّعوات "a derwish, whose prayers are answered;" so, مَرْدِ صادقِ القول "a man sincere in speech;" كريم النَّفس "generous of soul."

e. The Adjective Pronouns اين and آن precede their Substantives; and there are a few Adjectives of a pronominal nature which may optionally precede or follow; as, ديگر "other;" همه "all;" چند "some or several:" thus, همه مردُمان or مردُمانِ همه "all the people;" so, زنِ ديگر or ديگر زن "the other woman;" روزِ چند or چند روز "some or several days."

62. Our word *than,* after the comparative degree, is expressed in Persian by از; thus, روشنتر از آفتاب "more splendid than the sun;" so, اَي مِلك ما درين دُنيا بجَيش "O king, we are, در تُو كمتريم و بعَيش از تُو خُوشتر in this world, less than you as to pomp, but more happy in our enjoyments." The Adjective به "good," is often used in the positive form when denoting comparison, as in the following maxim from the گُلِستان of Shai<u>kh</u> Sa'dī; viz. دُروغِ مصلحت آميز به از راستيِ فتنه انگيز "Falsehood, fraught with good advice, is preferable to the truth, when tending to excite strife;" so, in the following sentence, خاموشِي به از سخُنِ بد است و سخُنِ نيك به از خاموشِي "Silence is better than evil speaking, but speaking well is better than silence."

a. The superlative degree, when used, governs the Genitive, as in our own language; thus, نيكترينِ مردُمان "the best of men;" so, گويند كه كمترينِ جانوران خر است "They say that the meanest of animals is the ass." The same rule applies to superlative forms from the Arabic; as, اشرفِ انبيا "the most illustrious of the prophets."

b. Sometimes the Superlative is employed merely in an intensive sense, like a simple Adjective; in which case the *izāfat* is not used, as in the couplet—

نکـویم گِرامیتریـن گوهری

سُپُردم بغامِیتریـن شوهري

" I will not say that I have given an exceedingly noble lady to a most highly-renowned husband."

63. In Persian, the Particles called Prepositions are, strictly speaking, very few in number, probably not more than those already given in § 51; viz. اَز "from;" با "with;" بر "on;" به "in," "into;" بی "without;" تا "till," "as far as;" جُز "except," "besides;" and در "in;" which invariably take the simple or Nominative form of a Noun or Pronoun after them; as, از بغُداد تا شِیراز "from Baghdād to Shīrāz;" با تو خواهم رفُت " I will go with thee." Such other words as are used like Prepositions are really Nouns, and in construction require the *izāfat*; as, نُزد وزیر "near the minister," which is an elliptical form of expression for به نُزد وزیر زیرِ زِمِین "in the vicinity of the minister;" so "under the earth;" بالاي سرش "above his head;" در پیشِ من پیشِ من "before me," that is, "in front of me." The student will do well in committing to memory the simple Prepositions, and in recollecting that the rest require the *izāfat* when they govern a Substantive.

a. It may be proper to observe that the Particle جُز is a species of Noun, denoting "other," "else," and consequently we should

M

expect it to be followed by the *iẓāfat*; which, however, is not the case; thus, in the following line from Sa'dī—

حَيف باشد كه جُز نِكو كويد

" Pity it were he should speak other than (what is) good "—

we know, from the metre, that جُز has no *iẓāfat*. We may farther mention, that the Particle تا is more generally used as a Conjunction, " till," or " until," " whilst;" تاكِه " so that," " in order that."

PRONOUNS.

64. We shall now treat more particularly of those classes of Pronouns, the explanation of which we passed over in § 39, the others having nothing peculiar in their construction. The following may be denominated *affixed,* because, with the exception of the 3d plural, they are always joined to some word or other in the sentence in which they are employed.

PERS.	SINGULAR.		PLURAL.
1.	مَ	" my *or* me."	مان " our *or* us."
2.	تَ	" thy *or* thee."	تان " your *or* you."
3.	شَ	{ " his, her, its," *or* " him, her, it." }	شان " their *or* them."

When these pronominal terminations are joined to Nouns, they generally correspond with our Possessives, *my, thy,* &c.; as, دِلم "my heart;" كِتابت "thy book;" سرش "his, her, *or* its head:" the plural terminations are very rarely used, their place being supplied by the nom. pl. of the Personal Pronouns employed in apposition as Nouns; thus, دِلهاي ما " our hearts," or " hearts of us;" اسْپانِ شُما " your horses," or

"horses of you;" حالِ ایشان "the condition of them."
When the Noun ends in ه imperceptible, the terminations
م, ت, ش, become ام, ات, and اش; as, جامه ام "my
robe," &c.: and if the Noun ends in ا or و long, they become,
in order to avoid a hiatus, یم, یت, یش; as, پایم "my
foot;" مویت "thy hair;" رویش "his *or* her face."
These are euphonic principles, similar in their nature to
those already detailed in § 48, *a.*, with respect to the verbal
terminations added to Substantives, Adjectives, and Participles.

65. When the terminations ش, ت, م, are joined
to the persons of a Verb, they correspond with the Dative or
Accusative Case of the Personal Pronouns; as, دیدمت
"I saw thee;" گفتمش "I said to him." It appears, then,
that these affixes may be employed to denote the Possessives
my, thy, his, &c., as well as the Dative and Accusative,
to me, to thee; or, *me, thee,* &c., according to circumstances.
When employed in the latter sense, they may be joined not
only to the Verb which governs them, but to any word in
the sentence, with the exception of the simple Prepositions,
already noticed, and a few of the Conjunctions, as وَ "and,"
یا "or," &c.; thus, دربانم رها نـکرد "the porter did not
admit me," or, verbatim, "the porter to me guidance not
made;" so, خاکش چنان بخورد "the earth has so much
consumed it." In instances of this kind the student must
be guided by the context; as, دربانم, in the first of the
above examples, when merely taken by itself, may also mean

"my porter:" but when Sa'dī (from whom the expression is taken) states, in the sentence immediately preceding, "that he went to wait on the *great man*," the true meaning of the expression will be obvious.

66. The invariable word خُود, in Persian, corresponds with our Reciprocal Pronoun *self;* as, مَن خُود "I myself;" تُو خُود "thou thyself," &c. It may also be the Nominative to any person of the Verb, the verbal termination sufficiently shewing the sense ; as, خُود رفتم "I myself went ;" خُود رفتند "they themselves went." The usage of the Persian language requires the employment of خُود, on certain occasions, as a substitute for a Possessive Pronoun ; thus, زرگر بہ خانہٴ خُود رفت "the goldsmith went to his own house," literally, "to the house of self ;" من از باغِ خُود مي آمدم "I was coming from my garden," or "from the garden of self."

a. The following is a general rule for the employment of خُود. If, in a simple sentence, a Personal Pronoun in an Oblique Case (as, *me, thee, of me,* or *my,* &c.) be required, and if it be of the same person with the Nominative of the sentence, the place of such Pronoun must be supplied in Persian by خُود; thus, "I am writing my letter," من خطِّ خُود مي نويسم, *i.e.* "I write the letter of (my) self ;" so, زید غُلام خُودرا زد "Zaid beat his (own) slave" (not another man's); مرُدمان بخانهاي خُود رفتند "the people went to their own houses." In recent Persian works composed in India this last sentence would be expressed مرُدمان بخانہٴ خودها رفتند. I have not, however, met with such an expression in any good Persian author.

b. It is almost unnecessary to state, that when the two Pronouns are not of the same person, or rather when the latter Pronoun does not belong to the Nominative of the sentence, خُود cannot be used; as, "Zaid beat your slave," زَيد غُلام شُمارا زد so, "Zaid beat his (meaning another person's) slave," زَيد غُلام اورا زد. We may observe, that instead of خُود, the words خويش, خويشتن and خوى are sometimes used: خُودش also occurs, but only in the 3d pers. sing.; as, زَيدرا در خانه خُودش ديدم "I saw Zaid in his own house;" literally, "I saw Zaid in the house of his self." This sentence, by the way, would at first sight seem to be at variance with part of the preceding rule; but the expression amounts to this, "I saw that Zaid was in his own house," or "I saw Zaid, who was in his own house."

c. We find in the last London edition of the Gulistān, Book III. 'Ap. 8, the following suspicious reading: يكي از حُكما پِسرشرا نهِي كرد "One of the sages made a prohibition to his son," where the use of the Pronoun ش is at variance with the general rule. We have consulted nine manuscripts of the original in our possession, not one of which has the Pronoun ش. In M. Semelet's edition of the Gulistān, printed at Paris, 1828, the same error is repeated, although the work pretends to great critical accuracy.

67. With regard to the Demonstrative Pronouns اين and آن, we have little further to add. When the name of an irrational being, or of an inanimate object, has been mentioned, and reference is made to it afterwards by a Pronoun, as *it* or *they,* اين and آن, with their plurals, are generally used, seldom اُو or ايشان; thus, in the apologue, شير گُفت مُصَوِّرِ اين اِنسانسْت "The lion said, The painter of it (alluding to a picture) is (was) a man;" so حُكما از تاويلِ آن عاجِز ماندند "The wise men were at a loss in the explaining of it" (viz. the dream).

a. The phrases از آنِ تُو, از آنِ من, or آنِ تُو, آنِ من, &c., are equivalent to our words *mine, thine,* &c.; as, مسندِ مصر آنِ تُوست "The throne of Egypt is thine;" so, in the *Akhlaki Muhsini,* we have the phrases این خانه اوّل از آنِ کِہ بُود؟ "Whose house was this originally?" کُفت از آنِ جدّم "He said, That of my grandfather's." چون او بکُذشت از آنِ کہ شُد؟ "When he died, whose did it become?" کُفت از آنِ پدرم "He said, That of my father's," &c.

68. The words کِہ and چہ, in Persian, generally correspond, in the Nominative Case, with our Relative Pronouns *who* and *which;* but Dr. Lumsden shews that they are merely *connectives,* and have the Personal Pronouns understood after them; thus, Sa'di has ملِک زادہ را دِیدم کِہ عقّل داشْت "I saw a prince who possessed wisdom:" after کِہ the Personal Pronoun او is understood; as, کِہ او عقّل داشْت "that he possessed wisdom." As the Personal Pronoun, however, is generally left out, the Particles کِہ and چہ have been considered, by some Oriental Grammarians, as *relatives.* The following sentence from the Gulistān, to which many others might be added, confirms Dr. Lumsden's views on this subject: ابلھی کو روزِ روشن شمّع کافورِي نِھد "The fool who burns (sets up) a camphor candle in a clear day;" where کو is a contraction of ہ او; literally, "The fool, that he burns," &c., where the mere کِہ, if it were a Relative, would have quite sufficed, and have equally preserved the metre.

a. When the Persians have occasion to express a sentence, containing what, in European Grammars, is called a Relative Pronoun in an Oblique Case, they employ the Particle کِه, together with the corresponding Personal Pronoun, as may be seen in the following examples from the Gulistān:—1st, In the Genitive Case:

بس نامَوَر کِه زیرِ زَمِین دفَن کرده اند

کزهسْتِیش بروِي زمینِ یك نِشان نماند

Many a renowned personage have they deposited beneath the dust, of whose existence (literally, that of his existence) no trace (now) remains on the face of the earth." Again, Sa'dī says—

آن نه من باشم کِه روزِ جنَگ بِینِي پُشتِ من

"I am not he whose back you will see in the day of battle," or, literally, "that you should see my back." 2dly, In the Dative:

اي که شخَصِ منَت حقیرِ نمُود

"O (thou) to whom my person appeared worthless!" literally, "that my person appeared to thee." 3dly, In the Accusative:

آن کِه چون پِستَه دِیدمش همه مغز

"He whom I beheld all fat, like the pistachio nut;" literally, "He that I saw him." 4thly, In the Ablative:

آنکِه در وَي مظِلنهء خطَر اسَت

"That (proceeding) in which there is suspicion of danger."

b. The compound terms هرکِه and هرچِه, when accompanied by a Substantive, correspond to our words *whosoever* and *whatsoever;* the former generally denoting rational beings, and the latter inferior animals, or lifeless matter; thus, in Sa'dī's Gulistān,

هرکِه دسَت از جان بِشوید

هرچِه دردِل دارد بِگـوید

"Whosoever shall wash his hands of life, the same will utter wnatever he has on his mind." If we could trust the genuineness of the following sentence from Sa'dī, it would appear that هرچِه may sometimes be applied to persons as well as things; thus, in the Second Book of the Gulistān (Ap. 37), an experienced old Doctor recommends to his pupil the following ingenious method of relieving himself of his friends, viz.:

هرچِه درُویشانند ایشانرا وامي بِدِه و آنچه توَنگرانَند از ایشان چِیزِي بخواه

"Whosoever are poor, to them give a small loan; and of those who are rich ask something:" but MSS. by no means agree in this reading; and our finest MS. has it thus,

درویشانرا وامي بِدِه و از توَنگران چیزي بخواه

"To the poor lend a little, and of the rich ask something."

c. When the Substantive is expressed after هر, the Particle کِه may follow, whether the Substantive be animate or inanimate; as, هرچیز کِه "every thing which." When the termination ي *majhūl* is added to a Noun, and کِه or چه follows, the Substantive is thereby rendered more definite or specific; thus, Shaikh Sa'dī says, "(Envy) (حسد) رَنجیسَت کِه از مشقّتِ آن جُز بمَرگ نتوَان رسَت is such a torment, that it is impossible to escape from its pangs, except by death." We may observe, in conclusion, on the subject of the Relative, or rather *the want of a Relative*, in Persian, that if کِه and چه are to be considered as mere connective Particles, it need not be wondered at that the rules respecting their agreement with their antecedents should be liable to many deviations.

69. We have already stated (§ 41) that کِه and چه are used as Interrogatives; the former applicable to persons, and the latter to irrational beings: but if the Noun be expressed, چه may be used in both instances; as, چهمَرد "What man?" The word کُدام is also used as an Interrogative: it is applicable to every gender and number; as, کُدام مَرد "What or which man?" کُدام کار "What or which business?" کِه and چه, when used interrogatively, are to be considered as Substantives, singular or plural, according to the Nouns which they represent; as, آن سپ کِه باشد "Whose horse may that be?" کِرا مِي گویند "To whom are they speaking?" ایشان کِینَد "Who are they?"

از بهْرِ چه آمدهٔ "On account of what are you come?"

چرا رفتِي "For what did you go?" The Interrogative

Particle آیا corresponds with the Latin *an, num,* &c.;

as, آیا بادشاه آمده است *An rex venit?* "Is the King

arrived?"

CONCORD OF VERBS.

70. If the Nominative to a Verb, in Persian, be expressive
of rational beings, or of living creatures in general, the Verb
agrees with it in number and person, as in our own language; also, two or more Nouns in the singular, denoting
animals, require the Verb to be put in the plural number;
as, برادران برنجیدنْد "The brothers were vexed;"

جانوران جنگل آواز نمُودنْد "The animals of the forest
made a noise;" زرگر ونجّار بُتانرا گرفْتنْد "The goldsmith
and the carpenter seized the images."

a. When two or more inanimate Nouns have a common Verb, the
latter is generally put in the singular, as in the following lines from
Sa'dī:

گرچِه سِیم و زر زِسنْگ آید همِي در همه سنْگي نباشد زرو سِیم

"Although silver and gold be produced from stone, yet every stone
will not yield gold and silver."

تامرْد سُخَن نگُفْته باشد عَیب وهُنرش نِهفْته باشد

"Until a man hath spoken his sentiments, his defects and his skill
remain concealed."

71. We have already mentioned, that when a Numeral
Adjective precedes a Noun, the latter does not require the

plural termination: but if the Noun denote rational beings, and be the subject of a Verb, the Verb is put in the plural; as, ده دُرویش در گِلیمي بِخُسپند "Ten darweshes will sleep on one blanket." Irrational animals, and especially inanimate things, generally take the Verb in the singular; as, صد هزار اسَپ حاضِر شُد "A hundred thousand horses were ready;" so, دو هزار غرفه وهزار اَیوان بُود "There were two thousand rooms and a thousand vestibules."

a. Arabic plurals, introduced into Persian, follow a similar rule; that is, if they denote animals, and more particularly rational beings, the Verb is put in the plural: but inanimate Nouns generally take the singular; as, حُكما گُفته اند "The wise men have said;" از آمدنِ بهار از رفتنِ دي اوراقِ حَياتِ ما میگردد طَي "By the approach of Spring, and the passing by of December, the leaves of our life come to a close."

b. Nouns of multitude, denoting rational beings, follow the same rule in Persian as in English; hence the Verb is sometimes in the singular and sometimes in the plural, according to the *unity* or *plurality* of the idea conceived in the mind of the speaker; thus, in the Gulistán, شاهنشاهِ عادِلرا رعیّت لشکر اسَت "To the just monarch the people is an army;" again, طائِقهٔ دُزدان عرب بر سرِ کوهي نِشسته بُودند "A gang of 'Arab thieves had settled on the summit of a certain mountain;" so, خلقي بتعصّب برو گِرد آمدند "The whole nation, through partiality, flocked around him." If the Noun of multitude applies to irrational animals or lifeless things, the Verb is more idiomatically used in the singular. Finally, Mirzá Ibrahím states in his Grammar (p. 146), that, "The Verbs belonging to this class of Nouns (*i.e.* all Nouns of multitude) are better always to be in the singular number, excepting when the Nouns themselves are used in the plural number." It is needless to add, that this last rule is utterly at variance with the practice of the best writers of the language.

c. The classical scholar will observe that there is a resemblance between the concord of a Persian Verb with its Nominative, and that of the Greek; the plurals of the neuter gender, in the latter language, requiring the Verb to be in the singular. The Persian has another peculiarity, not unlike the German; viz. when inferiors speak *to* or *of* their superiors, the Verb is employed in the plural, generally in the third person. Thus a servant, in speaking of his master, would say, صاحب خانه بیرون رفته اند " The master of the house is (are) gone out." So, in one of the anecdotes in our Selections, respecting the King and his Minister, we have a sentence of similar construction, viz. جهان پناه بسیار خوار هستند که نه تخم گذاشتند نه خرما " Your Majesty is a great glutton, having left neither dates nor stones;" literally, " The Asylum of the Universe *are* a great glutton," &c. This style, however, does not seem to have belonged to the classic period of the language.

GOVERNMENT OF VERBS.

72. The only peculiarity in the government of Verbs, in Persian, is, that a Transitive or Active Verb does not, as a general rule, require, as in Greek and Latin, that its Complement should have the termination of the Accusative Case; thus, ساقیا ساغرِ شراب بیار " O cup-bearer, bring a goblet of wine;" where ساغرِ شراب has not the sign of the Accusative Case affixed. So in the following lines from Sa'di:

عذرِ تقصیرِ خدمت آوردم ـ که ندارم بطاعت اِستِظهار ٭

عاصیان از گناه توبه کنند ـ عارفان از عبادت اِستِغفار ٭

" I have brought (only) an excuse for the defect of my service; for in my obedience I have no claim; the wicked express contrition for their sins; the holy beg forgiveness on the score of their (imperfect) devotions." In this extract the four words *excuse, claim, contrition,* and *forgiveness,* have not the sign of the Accusative Case added to any of them in the original. Again, in the following sentences the Accusative Case is accompanied by its appropriate sign: غُلام را بدریا انداختند "They threw the slave into the sea;" درویش سنگ را با خُود نِگاه می‌داشت " The darwesh preserved the stone in his possession." Lastly, in the following sentences from the first of our introductory Stories (§ 23), we have the same word used in different places, first without, and then with the sign را; thus, دِهقانی خری داشت ۰ مَردُمانِ باغ خر را میزدند "A certain villager had *an* ass. The people of the garden used to beat *the* ass." In the first sentence we have خری داشت, without the را; and in the second we have خر را میزدند, where the را is added. Hence we see that sometimes the object takes the termination را, and sometimes not; and the following appear to us to be the general principles that regulate the insertion or omission of that termination:

a. When we wish to render the object definite, emphatic, or particular, را is added; for instance, شراب بیار signifies, "Bring wine;" but شراب را بیار means, "Bring *the* wine." So in the Story, دِهقانی خری داشت "A villager had an ass," the را is not needed; but in the next sentence, مَردُمانِ باغ خر را میزدند " The people of the garden used to beat *the* ass," the را is used, because the object is now more definite. Sometimes we meet with an apparently superfluous Particle مر *prefixed* to the Noun or Pronoun to which the را is *affixed;* as, مر اورا دیدم "I saw him."

b. It is a general rule to add را to the Object of an Active Verb, whenever any ambiguity would arise from its omission; or, in other words, when the action described by the Verb is such as might be performed by either the Agent or Object; thus, زرگر نجّاررا بزد "The goldsmith struck the carpenter;" مرد شیررا کُشت "The man slew the lion;" اِسکندر داررا بیفکند "Iskandar overthrew Dārā," or, as the Latin Grammar hath it, *Alexander Darium vicit.* In these examples, if we omit the را we are left merely to infer the sense from the arrangement, which, in ordinary prose compositions, might form a sufficient criterion, but not in verse.

c. When the Object of an Active Verb is a Personal Pronoun, or its substitute خود, the termination را is always used; as, مرا نمی شِناسی "Dost thou not know me?" تُرا دیدم "I saw thee;" اورا گِرفتند "They seized him;" نگاهدار مارا ز راه خطا "Preserve us from the path of error;" فُلان شخص خودرا پِنهان کَرده است "Such a person has concealed himself."

d. Having stated what we consider the general principles which regulate the insertion of را as the sign of the Accusative Case, the rule for its non-insertion may be easily inferred; viz. the insertion of را is not necessary whenever the nature of the sentence is such as to enable the reader or hearer to comprehend the sense clearly without it, except when we wish to particularize or limit the Object, or when it is a Personal Pronoun. Lastly, in such Compound Verbs as we mentioned (§ 57, *o.*), like حُکم کَردن, &c., the را is never added to the Substantive.

73. The termination را is added to a Substantive to denote the Dative Case as well as the Accusative. On such occasions its insertion is indispensably necessary; thus,

"They relate a story with regard ظالِمِي را حكايت كُنند
to a certain oppressor;" so in the following sentence,
"For a thousand rupees هزار روپيه را اسپی خَرِيدم
I bought a horse."

a. When a Verb governs an Accusative, and at the same time a
Dative Case, the termination را is seldom, if ever, added to both
Cases; thus, if the Accusative be indefinite, or does not necessarily
require را, according to the principles already laid down, then the
Dative has the را added; as, آن مَردرا كِتابي دادم "I gave a book
to that man." So, هريك ضعيفهرا يك نيمه دِهند "Let them give
a half to each woman." If the Accusative necessarily require را,
the Dative must be formed by the Preposition به "to;" thus,
لَعل را به آن زن دِهند "Let them give the ruby to that woman;"
so, كتاب را بمن بِدِه "Give me the book." In these last examples,
the words كِتاب and لعل being definite, require the addition of را;
and the Dative Cases are formed by prefixing the Particle به *ba* to
the Pronouns آن and من.

74. When the Object is in a state of construction with
another Noun, or with an Adjective, and from its nature
requires را, that termination is added to the latter Noun or
Adjective, as follows: زَيد پِسرِ وزِير را دِيدم "I saw Zaid,
the son of the minister;" so, in this line from Ḥāfiẓ,
درجنّت نخواهِي يافت گُلگَشتِ مُصلّارا "In Paradise you
will not find the rosy bowers of Muṣallā." In this rule there
is much sound philosophy; for when one Substantive governs
another in the Genitive, the two are to be considered as
one modified Noun; thus, in the following sentence, from
the First Book of the Gulistān of Sa'dī, يكی از مُلُوك
خُراسان سُلطان مَحمُود سبكتِگِين را بخواب دِيد

"One of the kings of Khurāsān saw in a dream Sultān Maḥmūd (the son) of Sabaktagīn," the three words سُلْطَان مَحْمُودِ سبُکْتَـگِین are viewed as one modified Noun, and the termination را is very properly placed at the end. In like manner, a Substantive, accompanied by an Adjective, is to be considered as a single specified Noun; and, in construction, the termination را, when requisite, is placed at the end; thus, قَاضِي زِن هَمْسَايَهرا طَلب کرُد "The Judge summoned the neighbouring woman." So, however complex the Adjective may be, the را is placed at the end; thus, from Sa'dī, تَـنِي چند از مَرْدانِ واقِيه دِيدَه و جَنـگک آزمُودهرا بِفرِسْتادنُد "They sent forward several individuals from among men who had seen service and had experienced war:" here the Complement or Object of the Verb, بِفرِسْتادنُد, consists of the whole preceding sentence; and the را is affixed last of all, the more to define that complex object, now viewed as a single whole.

a. This last quotation from Sa'dī shews the importance of the few remarks we made (§§ 59 and 60) respecting the " Analysis of Sentences," &c.

75. It remains for us to notice a few verbal expressions which some Grammarians consider as tenses, and which we omitted in the paradigm, as of small importance. In Dr. Lumsden's Grammar, Vol. I. p. 93, &c., we have two tenses of a Potential Mood, present and past, formed respectively by adding the contracted Infinitive to the Aorist and Preterite of the Verb تَوَانِسْتن (root تَوان) "to be able;" as,

تَوَانِم رفت "I am able to go," or "I can go;" in like manner, تَوَانِستم رفت "I was able to go," or "I could go." But, in truth, we are more inclined to consider these as sentences than tenses. In a large and closely written Persian manuscript, which treats of the grammar of that language, called the *Miftāh-ut-tarkīb*, compiled, as the writer tells us, by *Shewā Rām*, poetically named *Jauhar*, there is a tense called the Continuative Imperative, or Imperative of Duration, formed by prefixing the Particle مِي to the Future Perfect; thus, from مِي رفته باشد "He may have gone," comes زفته باشد "Let him continue going." This tense is also called, according to Jauhar, *Istimrārī-e-Maznūn* (استِمْراري مظنون), which is a sort of Imperfect or Continuative Potential; as, "He may be going;" the meaning of it in Hindūstānī being given, جاتا هوئي وُه. The ordinary Imperative, by prefixing مِي, denotes continuity, as in the following sentence from Husain Va'īz: شبها برِدرگاهِ الِهي دادِ گدائي مِي دِه "Nightly at و روزها در بارگاهِ خُود بدادِ گدايان مِي رسَ the threshold of God continue giving forth the gift of thy unworthiness ; and daily in thine own court constantly attend to (the administration of) justice among the poor."

76. When the Verbs خواسْتن "to intend," or "to wish," تَوَانِسْتن "to be able," بايِستن and شايِسْتن "to be proper," or "fit," are followed by an Infinitive, the final ن—َ of the Infinitive is rejected; as, خواهم رفت "I will go," or "I intend to go;" تَوَانم نَوِشْت "I can write."

The Verbs بایِسْتَن and تَوَانِسْتَن are generally used impersonally, in the third person singular of the Aorist or Present; as, باید کرد "One ought to do." The mere root, تَوَان, of تَوَانِسْتَن is also used impersonally; as, تَوَان کرد "One may do." We have reason to believe, from observing the usage of the best writers of the language, that when the Infinitive precedes the above Verbs, the final ـن is not rejected; as, اِین کار کردن نِمِیتَوَانم "I cannot do this deed;" so, تُرا جائي فِرِسْتادن نِمِیخواهم "I do not intend to send you anywhere."

77. The Infinitive, in Persian, is to be considered merely as a Verbal Noun, and construed like any other Substantive. It corresponds more with the Verbal Noun of the Latin formed from the Supine by changing the *um* into *io* or *us*, than it does with the Infinitive, Gerund, or Supine of that language; thus, بادْشاهي به کُشْتَن اسِیري اِشارت کرد "A certain king made the signal for the killing of a captive;" which, by Gentius, is rendered into Latin, *Captivum interficere signum dederat;* but the literal rendering is, *Ad captivi interfectionem,* or *De captivi interfectione;* hence the Infinitive of an Active Verb, in Persian, governs a Genitive, and not an Accusative, as in most European tongues.

78. Conjunctions, in Persian, are applied as in English or Latin; that is, when any thing contingent, doubtful, &c. is denoted, the Conjunction is usually followed by the Sub-

junctive Mood (Aorist and Past Potential) ; as in the sentence
"Be به نانِي بِساز تا نكُنِي پُشْت به خِدْمت دوتا
satisfied with a single loaf (of bread), that you may not
bend your back in servitude ;" so, in the following sentence,
اگر روزِي بدانِش در فزُودي زِنادان تنگ‌روزتر نبُودي
"If the augmentation of wealth depended upon knowledge,
none would be so distressed as the ignorant."

79. When a person has occasion to relate what he has
heard from another, the usage of the Persian, like that of
most oriental languages, requires that it should be done in the
dramatic style.   This will be easily understood from the
following examples: "Zaid tells me that he will not come,"
زيد مرا مِيگويد كه نُخواهم آمد ; literally, "Zaid says to me
that 'I will not come.'"   From the employing of the
dramatic instead of the narrative style, it will often happen
that the Persian will differ widely from the English in the
use of the persons and tenses of the Verb, which may be
seen from the few following examples ; viz. "Zaid said that
his brother (meaning Zaid's brother) was not in the house,"
زيد گُفْت كه برادرِ من در خانه نِيسْت ; literally, " Zaid
said, 'My brother is not in the house.'"   So, "The king ordered
the executioner to put him to death in his (the king's) presence,"
پادشاه جلّادرا فرمُود كه رُو برُويِ من اورا بكُش ; i.e. "The
king ordered the executioner thus, 'Put him to death in
my presence.'"   It would be needless to add more examples
of this kind: the learner has merely to recollect, as a general

principle, that the person who relates a conversation that has occurred commonly gives the *ipsa verba* of the parties of whom he is speaking.

SECTION VI.

ON THE NATURE AND USE OF ARABIC WORDS INTRODUCED INTO THE PERSIAN LANGUAGE.

80. In all Muḥammadan countries, Arabic is the language of Religion and Science, just as the Latin was among us in Europe during the middle ages. In modern Persian, more than half the Substantives and Adjectives in use are pure Arabic; and it would appear that the introduction and employment of the latter are limited by no boundaries, except what the whim and caprice of individual writers may happen to affix. At the same time, this vast influx of foreign words does not in any degree affect the nature and genius of the Persian as one of the Indo-European family of languages. The Arabic words, thus admitted, are subject to the same laws as if they had been originally Persian; just as we, in English, have for the last six centuries made a free use of foreign words which have now become naturalized in our language.

81. The Persians, however, do not content themselves with the mere appropriation of an unlimited number of isolated Arabic words. In almost every page of even a popular Persian book, such as the Gulistān of Sa'dī, whole phrases and sentences from the Arabic are introduced *ad libitum*. The author seems to have taken for granted that his readers, as a matter of course, know Arabic as well as himself. Dr. Lumsden, in his Grammar, vol. i. p. 398, gives (from one of the Letters of the poet Jāmī) an extreme case of this kind of composition, to which, as he justly states, "the epithet *Persian* is but nominally applicable, since it exhibits a strange mixture of Arabic and Persian, which would be altogether unintelligible to a native of either country, who had not acquired, by study, the language of the other." The best illustration of this piebald kind of composition which at present occurs to me, will be found in "Burton's Anatomy of Melancholy," *passim*, which work, nevertheless, is one of the most entertaining in

the *English* language, if I may use so bold an expression. In the Introduction, Democritus Junior thus speaks of himself: "I am *aquæ potor*, drink no wine at all, which so much improves our modern wits; a loose, plain, rude writer; *ficum, voco ficum; et ligonem, ligonem*; and as free as loose; *idem calamo quod in mente*; I call a spade a spade; *animis hæc scribo, non auribus*; I respect matter, not words; remembering that *verba propter res, non res propter verba*; and seeking, with Seneca, *quod scribam, non quemadmodum.*"

82. It is evident, then, from what we have just stated, that the only sure means of acquiring any thing like a critical knowledge of the Persian language, consists in gaining, at least, an elementary knowledge of Arabic. For this purpose, a month or two devoted to the perusal of any good Arabic Grammar, together with some easy compositions in prose, will amply suffice; and the student will soon find that the two months thus bestowed will yield him an ample return. In the mean time, I shall here briefly endeavour to point out the more prominent peculiarities of such Arabic words as are of frequent occurrence in the Persian language. I do not intend to give even an abstract of Arabic Grammar, which would be inconsistent with the limits assigned to the present work. I confine myself chiefly to the mere mechanical formation of Arabic words, and their significations, as they gradually arise from the primary ROOT, which generally consists of three letters.

83. The Arabic stands at the head of that family of languages called "The Semitic." It is closely allied to the Hebrew, Syriac, and Ethiopic; the main difference being, that the three latter have been allowed to remain in a comparatively undeveloped state, whereas the former has been cultivated and polished almost to a fault. It is, actually, the most copious of human tongues; but, in addition to the words already formed by *use* or *prescription*, there appears to be no bounds to the extent to which, if necessary, other words may, by fixed laws, be evolved from such simple triliteral roots as already exist, or from any *newly-coined root*, if expediency should require it. Suppose, for example, that the Arabs adopted a new verbal root, say غرف (from γραφ), to denote the recently-discovered process called Lithography; then instantly, from this new root, would spring up, by fixed and unerring laws, some two or three hundred new words, all bearing more or less reference to the Lithographic

Art; thus, غارِف would denote "the lithographer;" مَغْروف "the thing lithographed;" مَغْرف "the time and place for lithographing;" مِغْراف "the lithographic apparatus;" غَرّاف "the professional lithographer," &c.

84. The radical words of the Arabic language generally consist of three letters; a few there are consisting of four, and a still smaller number of five letters. The greater portion of the triliteral roots are Verbs, the rest Substantives or Adjectives. There are a few verbal roots of four letters, but none of five, the latter being all Substantives. The mode adopted for the development of the triliteral roots of the Arabic language is highly ingenious and philosophic. This consists not so much in adding terminations to the simple root, as in expanding it by means of certain letters, either prefixed or inserted somewhere between the beginning and end of a word, so as to produce certain FORMS, bearing in general a definite relation to the original root. The letters thus employed are seven in number, and, for that reason, they are called SERVILE LETTERS. These are, ا, ت, س, م, ن, و, and ي, all contained in the technical word يتَسمَّنُوا, literally, "they fatten." The serviles ا and ت may occur either at the beginning, or in the interior, or, lastly, at the end of a word; the ن and the ي, either in the interior or at the end; the م always at the beginning; the و is employed in the interior of a word; and the س always as the second letter of a word, and it is preceded either by ا or م, and followed by ت. For example, let us take the verbal root قبل, which signifies "accepting;" we thence, by means of the servile ا alone, deduce the forms قَبَلا, and قِبال, قابِل, اقبَل. Then the various forms مقبُول, تَقْبِيل, and مُسْتَقبِل, اسْتقبال, قابِلِيَّت, قِبلتين, exhibit a few of the other serviles in their mode of application, of which more hereafter. It is evident, then, as a general rule, that if we strip every Arabic word of its servile letters, we at once come to the ROOT: thus, in the words انفِعال, مُتَفارِق, and استَغْفار, we see at once that the roots are فعل, فرق, and غفر respectively. We must observe, however, that the seven serviles, conjointly or severally, may be employed as radical letters of the triliteral root. Thus the word مفتُون "tried," or "tested" (as

gold in the fire), contains no fewer than four servile letters, and only one letter strictly radical, viz. ف‍. Now, out of these four serviles, two *must* belong to the root. We see, however, that the word is of the form مَقْبُول, already cited; hence we infer that the root is فتن, just as that of مَقْبُول is قبل. A little practice, however, will enable the learner to get over difficulties of this sort; at the same time had it been possible for the Arabs, when manufacturing their very artificial language, to have excluded the servile letters altogether from the primitive triliteral roots, Arabic would have been the most perfect of human tongues.

85. All the Arabic words, with the exception of a few Particles, introduced into Persian are to be considered as Nouns, in the *Oriental* sense of that term (v. § 25), that is, they are Substantives, Adjectives, Infinitives, or Participles. Hence it will be proper here to give a brief sketch of the Arabic Declension; premising, at the same time, that the language has only two Genders—the Masculine and the Feminine. It has three Numbers, like the Greek—the Singular, Dual, and Plural; also three Cases—the Nominative, the Genitive (which also includes the Dative and Ablative), and the Accusative. As a specimen of the regular Arabic Declension, let the following words suffice:—

1st.—*Declension of a Masculine Noun.*

SINGULAR.	DUAL.	PLURAL.
Nom. وَالِدٌ a father.	وَالِدَانِ two fathers.	وَالِدُونَ fathers.
Gen. وَالِدٍ of a father.	وَالِدَيْنِ of two fathers.	وَالِدِينَ of fathers.
Acc. وَالِدًا a father.	وَالِدَيْنِ two fathers.	وَالِدِينَ fathers.

2nd.—*Declension of a Feminine Noun.*

SINGULAR.	DUAL.	PLURAL.
Nom. وَالِدَةٌ a mother.	وَالِدَتَانِ two mothers.	وَالِدَاتٌ mothers.
Gen. وَالِدَةٍ of a mother.	وَالِدَتَيْنِ of two mothers.	وَالِدَاتٍ of mothers.
Acc. وَالِدَةً a mother.	وَالِدَتَيْنِ two mothers.	وَالِدَاتٍ mothers.

When a Noun is rendered *definite*, by prefixing the Article ال,
the *nūnation* (§ 22) which appears at the end of some of the Cases
is dropt, and the simple short vowel retained; thus, Nom. اَلْوَالِدُ
"the father;" Gen. اَلْوَالِدِ "of the father;" Acc. اَلْوَالِدَ "the father;"
so اَلْوَالِدَةُ "the mother;" اَلْوَالِدَةِ "of the mother;" اَلْوَالِدَةَ "the
mother." In like manner, the nūnation is rejected when one Noun
governs a Noun following in the Genitive; thus, اَمِيرُ الْمُومِنِينَ
"Commander of the Faithful;" اِقْبَالُ الدَّوْلَةِ "Dignity of the State."
It is a rule in Persian, on introducing an expression of this sort,
always to reject the final short vowel of the word governed; hence they
say, "*Amīru-l-mūminīn,*" and "*Ikbālu-d-Daulat,*" or "*Ikbālu-d-
Daula.*" The Arabic Dual is sometimes introduced into Persian, but
always in the Oblique Case, the final vowel being rejected; thus,
مَشْرِقَيْن "The East and West;" مَدِينَتَيْن "the two cities;" وَالِدَيْن
"the two fathers," meaning the two parents. In a similar manner
the regular Oblique plural of masculine Nouns is sometimes introduced
into Persian; thus, عُلُومِ اوَّلِين و آخِرِين "the sciences of the
ancients and moderns!" The regular feminine plural ending in
ات—, without the nūnation or vowel-point, is of frequent occurrence
in Persian; thus, تَوَجُّهَاتِ دوسْتَان "the kind attentions of friends;"
تَكْلِيفَاتِ مَزْبُور "the aforesaid difficulties."

86. Besides the regular plurals exemplified in the words والِد and
وَالِدَة, the Arabs have adopted several modes of forming *artificial,*
or, as they call them, BROKEN PLURALS. Of these, some half-dozen
are of very common occurrence in Persian. 1st, From the triliteral
root a plural may be formed, of frequent occurrence, by means of
two *alifs,* thus حُكْم "an order," plur. اَحْكَام "orders;" so مِلْك
"property," plur. اَمْلَاك "goods" or "chattels." 2nd, From a triliteral root, with or without the additional ة (vide § 89), may
be formed a broken plural of the measure قِبَال; thus, جَبَل "a
mountain," plur. جِبَال "mountains;" so رَجُل "a man," رِجَال "men;" خَصْلَة "disposition," خِصَال "dispositions." 3rd, From the

triliteral root another plural, of frequent occurrence in Persian, may be formed on the measure قُبُول; thus, مَلِك "a king," plur. مُلُوك "kings;" so عِلْم "science," plur. عُلُوم sciences." 4th, Another broken plural, of frequent occurrence in Persian, is formed on the measure قُبَلَاء; thus, حَكِيم "a sage," حُكَمَاء "sages;" so شاعِر "a poet," plur. شُعَرَاء "poets." This form of plural arises from singular Nouns of the measure قَابِل or قَبِيل. 5th, Another broken plural is formed by inserting ا and ي in the penult and final syllables of a word respectively; thus, سُلْطان "a king," plur. سلاطِين "kings;" so شَيطان "the devil," plur. شَياطِين. There are several other modes of forming broken plurals, which shall be noticed as we proceed, but it is impossible to reduce them to any general rule. The student cannot *à priori* determine what kind of broken plural any individual triliteral root may form, consequently he must be guided entirely by usage or prescription. The converse process, however, is much more manageable: the learner, on meeting with any broken plural, can be at little or no loss in determining the root or singular number from which it may have sprung.

87. Let us now proceed to describe the more common and useful derivatives that may arise from a simple triliteral root. With a view to precision, I adopt the term FORM to denote the mere outward appearance of a word as consisting of so many consonants, independent of the short vowels by which such consonants may become moveable. The various modifications or changes which a FORM may undergo by the application of the short vowels, together with the *jazm*, I call the MEASURES of such form. For example, the primitive *form* قبل is susceptible of twelve different *measures*, according as we apply the three short vowels and the *jazm*. Supposing the student to meet with the root قبل for the first time, in a book without vowel-points, he has the comfort of knowing that the word may be pronounced in twelve different ways or *measures*, though it remains all along under one and the same *form*. Thus it may be قَبْل, قِبْل, or قُبْل, by using the *jazm* on the middle letter; or it may be any of the following nine measures as dissyllables, viz. قَبَل, قَبِل, قَبُل, with *fatḥa* on the first letter;

also قِبَل ,قِبِل ,قِبِل, with *hasra* for the first vowel; or, lastly, it may be قُبَل ,قُبُل, or قُبُل, with *zamma* on the first letter.

88. The Semitic Grammarians, both Arabs and Jews, have adopted, *as a special favourite*, the triliteral root فعل, with a view to exemplify the various *forms* and *measures* of their words. This root, however, is utterly unsuitable to Europeans, not one in a thousand of whom ever can realize the true sound of the letter ع as the middle consonant. I therefore adopt here, as *my model*, the root قبل, which has the advantage of being more manageable; but the student must not suppose that either فعل or قبل, or any other root in the language, furnishes us with *all* the *forms* and *measures* we are about to detail. Some roots furnish us with a certain number of forms and measures which must be determined merely by *prescription*; others may give out different forms and measures, to be determined in like manner; but no single root in the language has ever furnished *all* the forms and measures assigned by the Grammarians to the root فعل. A similar instance occurs in the Greek Grammar, in the case of the verb τυπτω, where we are treated to some hundred different moods and tenses, &c., whilst it is perfectly understood that no single Greek Verb ever exhibited the *whole* of them.

PRIMARY FORM OR ROOT, قبل.

89. We have just shewn, in § 87, that the triliteral *root* is susceptible of twelve distinct *measures*. Of these, nine may occur in Persian; viz. 1st, قَبَل, which may be either a Substantive or an Adjective; thus, دَخُل "entrance;" حَمَد "praise;" صَعَب "difficult;" سَهَل "easy." 2nd, قِبَل (Substantive or Adjective); thus, عِلم "knowledge;" ذِكر "remembrance;" صِرف "pure;" حِتّ "friendly." 3d, قُبَل (Substantive); thus, حُسَن "beauty;" شُغَل "occupation." This measure may also be a broken plural; thus, أَسَد "a lion;" pl. أَسَد "lions." 4th, قَبَل (Subst. or Adj.); thus, طَلَب "search;" عَمَل "action;" حَسَن "beautiful;" بَطَل "bold." 5th, قِبَل (Adj.); thus, فَطِن "intelligent;" نَجِس "impure." 6th, قُبَل (Subst.); thus,

رَجُل "a man;" سَبُع "a beast of prey."   7th, قِبَل (Subst.); thus, عِظَم "greatness;" صِغَر "childhood." This measure may also be a broken plural; thus, حِرْفة "trade," pl. حِرَف "trades."   8th, قُبَل (Subst.); thus, هُدَي "guidance;" لُقَي "seeing."   9th, قُبُل (Subst.); thus, قُدُس "holiness;" رُحُم "tenderness." This last measure may also represent one of the broken plurals; thus, كِتاب "a book;" pl. كُتُب "books."

a. Most, if not all, of the preceding measures admit of a further modification, by the addition of the syllable ﻩـَـ, or ﺓـَـ, or ﺕـَـ; the effect of which is, either to render their meaning more definite, or, at the same time, to denote that words so ending, whether Substantives or Adjectives, are, as a general rule, of the feminine gender.

SECOND FORM, قابِل.

90. This form has two measures: viz. 1st, قابِل, which is the measure of the *Present Participle*, or *Noun of Agency*, of the triliteral verbal root. It is of very frequent occurrence in Persian; and from its nature it may be either a Substantive or an Adjective; thus, غالِب "prevailing," or "a conqueror;" قاتِل "a slayer;" قادِر "powerful." 2d, قابَل (a Substantive, and of rare occurrence); thus, خاتَم "a signet ring;" قالَب "a mould." These, like the preceding measures, may all assume the additional terminations ت, or ة, or ﻩ; thus, عاطِفَت "kindness;" فاصِلَة "distance;" فائِدﻩ "gain;" خاتِمَت "sealing up," or "conclusion" (of a book or epistle, &c.).

THIRD FORM, قبال.

91. This form has three measures: viz. 1st, قَبَال (Subst. or Adj.); thus, كَمَال "perfection;" قَرَار "rest;" حَرَام "unlawful;" خَرَاب "desolate." 2d, قِبَال (Subst.); thus, حِسَاب "reckoning;" فِرَار "flight." This measure is also that of one of the broken plurals, of

not unfrequent occurrence ; thus, عَبْد "a slave *or* servant;" pl. عِبَاد "slaves;" رَجُل "a man;" pl. رِجَال "men."   3d, قُبَال (a Subst.); thus, غُلَام "a boy *or* slave;" بُشَار "the lowest of the people." Like the preceding measures, the singular Nouns may assume the final ت, or ة, or ه ; thus, تِجَارت "traffic;" دَلَالت "guidance;" بُشَارت "glad tidings."

FOURTH FORM, قبول.

92. This form has two measures : viz. 1st, قَبُول (Adj. or Subst.); thus, قَبُول "acceptance." شَكُور "grateful;" ضَرُور "necessary;" 2d, قُبُول (Subst.); thus, دُخُول "entrance." ظُهُور "appearance;" This is also the measure of one of the broken plurals, as we have mentioned in No. 7; thus, حَرْف "a letter;" pl. حُرُوف "letters," &c. These measures (the broken plurals excepted) may assume the additional ت, or ة, or ه, as before ; thus, ضَرُورت or ضَرُورة "necessity."

FIFTH FORM, قبيل.

93. This form has two measures: viz. قَبِيل (Subst. or Adj.); thus, رَحِيل "marching;" دَلِيل "a guide;" حَسِين "beautiful;" كَرِيم "generous."   2d, قُبَيل (a diminutive Noun); thus, عَبْد "a slave;" عُبَيد "a little slave."   They may further assume the final ت, or ة, or ه ; thus, فَضِيلت "excellence;" نَصِيحت "admonition," &c.

SIXTH FORM, قبّال.

94. This form has two measures : viz. قَبَّال (Subst. or Adj.).   As a Substantive, it indicates the trade or profession of a person ; as, صَرَّاف "a banker *or* money-changer;" بَقَّال "a greengrocer;" جَلَّاد "an executioner."   As an Adjective it indicates an intensive degree,

called by the Arabs the Noun of Excess; thus, عَلَّام "very learned;" وَهَّاب "very bountiful." 2d, قُبَّال, which is the measure of one of the broken plurals; thus, جاهِل "a fool;" pl. جُهَّال "fools;" عامِل "an agent;" pl. عُمَّال "agents."

SEVENTH FORM, قَبِّيل.

95. This form has only one measure: viz. قَبِّيل, and it always indicates an intensive Adjective, or Noun of excess; thus, صِدِّيق "very sincere;" عِرِّيف "very knowing." It is not of very frequent occurrence in the Persian language.

EIGHTH FORM, قَبْلاء.

96. This form has two measures: viz. 1st, قَبْلاء; thus, باساء "calamity;" بغضاء "enmity." 2d, قُبَّلاء, a very frequent form of one of the broken plurals, as we stated in No. 7; thus, وَكِيل "an agent;" pl. وُكَلاء "agents;" نَدِيم "a courtier;" pl. نُدماء "courtiers." In general the final *hamza* is omitted in Persian.

NINTH FORM, قبلي.

97. This form has three measures: viz. 1st, قَبْلي (Subst.); thus, دَعْوي "a decree" (of a judge, &c.); دَعْوي "a demand." 2d, قِبْلي (Subst.); thus, فِكْري "reflection;" ذِكْري "mention." 3d, قُبْلي; thus, قُرْبي "proximity;" بُشْري "good news." This last measure may also indicate the feminine form of an Adjective of the comparative or superlative degree; thus, كبري "greater;" عُلْيا "higher;" دُنْيا "lower," &c. In Persian the final ي is generally changed into ا; thus دعوا and فتوا are much more common than دعوي and فتوي.

TENTH FORM, قبلان.

98. This form has four measures, most of them Substantives: viz.
1st, قَبَلَان (Adj.); thus, حَيْرَان "astonished;" سَكْرَان "intoxicated."
2d, قِبَلَان (Subst.); thus, حِرْمَان "disappointment;" عِرْفَان "knowledge." 3d, قَبَلَان (Subst.); thus, دَوَرَان "revolution;" طَيَرَان
"flying." 4th, قُبَلَان (Subst.); thus, كُفْرَان "ingratitude;" سُلْطَان
"a king or sovereign." This last measure may also be one of the
broken plurals; thus, بَلَدَ "a city;" pl. بُلْدَان "cities;" عَبْد " a
slave;" pl. عُبْدَان "slaves."

ELEVENTH FORM, اقبل.

99. This form has only one measure, viz. اَقْبَل, which is an
Adjective, and may be of any of the three degrees of comparison;
thus, اَكْبَر "greater;" اَبْكَم "dumb;" اَبْلَق "piebald;" اَحْسَن
"more or most beautiful."

TWELFTH FORM, اقبال.

100. This form has two measures: viz. 1st, اَقْبَال, which, as we have
already stated, is one of the broken plurals of most frequent occurrence
in Persian; thus, لُوح "a tablet;" pl. اَلْوَاح "tablets;" لُطف " a
favour," pl. اَلْطَاف "favours." 2d, اِقْبَال, which is the Infinitive
of the third FORMATION, or "derivative form," of the Verb from the
triliteral root, vulgarly and improperly called by our Grammarians
"the fourth conjugation," as if there were more conjugations than one
in the Arabic language; thus, اِخْرَاج "expulsion," or "expelling;"
اِخْلَاص "purifying;" اِقْرَار "confirming."

THIRTEENTH FORM, مقبل.

101. This form has four measures: viz. 1st, مَقْبَل and مِقْبَل

called by the Arabs the " Noun of Place and Time," because it generally denotes the *place where* or the *time when* the action indicated by the simple triliteral root is performed ; thus, مَعْبَر "a ferry" (place of crossing) ; مَكْتَب "a school" (place of writing) ; مَجْلِس "an assembly" (place of sitting) ; مَنْزِل "an inn" or "stage" (place of alighting). 2nd, مِقْبَل, called the "Noun of Instrument," because it generally indicates the "means or instrument" we employ in performing the action denoted by the simple triliteral root ; thus, مِحْلَب "a milk-pail," from حَلَب "milking ;" مِنْفَخ "a pair of bellows," from نَفَخ "blowing." 3rd, مُقْبِل, the Active Participle, or agent of the third derived form of the Verb from the triliteral root ; thus, مُخْرِج "expelling ;" مُخْلِص "purifying." 4th, مُقْبَل, the Passive Participle of the last mentioned measure ; thus, مُخْرَج "expelled ;" مُخْلَص "purified."

FOURTEENTH FORM, مقبال.

102. This form has only one measure, viz. مِقْبَال, which may either be a Noun of instrument or of excess ; thus, مِفْتَاح "a key ;" مِيزَان "a balance ;" مِنْعَام "very bountiful ;" مِخْلَاف "a great opposer."

FIFTEENTH FORM, مقبول.

103. This form has only one measure, viz. مَقْبُول. It is the Passive Participle of the triliteral verbal root, and from its nature it may be either a Substantive or an Adjective, as is the case in Latin and Greek ; thus, مَكْتُوب "written," or any "written production ;" مَنْشُور "published " or "divulged," hence, as a Substantive, "a proclamation" or "mandate."

(*a.*) The preceding forms and measures, all springing from the triliteral root, comprehend such only as will be found most useful to the Persian student. For a more detailed view of the subject he may have recourse to "Lumsden's Persian Grammar," or " Baillie's Arabic Tables."

104. It remains for us now to describe briefly the nature and peculiarities of the Derivative Forms of the Verb which may be deduced
from the primitive triliteral root. These are generally reckoned to
be *twelve* in number, or, according to some Grammarians, *fourteen*.
They have all the same terminations or inflections as the primitive Verb.
Grammarians very improperly call them CONJUGATIONS; but this term
is apt to mislead the student, whose ideas of a conjugation are already
formed on the Latin and Greek Grammars, to say nothing of French, &c.
Let not the student be alarmed, then, when he hears of the fifteen
conjugations of the Arabic language, for there is in reality but *one*
conjugation, according to our notions of the term. Instead of *conjugations*, then, I shall here use the term FORMATIONS; and of these only
eight occur in the Persian language, merely as Infinitives or Verbal
Nouns, and as Active or Passive Participles.

TABLE OF THE EIGHT DERIVED FORMATIONS OF VERBS.

Pas. Part.	Active Part.	Infinitive.	Basis.	No.
مُقَبَّل	مُقَبِّل	تَقْبِيل	قَبَّلَ	1.
مُقَابَل	مُقَابِل	مُقَابَلَة	قَابَلَ	2.
مُقْبَل	مُقْبِل	اِقْبَال	اَقْبَلَ	3.
مُتَقَبَّل	مُتَقَبِّل	تَقَبُّل	تَقَبَّلَ	4.
مُتَقَابَل	مُتَقَابِل	تَقَابُل	تَقَابَلَ	5.
مُنْقَبَل	مُنْقَبِل	اِنْقِبَال	اِنْقَبَلَ	6.
مُقْتَبَل	مُقْتَبِل	اِقْتِبَال	اِقْتَبَلَ	7.
مُسْتَقْبَل	مُسْتَقْبِل	اِسْتِقْبَال	اِسْتَقْبَلَ	8.

105. The Arabian Grammarians consider the third person singular
masculine of the past tense of every Verb or Formation as the source

or basis of such Verb; and this is the part given in Arabic Lexicons in those instances where the Latin or Greek Dictionaries give the first person of the present tense, and the German and French the Infinitive; thus, in the Arabic Lexicon of Golius, the leading word is the Verb قَبِلَ, for example, means "he received," or "he accepted;" not "to receive," or "to accept," as in European Dictionaries: and the same rule holds of all other Verbs. In the foregoing table we have given the leading word or *basis* of the eight derivative formations in their order, together with their Infinitives and Participles, Active and Passive. It will be observed, at the same time, that all the Participles of the eight formations, both Active and Passive, commence with م *mīm* moveable by the vowel *zamma*, and that the difference between the Active and Passive Participles is simply this, that all the Active Participles have *kasra* as the vowel of their last syllable, whilst the corresponding Passive has always *fatha*.

106. In conclusion, we may notice two classes of Arabic Nouns of frequent occurrence in Persian, viz. the Relative Noun (Subst. or Adj.), derived from any other Noun by the addition of the termination ـِيّ ; thus, شَمْسِيّ "solar," from شَمْس "the sun;" so دِمَشْقِيّ "a native of Damascus;" مِصْرِيّ "an Egyptian," &c. These, when adopted into Persian, dismiss the *nūnation* and undouble the final ي ; thus, مِصْرِي, دِمَشْقِي, شمسي, &c. 2nd, Abstract Nouns, formed in a similar manner by adding ـِيَة or ـِيّة ; thus, كَرَاهِيَة "aversion;" رَجُلِيَّة "manhood," طُفُولِيَّة "infancy."

107. The *source*, or third person singular, past tense, of the primary Verb, consists of three consonants, the first and last of which have always *fatha* for their vowel; and the middle letter has *fatha*, as a general rule, when the Verb is transitive or active, and either *kasra* or *zamma* when neuter or intransitive; thus, كَتَبَ "he wrote," حَزِنَ "he was sad," عَظُمَ "he was great."

(*a.*) The first derivative formation doubles the middle letter of the primitive root, and its vowels are always three *fathas*, as in the preceding table. If the primitive root is transitive, the first formation is *causal*; thus, كَتَبَ "he wrote," becomes in the first formation كَتَّبَ, which means "he caused to write," or "taught writing." Again, when the root is a Neuter or Intransitive Verb, the first formation is transitive; thus, حَزِنَ "he was sad," حَزَّنَ "he saddened," or "he afflicted." A few Verbs of this formation are derived from Nouns, and signify to *form* or *produce* whatever the Noun signifies; thus, from خُبْز "bread," is formed خَبَّزَ "he baked." Another peculiarity of this formation is the ascribing of the sense of the primitive root to a given object; thus, from كُفْر "infidelity," comes the infinitive تَكْفِير, which signifies "calling one an infidel;" so from كِذْب "lying," comes تَكْذِيب "giving one the lie."

(*b.*) The second formation inserts *ālif* after the first radical, and its vowels are always three *fathas*, as in the table. It is generally transitive, and often denotes a reciprocal action; thus, كَاتَبَ "he wrote to" or "corresponded with" (another person).

(*c.*) The third formation prefixes *alif*, and it has always for its vowels three *fathas*, as in the table. Like the first formation, it gives a causal or active signification to the primitive; thus, أَكْتَبَ "he taught writing," or "he dictated," or "made another write;" so, from عَظُم "he was great," comes أَعْظَم "he deemed (another) to be great," that is, "he honoured," or "respected" (another.) It will be observed, then, as a general rule, that the first and third formations are the causals of the primitive triliteral root, similar to the class of Persian Verbs in ـَانِيدن or ـَاندن, described in § 47.

d. The fourth formation, which prefixes the letter ت, with a *fatha*, to the first formation, is generally of a passive or submissive sense; thus, عَلِم "he knew;" عَلَّم "he taught;" تَعَلَّم "he was taught," or "he learned." So, from أَدَب "manners," "morals," or "polite literature," comes the Infinitive of the first formation تَأْدِيب "teaching manners," "chastisement;" and thence the Infinitive of the fourth formation تَأَدُّب "submitting to be taught manners."

e. The fifth formation prefixes ت, with a *fatḥa*, to the second. It generally denotes reciprocity, co-partnership, or association; thus, مُضَارَبَت "beating each other;" مُقَاتَلَه "slaying each other;" مُحَارَبَه "fighting together," &c. So تَكَاتَب "he corresponded by writing;" تَلَاعَب "he played with" (some one). Lastly, it may denote "pretending," the sense of the primitive; thus, تَمَارَض "he feigned sickness," or, as they say at sea, "he shammed Abram;" so from جَهِل "ignorance," comes تَجَاهُل "pretending ignorance."

f. The sixth formation prefixes the syllable اِنْ to the triliteral root, which is then pronounced with three *fatḥas*, whatever it may have originally been. This formation is always of a passive signification; hence, strictly speaking, it is never used in the Passive Participle; thus, كَسَر "he broke;" اِنْكَسَر "it was broken;" so the Infinitives, اِنْقِلَاب "being changed," اِنْكِسَار "being broken," are altogether passive in signification.

g. The seventh formation prefixes اِ, and inserts ت (sometimes د or ط) between the first and second radical of the triliteral, as may be seen in the table. Generally speaking, it denotes the passive or reflexive sense of the primitive triliteral root; thus, فَرَق "he divided;" اِفْتَرَق "it went to pieces;" ضَرَب "he beat;" اِضْطَرَب "he beat himself" (in agitation, &c.); hence the Infinitive اِضْطِرَاب "perplexity." Sometimes it denotes reciprocity, &c., like the fifth formation; thus, اِخْتِصَام "mutual contention;" اِجْتِمَاع "collecting together."

h. The eighth formation prefixes اِسْت to the primitive root, as shewn in the table. Its general property is, *asking, wishing,* or *demanding* the state or action expressed by the primitive; thus,

غَفَرَ "he pardoned ;" اِسْتَغْفَرَ "he begged pardon."   This formation agrees nearly with the Latin "Desiderative Verbs," formed from the second supine by adding *rio*, such as *esurio*, "I desire to eat," from *esu*; so *cœnaturio*, "I wish I had my supper," from *cœnatu.*   For a full account of the various shades of meaning peculiar to the eight derived forms of the Verb, the reader may consult Dr. Lumsden's Persian Grammar, where the subject is absolutely exhausted.

OF THE FORMS UNDER WHICH ARABIC WORDS ARE USED IN THE PERSIAN.*

108. All Arabic Infinitives, Participles, Substantives, and Adjectives, are introduced into the Persian in the form of the Nominative, which throws away from the last letter every species of nunation, such as ـٌ , ـً , ـٍ , as well as all short vowels, which they may have possessed as Arabic words; but when their construction in the Persian requires them to assume the *iẓāfat*, or sign of the word governing the Genitive Case, they receive it in the same manner as if they were originally Persian words, with the following exceptions :—

a. When an Arabic word terminating in ىٰ , that must be pronounced as ا , becomes the first Substantive in construction with another Substantive following it, ىٰ is actually changed into ا , to which short ى is afterwards affixed to shew the construction : thus تَمَنّىٰ in construction becomes تَمَنّاى ; as, تَمَنّاى شِفَاعَت "the petition of intercession ;" and so also مَولىٰ, دَعْوىٰ, مَعْنىٰ, &c.

b. Feminine Arabic Substantives terminating in ة , when introduced into the Persian, change ة sometimes into ه , and sometimes into ت ; thus, مُحَبَّت "friendship," being found written by the same author مُحَبّه and مُحَبَّت.

---

* The paragraphs from No. 108 to 116 inclusive are extracted, with numerous corrections and alterations, from a valuable article on the subject, which will be found in the second volume of the "Asiatic Researches."

c. Feminine Arabic Adjectives and Participles terminating in ة, wnen introduced into the Persian, always change ة into ه; viz. خالِصَة "pure," is always written خالِصَه; thus, مُحَبَّتِ خالِصَه "sincere friendship."

OF ARABIC VERBAL NOUNS.

109. Their masculines singular are used in the Persian as Substantives, and in every respect serve the same purposes, and are subject to the same rules of construction as Substantives originally Persian; thus, اِظْهارِ يكَانكِي "demonstrations of unanimity"—اسْتِعْجالِ تَمام "great haste"—تَحْرِيرِ مَسْطُور "the said writing"—نظر بر اِين بُود "my view was this"—اِحْتِظاظِ وافِر يافت "he received great delight"—بعد از تَقْدِيم مراسِم "after performing the duties"—اِقْبال و اِجْلال "prosperity and splendour"—اِتِّحادي كه در مِيانِ ايشان بُود "the union that was between them."

a. Their masculines plural are used in the Persian as Substantives; and in every respect serve the same purposes, and are subject to the same rules of construction as Substantives originally Persian; thus, افعالِ نيك "good actions"—اخْلاقِ مَرْدُم "the dispositions of men"—اطْوارِ مَسْطُور "the qualifications described."

b. Their feminines singular are used in the Persian as Substantives, and in every respect serve the same purposes, and are subject to the same rules of construction as Substantives originally Persian; thus, مُعامِلتِ مُلْك "the business of the empire"—اِجازَت اسْت "there is permission"—مُقاتلهٌ عظيمه "enormous mutual slaughter"—مُكاتبهٌ مَرْقُومه بدوسْتِي "a letter written in friendship."

c. Their feminines plural are used in the Persian as Substantives, and in every respect serve the same purposes and are subject to the

same rules of construction as Substantives originally Persian; thus,
مُعاملاتِ كُلِّي "public affairs"— توجُّهاتِ دوسْتان "the civilities of friends"— تكْلِيفاتِ مزْبور "the aforesaid difficulties."

OF ARABIC PARTICIPLES ACTIVE.

110. Their masculines singular are used in the Persian as Participles, as Substantives, and as Adjectives; thus, مُنْتَظِر ماند "he remained expecting"— طالِع و لامِع باد "may it be shining and blazing"— حاكِمِ شهر "governor of the city"— مُوجِبِ خُوشْنُودِي "causing gladness," or "the cause of gladness"— مُصَنِّفِ اِين كِتاب "composing this book," or "the author of this book"— مُطابِقِ شَرْعِ شرِيف "following the noble law," or "follower of the noble law"— مَرْدُمِ قابِل "an able man"— عامِلِ نيك "a good agent"— حضْرتِ خالِق "God the Creator"— قاتِلرا كُشْت "he put the murderer to death"— حاكِمِ مُستَقِلّ "absolute judge"— اگر عاشِق صادِق اسْت "if the lover is sincere"— مُشْتَمِل بر مصادقت "containing friendship."

a. Their masculine perfect plurals are used in the Persian as Substantives, in the form of the Oblique Case which terminates in ـين; but they do not seem to be used in the form of the Nominative which terminates in ـُون; thus, عِلْمِ اوَّلِين و آخِرِين "the knowledge of the ancients and moderns"— قومِ مُسْلِمِين "the sect of the faithful."

b. Their masculine imperfect plurals are used in the Persian as Substantives; thus, حُكّامِ حال و اسْتِقْبال "officers of the present and future"— عُمّالِ جدِيد و قدِيم "the new and old agents."

c. Their feminines singular are used in the Persian as Participles, as Substantives, and as Adjectives; thus, حامِلِه اسْت "she is

a " زنِ حاملہ "queen of the empire"—مالکہُ مُلَک "a pregnant"—صاحبۃٌ مَوصُوفہ "kind friend"—مُشفِقۃٌ مِهربان "pregnant woman"—
"accomplished lady."

d. Their feminine perfect plurals are used in the Persian as Substantives when they express things without life; thus, واقِعاتِ زمان "the incidents of time"—واردَاتِ ناگهاني " unforeseen events."

OF ARABIC PARTICIPLES PASSIVE.

111. Their masculine singular is used in the Persian as Participles Passive, as Substantives, and as Adjectives; thus, جُملگئ هِمَّت "the sum of my desire is bestowed on that"—مَصرُوف بران اسْت "be the shade of clemency extended"—ظِلِّ شفقَت ممدُود باد "He makes it the perception (i. e. the thing perceived) of your enlightened soul;" i. e. "I represent it," &c.—مشهُود ضمير مُنير ميگردانَد "the desire (i. e. the thing desired) of the souls"—مرغُوب طبائِع "the injured slave"—بندۀ مظلُوم "intention and design"—مقصُود و مُراد "let them make the people glad"—خلائِق را محظُوظ گردانند "their intention was this.'"—مَقصُود ایشان بر این بُود

a. Their masculine perfect plural does not seem to be used in the Persian, either in the form of the Nominative or the Oblique Case.

b. Their feminines singular are used in the Persian as Substantives and as Adjectives; thus, مَعشُوقۃ من "my sweetheart," i. e. "the beloved of me"—مَعشُوقۃ مَذکُورہ "the said beloved woman"—والدۃُ مخدُومہ "respected mother."

c. Their feminine perfect plurals are used in the Persian as Substantives, to express things without life; thus, مطلُوباتِ آن مِهربان "the demands of that friend"—مُقدّماتِ شرعي "law affairs."

d. The Active and Passive Participles of Transitive Verbs, with a following Substantive having the article ال prefixed to it, form expressions corresponding to such Persian compounds as خُوب‌رُوي, which are used both as Substantives and as Adjectives; thus, شَخْصٍ واجِبُ ٱلتَّعْظِيم " he evades a decision "—مُتَعَذِّرُ ٱلفَصْلِ است " a person deserving respect "—قلمٍ مَقْطُوعُ ٱللِسان " a pen cut short in the point."

OF ARABIC ADJECTIVES RESEMBLING PARTICIPLES.

112. The forms قَبِيل, قَبِل, and قَبَل, represent three species of Arabic words which are derived from Intransitive Verbs; and called by Arabian Grammarians, Adjectives resembling Participles. The singulars of these forms are used in the Persian both as Adjectives and Substantives.; as, آن عزِيز "that respectable person"—شرِير است "he is wicked"—دوستِ قدِيم "an old friend."

a. Their plurals are used in the Persian as Substantives; thus, شُرَفاي پاك‌نِهاد "the learned men of Greece"—حُكَماي يُونان "noblemen of integrity."

b. These three forms of Adjectives resembling Participles, with a following Substantive having the article ال prefixed to it, form expressions corresponding to such compounds as حُوب رُوي, which are used in the Persian both as Substantives and Adjectives; thus, آن حَسَنُ ٱلوَجْهِ "that (person) beautiful, as to countenance"—قدِيمُ ٱلخِدْمَت "the said old servant"—مرْكِم قدِيمُ ٱلخِدْمَت مذكُور "a man of long service."

OF PARTICIPLES EXPRESSING THE SENSE OF THEIR PRIMITIVES IN A STRONGER DEGREE.

I. The forms قَبُول قَيّال, قَبِيل, قَبِل, and مِقْبال are sometimes Participles which express the sense of their primitives in a stronger degree, and are sometimes used in the Persian as Adjectives; thus, أَدْوِيَةٌ قَتَّالَه "a poisonous" or "highly poisonous medicine"—صَبُور است "he is full of patience."

OF ARABIC SUBSTANTIVES.

113. The Arabic Nouns of time and place are frequently employed in the Persian; and the following list exhibits the forms of such as are derived from the primitive roots of the different species of triliterals; thus, from كتب comes مَكْتَبٌ "the time and place of writing"—from قرّ comes مَقَرّ "a place of rest, residence"—from امن comes مَأْمَن "a place of safety"—from بداء comes مَبْدَأ "the place and time of beginning"—from وضع comes مَوْضِع "place, opportunity"—from قوم comes مَقَام "the place and time of standing"—from دعو comes مَدْعَا "the place or object of desire"—from بيع comes مَبِيع "the time and place of selling"—from رمي comes مَرْمَا "the place and time of throwing"—from اوب comes مَآب "the place of return, the centre"—from حي comes مَحْيَا "the time and place of living." To express the *place* more particularly, ة or ه is sometimes added to the common form; as, مَقْبَرَة "burying-place."

a. The Noun of time and place from the derivative forms is exactly the same with the Participle Passive, and is also used in the Persian; thus, مُسْتَوْدَع "deposited," also "a place of deposit."

b. The Persian language also makes free use of the Arabic instrumental Noun, which is represented by the forms مِقْبَلَة, مِقْبَل, and مِقْبَال (vide §§ 101 and 102); thus, بِمِيزانِ عقل سنجيد "he weighed in scale of reason"—مِفْتَاحِ مقصُود "the key of intention."

c. All Arabic names of persons and things in general are introduced into Persian at pleasure; thus, مَرْيَم "Mary," مَكَّة "Mecca," عَين "the eye," لَحْم "flesh," جَدّ "an ancestor," &c.

OF ARABIC ADJECTIVES.

114. Besides the Arabic Participles which we have already observed are used as Adjectives, there is also a plentiful source of real Adjectives formed by affixing ي ـــ to Substantives of almost every denomination, which are freely introduced into the Persian; thus, اِنْسَانِي "human," ارْضِي "earthly," مِصْرِي "Egyptian," &c.

a. The masculines singular of Arabic Superlatives are used in the Persian both as Substantives and Adjectives; thus, اَسْعَدِ زمان " the most fortunate of times ;" در وقْتِ اَحْسَن "at a most lucky time."

b. The masculines plural of Arabic Superlatives are used in the Persian both as Substantives and Adjectives; thus, اكابِر وقْت "the great men of the age ;" اشْخاصِ اكابِر "most illustrious personages."

c. The feminines singular of Arabic Superlatives are used in the Persian as Adjectives; thus, دَولَتِ عُظْمٰى "prosperity most great."

d. Arabic Ordinal Numbers are used in the Persian as Adjectives; thus, باب اوّل "the first chapter." With respect to phrases purely Arabic, and whole sentences, which are often met with in Persian authors, they require an elementary knowledge of the Arabic language, and do not belong to this place.

OF THE CONSTRUCTION OF ARABIC INFINITIVES, PARTICIPLES, SUBSTANTIVES, AND ADJECTIVES.

115. In the Persian language, when Arabic Adjectives or Participles are made use of to qualify Arabic or Persian Substantives singular, they agree with them in gender and number; thus, عاشِقِ مَذْكُور "the said lover ;" والِدهٔ مُكَرّمه "respected mother ;" دوستِ قديم "an old friend ;" هَمْشِيرهٔ عزيزه "dear sister."

a. When Arabic Adjectives and Participles are made use of to qualify Arabic and Persian Substantives masculine and plural, they remain in the form of the masculine singular; thus, حُكَّام مَذْكُور "the said officers;" برادران مَفْقُود "the lost *or* missing brethren."

b. When Arabic Adjectives and Participles are made use of to qualify Arabic or Persian Substantives feminine and plural, they are put in the feminine singular; and often, though not so properly, in the masculine singular; thus, تَكْلِيفاتِ مَذْكُورة or تَكْلِيفاتِ مَذْكُور "the said difficulties;" زَنانِ مَوْصُوف or زَنانِ مَوْصُوفه "accomplished women."

c. An Arabic Substantive, in the Persian, is often rendered definite by a following Arabic Adjective or Participle having the article ال prefixed; thus, نبِيُّ ٱلْمُخْتار "the prophet elect."

OF THE INTRODUCTION OF ARABIC WORDS INTO THE LANGUAGE OF HINDŪSTĀN.

116. All the different species of Infinitives, Participles, Substantives, and Adjectives, which we have enumerated, are introduced into the Hindūstānī language, in the same form, for the same purposes, and with the same freedom as in the Persian: submitting themselves to the different rules of regimen and concord that are peculiar to the Hindūstānī language, in the same manner as if they were words originally belonging to it. Arabic Adverbs, Prepositions, and Conjunctions, are also used in the language of Hindūstān, but perhaps less frequently than in the Persian.

a. Arabic Prepositions occur both in Persian and Hindūstānī, but they are used only with Substantives admitted from the former language. The principal Arabic Prepositions are, عَلَى "upon," or above;" عَن "from;" عِنْد "near," "with," (Latin, *apud*); فِي "in;" كَ "like;" لَ or ل "to," "for;" مَعَ "with," and مِن "from;" thus, عَلَي ٱلصَّباح "in *or* upon the morning;" فِي ٱلْجُمْله "in short," or "upon the whole," &c.

117. The following judicious remarks, from the Preface to " Richardson's Arabic Grammar," 4to, London, 1811, contain all that need be said in proof of the impossibility of acquiring an accurate knowledge of Persian without studying the genius of the Arabic, on which it so much depends. In page x, the author expresses himself as follows, viz. :—

a. " Exclusive of the Arabic sentences, which occur in almost every Persian book, three-fourths perhaps of the component words of this tongue are either adopted or derived from that language; so that it is equally impossible to compile a Persian Dictionary without the assistance of the Arabic, as to confine the English language to words of mere Anglo-Saxon* origin, to the exclusion of every derivation from the Greek, Latin, French, and other dialects. On a superficial view, it may be supposed, perhaps, that as the genius of the two languages is so different, a perusal of Arabic Grammar can throw no light on that of the Persian : but two things essentially foreign to each other may often have a tendency to the same point; for though Astronomy can never teach the practical method of working a ship, yet is it to the highest degree necessary to the safety of navigation; so Arabic Grammar, though not absolutely teaching the elements of the Persian, will be found to throw most satisfactory lights on the study, especially by enabling the student to discover the roots of those Arabic words which are so copiously blended with that language; of which being once possessed, and of the mode of forming from them the derivative inflexions, he may with ease fix in his memory twenty words perhaps for one which he could acquire without such assistance. Upon the whole, therefore, I will not hesitate to assert, that the reading of Arabic Grammar with the least attention will give a gentleman already acquainted in some degree with the Persian, a more critical knowledge of that tongue, than twice the time directed to any other branch of the study."

118. As an apt illustration of the soundness of the preceding remarks by Mr. Richardson, I conclude this Section with an example of an

---

* The original, instead of " Anglo-Saxon," reads " Celtic," an extraordinary slip of the *pen*; for, let us " give the *devil* his due," I cannot suppose it to be an *error of the printer's*.

Arabic triliteral verbal root, together with the various *forms* and *measures* thence derived and in actual use. These it will be seen amount to *fifty-one in number :* supposing, however, that each Arabic root yields at an average only *thirty* derivatives, it is evident that, by getting by heart one thousand such roots, joined to a knowledge of forming the derivatives, a Persian student may easily gain an acquaintance with *thirty thousand* useful words, which otherways no common memory could either acquire or retain.

a. The Arabic root نَظَرَ, as a Verb, denotes " he looked," or " surveyed with his eyes ;" hence, figuratively, " he viewed mentally," or " pondered in his mind." Now from this single root result the following derivatives, all of more or less frequent occurrence in the Persian language ; viz. ناظِر " an inspector," " superintendant "— ناظِرة " the eye," " vision," " reading "— نِظَّار " physiognomy," " penetration "— ناظُور " a watchman "— ناظُورة " looked at," " respectable," " venerated "— نَظَّار (Adj.) " noble spirited," (Subst.) " a scrutineer," " an overseer "— نَظَارة " inspection," " superintendency "— ناظِرَين " the two lachrymal ducts from the inner corner of the eye "— نَظَّارة " spectators "— نَظَّارِي " seeing," " a sight "— نَظَائِر (plur.) " eminent," or " respected men "— نَظِر " expecting "— نِظْر " like," " resembling "— نَظَر " looking," " considering," " pondering," &c.— نُظَرَاء (plur.) " equals "— نَظَرَات (plur.) " looks," " appearances "— نَظَران " looking at," " viewing "— نَظْرة " one look," " look of a demon," " evil eye "— نُظْرة and نَظِرة " delay," " postponement "— بَنُو نَظَرِي " those who are fond of, and polite to ladies "— نَظَرِي " visionary," " speculative," " ideal "— نَظُور " one who attentively looks at another "— نَظُورة and نَظِيرة " one who is looked upon or revered above others ;" also, " the first line or van of an army"—نَظِير "alike," "equal to"—اَنْظَار (plur.) "looks," "eyes"—اِنْظَار "listening," "considering"—اِنْتِظَار "expectation," "anxiously waiting for one"—اِسْتِنْظَار "desiring one to wait or delay"—تَنْظَار "looking," "viewing"—تَنَظُّر "granting a delay," "waiting"—تَنْظِير "waiting," "granting a delay," hence "selling on credit"—تَنَاظُر "looking at one another," "facing"—مِنْظَار "a mirror," "looking-glass"—مَنْظَر "looking," "the face," "aspect"—مَنْظَر "waited for"—مَنْظَرَانِي or مَنْظَرِي "beautiful of face," "a theatre," "scene," &c.—مَنْظَرَة "looking at," "beholding," "a place where one may have an extensive view"—مَنَاظِر (pl.) "shows," "spectacles," "exhibitions," "high places whence an extensive view may be had," &c.—مُنَاظِر "like," "resembling," (Subst.) "a rival," "an opponent"—مُنَاظَرَة "disputing," "arguing," "making one thing look like another"—مُنْتَظِر "one who waits or expects impatiently"—مَنْظَرَة "a place of show," "theatre," &c.—مَنْظُور "looked at," "approved of," "agreeable"—مَنْظُورَة "a misfortune"—مُسْتَنْظِر "one who craves delay"—مُنْتَظَر "time or place of waiting."

SECTION VII.

PROSODY.

119. The Prosody of the Persians, the Turks, and the Musalmāns of India, is founded on that of the Arabs. They, all of them, possess a variety of *feet* and *metres*, much resembling that which prevailed of old among the Greeks and Romans. There are, however, certain

metres, of general use among the Arabs, which the Persians very rarely employ, and *vice versâ*. I here take slight note of the metres purely Arabian, which are five in number, and confine myself to those peculiar to the Persians, which I shall endeavour to describe in as plain and concise a manner as the short limits assigned to this Section will permit.

120. In order to form a clear conception of the very simple principles on which the Persian metres are founded, the student must bear constantly in mind what we stated in our first page, viz. that *the thirty-two letters of the Alphabet are* ALL *to be viewed as* CONSONANTS. In the second place, it is a law of the language that the initial letter of every word must be followed by one or other of the three primitive vowels, ـَ, ـِ, or ـُ (vide §§ 4, 5, & 6); which vowels are uniformly *short* when succeeded by a single moveable consonant in the next syllable, but they become *long by position* if the following consonant be inert; and this rule holds from the beginning to the end of every word. Lastly, the final letter of every word in Persian is *inert*, with the sole exception of Substantives accompanied by an *iẓāfat* (§ 29), or in regimen with the word following (§ 61); hence, in poetry, *the last syllable of every Persian word is long by position*, because the word following must necessarily begin with a consonant.

121. We mentioned in a former Section (§ 88), that the Arabian Grammarians adopted the verbal root فعل as a mere formula or model for exhibiting the various *forms* and *measures* of Nouns and Verbs; but this is not all, they have applied the same root and its formations as models for exemplifying the اركان or FEET in Prosody. Thus instead of saying that the word جَلَال, for example, is an *Iambus*, they simply say that it is of the measure فَعُول, and thus of all other feet. The Arabian method, then, of exhibiting the various poetic feet is exceedingly clear and simple, as it speaks at once to the *ear* and to the *eye*. The only objection to it is, that the root فعل, selected as a formula, is, as we formerly stated, unsuitable to European students, however satisfactory it may prove to the Arabs. I here, therefore, select as my formula the root فضل, which bears a close resemblance in form to فعل, with the important advantage of having for its middle consonant a letter that is quite perceptible to a European

ear. In the Roman character I represent this middle consonant by our letter *d*, which is the sound given to it by the Arabs (vide page 6). Thus, what the Romans would call an Iambus will here be represented by the measure فَضُول, pronounced *Fadūl*, not *Faẓūl*. Perhaps I am a little fastidious; but my reason for avoiding the *z* is that the Greeks and Romans viewed it as a *double consonant*, hence with them the short vowel preceding it becomes long by position; and the classical scholar might be apt to fancy that *a* in *Faẓūl* is also long, an error into which he is not likely to fall when we write it *Fadūl*.

122. Before we come to describe the *Feet* and *Metres* (بُحُور) employed in Persian Poetry, the student is once more requested to bear constantly in mind the peculiar principles on which the Prosody of the language is founded, as explained in § 120. For the sake of simplicity and perspicuity, we intend to make a free use of the Roman character in this Section; and in so doing let it be observed that the three vowels *a*, *i*, and *u*, when unaccented, represent the *zabar* ـَ, *zer* ـِ, and *pesh* ـُ of the Persians. These are naturally short when followed in the next syllable by a single moveable consonant, and they become long by position when followed by two or more consonants; hence it will not be necessary for us to perplex the student with a superfluity of long and short marks, very ridiculously applied as they are in every work on Eastern Prosody which we have yet seen. The vowels *ā*, *ī*, and *ū* are always understood to be long, and indicate the presence of the three letters of prolongation, *alif* ا, *ye* ي, and *wāw* و respectively, each being preceded by its own homogeneous short vowel.

OF THE اَرْكَان, *i. e.* STANDARD MEASURES, OR FEET.

123. The poetic feet or measures in Persian may be reckoned at about twenty-one in number. So far as they extend they are the same as those employed in Greek and Latin, with this peculiarity, that the feet in Arabic and Persian have no specific name, being all represented by the *unmeaning* word or standard which gives their exact sound. They are divided into two classes, six of which are called Perfect and fifteen Imperfect Feet, a distinction of no great practical utility, for few compositions of any length consist solely of Perfect Feet.

The following are the six PERFECT FEET—

NO.	MEASURE.		LATIN NAME.	QUANTITY.
1.	فَضُولُن	Fadūlun	Bacchius	◡ — —
2.	فَاضِلُن	Fādilun	Amphimacer	— ◡ —
3.	مَفَاضِيلُن	Mafādīlun	Epitritus primus	◡ — — —
4.	فَاضِلَاتُن	Fādilātun	,, secundus	— ◡ — —
5.	مُستَفضِلُن	Mustafdilun	,, tertius	— — ◡ —
6.	مَفضُولَاتُ	Mafdūlātu	, quartus	— — — ◡

The IMPERFECT or ARTIFICIAL FEET are—

NO.	MEASURE.		LATIN NAME.	QUANTITY.
1.	فَاضِ or فَضْ	Fad or Fād	Cæsura	—
2.	فَضَلُ	Fadlu	Trochæus	— ◡
3.	فَضُول	Fadūl	Iambus	◡ —
4.	فَضلُن	Fadlun	Spondæus	— —
5.	فَضُولُ	Fadūlu	Amphibrachys	◡ — ◡
6.	فَضَلُن	Fadalun	Anapæstus	◡ ◡ —
7.	مَفضُولُ	Mafdūlu	Antibacchius	— — ◡
8.	مَفضُولُن	Mafdūlun	Molossus	— — —
9.	فَضِلَاتُ	Fadilātu	Pæon tertius	◡ ◡ — ◡
10.	فَضَلَتُن	Fadalatun	Pæon quartus	◡ ◡ ◡ —
11.	فَضِلَاتُن	Fadilātun	Ionicus minor	◡ ◡ — —
12.	فَاضِلَاتُ	Fādilātu	Ditrochæus	— ◡ — ◡
13.	مُفَاضِلُن	Mufādilun	Diambus	◡ — ◡ —
14.	مُفَاضِيلُ	Mufādīlu	Antispastus	◡ — — ◡
15.	مُفتَضِلُن	Muftadilun	Choriambus	— ◡ ◡ —

124. We shall now proceed to lay before the reader a Table of the Fourteen Standard Metres employed in Persian verse. These, it may be observed, are wholly composed of Perfect Feet, and are thence called Perfect Metres; otherwise, they are Imperfect. Here again the distinction is whimsical and useless; for the great body of the poetry of the language, especially poems of any length, are found to prefer the Imperfect Metre, probably because the Perfect would prove too monotonous by long continuance. It would occupy too much of our space to insert in the Table the translation of the Arabic names of the various Metres; nor would it be of any great use if we did, for in most instances the aptness of the name is not very perceptible.

a. The Arabs and Persians consider a verse as consisting of two equal members; in fact, what we call a couplet is, with them, a single verse, as will be seen in the following extract (a little corrected) from Gladwin, viz.—

"It is generally allowed that a *Bait*, or verse, cannot consist of less than two hemistichs; and each of these hemistichs is called *Miṣrā'*, a word which literally signifies *the fold of a door:* and the resemblance between a distich and a door of two folds is in this, that in the same manner as with a door of two folds you may open or shut which you please without the other, and when you shut both together it is still but one door; so also of a distich, you may scan which of the hemistichs you please without the other, and when you read both together they will form but one verse. The first foot of the first hemistich is called *Ṣadr*, and the last foot thereof *'Arūẓ*. Of the second hemistich, the first foot is called *Ibtidā* and the last *Ẓarb*. The intermediate feet of both have the general name *Ḥashw*. The meaning of *Ṣadr* is the *first*, and *Ibtidā* signifies *commencement*; the first beginning the distich, as the other does the second hemistich. The last foot of the first hemistich is called *'Arūẓ*, signifying the *pole of a tent;* for, as the pole is the support of the tent, so is the distich founded on this prop; for until this foot is determined, the hemistich is not complete, nor its measure known. The last foot of the second hemistich is called *Ẓarb*, i.e. *of one kind*, or *alike*, it resembling the *'Arūẓ* in that both are at the end of a hemistich, and that the conclusion of verses are alike by the observance of rhyme. *Ḥashw* is the stuffing of a cushion, and on account of their situation the intermediate feet are so called.

"Feet are either *Sālim* or *Ghair-Sālim*, i.e. "perfect" or "imperfect." The perfect foot is that in which the verse is originally composed, without excess or diminution. The Imperfect Foot is that wherein some change has happened, either by adding something to it, or taking something from it; as, for example, if in the word مفاضِيلُن *mafadilun*, between ل and ن you introduce an *alif* ا, and read مَفاضيلان *mafadilan* ; or if from the same word you take away ن and the short vowel of the ل, and say مفاضيل *mafadil*. The Imperfect Foot is called *Muzāḥif*, and the alteration is called *Ziḥāf*, or *Muzāḥaf*, derived from the root *Zaḥf*, or *Zaḥaf*, literally signifying "departing from its original intention," as we say *Sahmi Zāḥif*, "an arrow that errs from the mark."

TABLE OF PERFECT PERSIAN METRES

CLASS I.—*Hemistich of Four Feet, each Four Syllables.*

NO.	NAME.	MEASURE.	AFFINITY.
1.	*Baḥri Hazaj.*	Măfādīlun, Măfādīlun, Măfādīlun, Măfādīlun . . .	ᴗ – – –|ᴗ – – –|ᴗ – – –|ᴗ – – –|
2.	— *Rajaz.*	Mustafdīlun, Mustafdīlun, Mustafdīlun, Mustafdīlun . . .	– – ᴗ –|– – ᴗ –|– – ᴗ –|– – ᴗ –|
3.	— *Ramal.*	Fādīlātun, Fādīlātun, Fādīlātun, Fādīlātun	– ᴗ – –|– ᴗ – –|– ᴗ – –|– ᴗ – –|

CLASS II.—*Hemistich of Four Feet, each Three Syllables.*

NO.	NAME.	MEASURE.	AFFINITY.
4.	*Baḥri Mutaḳārib*	Fădūlun, Fădūlun, Fădūlun, Fădūlun	ᴗ – –|ᴗ – –|ᴗ – –|ᴗ – –|
5.	— *Mutadārik.*	Fādīlun, Fādīlun, Fādīlun, Fādīlun	– ᴗ –|– ᴗ –|– ᴗ –|– ᴗ –|

TABLE OF PERFECT PERSIAN METRES—*continued*.

CLASS III.—*Hemistich of Three Feet, each Four Syllables.*

NO.	NAME.	MEASURE.	AFFINITY.
6.	*Baḥri Munsariḥ*	Mustafdīlun, Mafdūlātŭ, Mustafdīlun	
7.	—— *Khafīf*	Fadīlātun, Mustafdīlun, Fadīlātun	
8.	—— *Muẓāri'*	Măfadīlun, Fādīlātun, Măfadīlun	
9.	—— *Muḳtaẓab*	Mafdūlātŭ, Mustafdīlun, Mustafdīlun	
10.	—— *Mujtass*	Mustafdīlun, Fādīlātun, Fādīlātun	
11.	—— *Mushāḳil*	Fadīlātun, Măfadīlun, Măfadīlun	
12.	—— *Sarī'*	Mustafdīlun, Mustafdīlun, Mafdūlātŭ	
13.	—— *Jadīd*	Fādīlātun, Fādīlātun, Mustafdīlun	
14.	—— *Ḳarīb*	Măfadīlun, Măfadīlun, Fādīlātun	

(*a.*) Out of the preceding fourteen Metres, three are peculiar to the Persians, and never used by the Arabs, viz. the *Baḥri Mushāḳil*, No. 11, and the *Jadīd* and *Ḳarīb*, Nos. 13 and 14. The remaining eleven are common to both nations.

125. In the arrangement and classification of the Persian Metres, I have adopted an entirely new plan of my own, which, I flatter myself, will be found far more conspicuous than the clumsy method followed by the natives of the East and their servile imitators in Europe. In the first place, I have adopted the Roman character throughout, which is a great saving of space. Secondly, I have carefully marked the quantities of the vowels, but only in those cases where there might possibly occur a mistake. For instance, when a vowel is followed by two consonants, or by a single consonant at the end of a word, as in the foot *Mustafdilun*, it is quite superfluous to mark the quantities of the first, second, and fourth vowels, and to write the word *Mūstāfdīlūn*, or, more absurdly, *Mūstāfīlūn*, as we have seen it figure in some recent works on the subject. Lastly, in exhibiting the affinity or relationship that holds between the various Metres of each class, I have made use of the *straight line*, which leads *more directly to the point* than the *circles* used by the Prosodians of the East. Take, for example, CLASS I.: we see at a glance, that by taking the two first syllables of the *Bahri Hazaj* from the *beginning* of the hemistich, and placing the same at the *end*, we have the *Bahri Rajaz*, which comes next. In like manner, if we transfer the first syllable of the *Bahri Rajaz* from the beginning to the end of the hemistich, we have the *Bahri Ramal*, and so on with all the rest. In CLASS III. I have adopted an arrangement of my own, which has enabled me to exhibit nine Metres at once. These are all made up of the four *Epitriti* Feet of the ancients, and it is a wonder that no one has been hitherto led to classify them as I have done.

(*a.*) In the three preceding classes of Persian Metres, it is curious to observe the prevalence of the long syllables over the short. In Classes I. and III., for instance, the *long* is to the short as *three* to *one*, and in Class II. as *two* to *one*. In a very good Persian Grammar (barring the paper and typography), published some fifteen years ago, at Helsingfors, the author, who, like his Teutonic neighbours, is evidently fond of a *theory*, says that " the Persians and Arabs, like the Greeks and Romans, rejoice in a great variety of Metres, but that the Asiatic Metres differ mainly in this, viz. the long syllables far exceed the short. All this (quoth he) is quite in conformity with the character of the Oriental people, who are distinguished by a certain degree of gravity and sobriety in their conversation and gestures, combined with dignity and stateliness in all their movements."

126. We shall now notice the five Metres used chiefly by the Arabs, and very rarely by the Persians. The Arabian Metres are divided into two classes, in the first of which we have two additional Feet, viz. *Mŭfādĭlătun* and *Mŭtă-fādĭlun*, consisting each of five syllables, and for neither of which have we a Greek or Latin name. In Class II. the Feet are the same as in the preceding Table, and the Metres differ merely in their arrangement or disposition.

TABLE OF ARABIAN METRES.

CLASS I.—*Hemistich of Four Feet, each Five Syllables.*

NO.	NAME.	MEASURE.	AFFINITY.
1.	*Baḥri Wāfir.*	Mŭfādĭlătun, Mŭfādĭlătun, Mŭfādĭlătun, Mŭfādĭlătun,	
2.	—— *Kāmil.*	Mŭtăfādĭlun, Mŭtăfādĭlun, Mŭtăfādĭlun, Mŭtăfādĭlun,	

CLASS II.—*Hemistich of Four Feet, each Three and Four Syllables alternately.*

NO.	NAME.	MEASURE.	AFFINITY.
3.	*Baḥri Ṭawīl.*	Fădūlun, Măfādĭlun, Fădūlun, Măfādĭlun	
4.	—— *Madīd.*	Fădĭlātun, Fādĭlun, Fādĭlātun, Fādĭlun	
5.	—— *Basīṭ.*	Mustafdĭlun, Fādĭlun, Mustafdĭlun, Fādĭlun	

(a.) It will be observed that in the above five Metres, peculiar to the Arabs, the short syllables are more nearly on a par with the long; whereby we are to infer, according to Herr Geitlin's theory, that the roving Arabs are less grave and sober in their conversation and gestures than their neighbours of Persia.

127. We shall now proceed to exhibit in their order the whole of
Muzāhafāt, or " Deviations," peculiar to each of the Perfect Metres,
following the same order as that adopted in the Table. We may premise
that, as a rule, every hemistich in Persian consists either of *three* or of
four feet; hence the *Bait*, or complete verse, must necessarily consist
either of *six* or of *eight* feet; the former being called *Musaddas* (Hexameter), and the latter *Musamman* (Octameter).

I.—BAHRI HAZAJ.

Standard.—*Mặfādĭlun, Mafādĭlun, Mặfādĭlun, Mặfādĭlun.*

128. Of this Metre there are eighteen Deviations, or Variations, eight
of them Octameter and ten Hexameter, viz.—

Var.	1.	Māfādīlun,	Māfādīlun,	Māfādīlun,	Māfādīlān.
	2.	Māfādīlun,	Māfādīlun,	Māfādīlun,	Māfādīlun.
	3.	Māfādīlun,	Māfādīlun,	Māfādīlun,	Māfādīlān.
	4.	Fādīlun,	Māfādīlun,	Fādīlun,	Māfādīlun.
	5.	Mafdūlŭ,	Māfādīlun,	Mafdūlŭ,	Māfādīlun.
	6.	Mafdūlŭ,	Māfādīlŭ,	Māfādīlŭ,	Māfādīl.
	7.	Māfdūlŭ,	Māfādīlŭ,	Māfādīlŭ,	Fādūlun.
	8.	Māfādīlŭ,	Māfādīlŭ,	Māfādīlŭ,	Fādūlun.
	9.	Māfādīlun,	Māfādīlun,	Māfādīl.	
	10.	Māfādīlun,	Māfādīlun,	Fādūlun.	
	11.	Māfādīlŭ,	Māfādīlŭ,	Māfādīl.	
	12.	Māfādīlŭ,	Māfādīlŭ,	Fādūlun.	
	13.	Mafdūlŭ,	Māfādīlun,	Māfādīlun.	
	14.	Mafdūlŭ,	Māfādīlun,	Māfādīl.	
	15.	Mafdūlŭ,	Māfādīlun,	Fādūlun.	
	16.	Mafdūlŭ,	Māfādīlŭ,	Fādūlun.	
	17.	Fādīlun,	Fādīlun,	Māfādīlun.	
	18.	Mafdūlun,	Fādīlun,	Māfādīlun.	

129. We may here appropriately add a Table of the twenty-four Metres
peculiar to the *Rubā'i* or Tetrastich, all of which are deviations from
the last of the above Metres.

Rubā'i Metres.—Class I., beginning with *Mafdūlun.*

	1.	*Mafdūlun,*	Fādīlun,	Mafādīlun,	Fād.
	2.	——	Mafdūlun,	Māfādīlun,	Fād.

Rubā'i Metres—continued.

3.	*Mafdūlun,*	Fādĭlun,	Măfādĭlu,	Fădal.
4.	——	Mafdūlun,	Mafdūlun,	Fād.
5.	——	Mafdūlun,	Mafdūlun,	Fad.
6.	——	Fādĭlun,	Măfādĭlun,	Fad.
7.	——	Mafdūlŭ,	Măfādĭlŭ,	Fădūl.
8.	—— .	Mafdūlŭ,	Măfādĭlŭ,	Fad.
9.	——	Mafdūlun,	Mafdūlŭ,	Fădal.
10.	——	Mafdūlŭ,	Măfādĭlŭ,	Fădal.
11.	——	Fādĭlun,	Măfādĭlŭ,	Fădūl.
12.	——	Mafdūlun,	Mafdūl,	Fădūl.

Class II., beginning with *Mafdūlŭ.*

1.	*Mafdūlŭ,*	Măfādĭlun,	Măfādĭlun,	Fad.
2.	——	Măfādĭlŭ,	Măfādĭlun,	Fad.
3.	——	Măfādĭlun,	Mafdūlŭ,	Fădūl.
4.	——	Măfādĭlun,	Mafdūlun,	Fad.
5.	——	Măfādĭlun,	Mafdūlŭ,	Fădal.
6.	——	Măfādĭlŭ,	Măfādĭlŭ,	Fădūl.
7.	——	Măfādĭlun,	Măfādĭlŭ,	Fădūl.
8.	——	Măfādĭlun,	Măfādĭlŭ,	·Fădal.
9.	——	Măfādĭlun,	Măfādĭlun,	Fād.
10.	——	Măfādĭlŭ,	Măfādĭlun,	Fād.
11.	——	Măfādĭlŭ,	Măfādĭlŭ,	Fădal.
12.	——	Măfādĭlun,	Mafdūlun,	Fād.

II.—BAḤRI RAJAZ.

Standard.—*Mustafdĭlun, Mustafdĭlun, Mustafdĭlun, Mustafdĭlun.*

130. Of this Metre there are seven Variations, five of them Octameter and two Hexameter, viz.—

Var. 1.	Mustafdĭlun,	Mustafdĭlun,	Mustafdĭlun,	Mustafdĭlān.
2.	Muftădĭlun,	Muftădĭlun,	Muftădĭlun,	Muftădĭlun.
3.	Muftădĭlun,	Măfādĭlun,	Muftădĭlun,	Măfādĭlun.
4.	Măfādĭlun,	Muftadĭlun,	Mufādĭlun,	Muftădĭlun.
5.	Mustafdĭlun,	Măfādĭlun,	Măfādĭlun,	Fădal.
6.	Muftădĭlun,	Muftădĭlun,	Muftădĭlun.	
7.	Măfādĭlun,	Măfādĭlun,	Măfādĭlun.	

III.—BAHRI RAMAL.

Standard.—*Fādilātun, Fādilātun, Fādilātun, Fādilātun.*

131. Of this Metre there are seventeen Variations, eleven of them Octameter and six Hexameter, viz.—

Var. 1. Fādilātun, Fādilātun, Fādilātun, Fādilaiyān.
2. Fādilātun, Fādilātun, Fādilātun, Fādilātun.
3. Fādilātun, Fādilātun, Fādilātun, Fādilāt.
4. Fādilātun, Fādilātun, Fādilātun, Fādilun.
5. Fādilātun, Fādilātun, Fādilātun, Fadlun.
6. Fādilātŭ, Fādilātun, Fādilātŭ, Fādilātun.
7. Fādilātun, Fādilātun, Fādilātun, Fādilāt.
8. Fādilātun, Fādilātun, Fādilātun, Fādilun.
9. Fādilātun, Fādilātun, Fādilātun, Fādilun.
10. Fādilātun, Fādilātun, Fādilātun, Fadlun.
11. Fādilātun, Fādilātun, Fādilātun, Fadlān.
12. Fādilātun, Fādilātun, Fādilāt.
13. Fādilātun, Fādilātun, Fādilun.
14. Fādilātun, Fādilātun, Fādilāt.
15. Fādilātun, Fādilātun, Fādilun.
16. Fādilātun, Fādilātun, Fadlun.
17. Fādilātun, Fādilātun, Fadlān.

IV.—BAHRI MUTAKĀRIB.

Standard.—*Fādūlun Fādūlun, Fādūlun, Fādūlun.*

132. Of this Metre there are four Variations, all of them Octameter, viz.—

Var. 1. Fādūlun, Fādūlun, Fādūlun, Fādūl.
2. Fādūlun, Fādūlun, Fādūlun, Fādal.
3. Fadlun, Fādūlun, Fadlun, Fādūlun.
4. Fadūlŭ, Fadlun, Fādūlŭ, Fadlun.

V.—BAHRI MUTADĀRIK.

Standard.—*Fādilun, Fādilun, Fādilun, Fādilun.*

133. Of this Metre there are only three Variations, all Octameter. viz.—

Var. 1. Fādilun, Fādilun, Fādilun, Fādilun.
2. Fadlun, Fadlun, Fadlun, Fadlun.
3. Fādilun, Fādal, Fādilun, Fadal.

VI.—BAHRI MUNSARIH.

STANDARD.—*Mustafdilun, Mafdulatu, Mustafdilur.*

134. Of this Metre there are six Variations, four Octameter and two Hexameter, viz.—

Var. 1.	Muftădĭlun,	Fādĭlătŭ,	Muftădĭlun,	Fādĭlāt.
2.	Muftădĭlun,	Fādĭlun,	Muftădĭlun,	Fādĭlun.
3.	Muftădĭlun,	Fādĭlătŭ,	Muftădĭlun,	Făd.
4.	Muftădĭlun,	Fādĭlătŭ,	Muftădĭlun,	Fad.
5.	Muftădĭlun,	Fādĭlătŭ,	Muftădĭlun.	
6.	Muftădĭlun,	Fādĭlătŭ,	Mafdūlun.	

VII.—BAHRI KHAFĪF.

STANDARD.—*Fādĭlātun, Mustafdilun, Fādĭlātun.*

135. Of this Metre there are four Variations, all of them Hexameter, viz.—

Var. 1.	Fādĭlātun,	Măfādĭlun,	Fādĭlātun.
2.	Fādĭlātun,	Măfādĭlun,	Fădĭlāt.
3.	Fādĭlātun,	Măfādĭlun,	Fădĭlun.
4.	Fādĭlātun,	Măfādĭlun,	Fadlun.

VIII.—BAHRI MUZĀRĪ'.

STANDARD.—*Măfādĭlun, Fādĭlātun, Măfādĭlun.*

136. Of this Metre there are eight Variations, six of them Octameter and two Hexameter, viz.—

Var. 1.	Mafdūlŭ,	Fādĭ-lātun,	Mafdūlŭ,	Fādĭ-lātun.
2.	Mafdūlŭ,	Fādĭ-lātun,	Mafdūlŭ,	Fādĭlaiyān.
3.	Mafdūlŭ,	Fādĭ-lātŭ,	Măfādīlŭ,	Fādĭ-lātun.
4.	Mafdūlŭ,	Fādĭ-lātŭ,	Măfādīlŭ,	Fādĭ-lāt.
5.	Mafdūlŭ,	Fādĭ-lātŭ,	Măfādīlŭ,	Fādĭlun.
6.	Măfādīlŭ,	Fādĭ-lātŭ,	Măfādīlŭ,	Fādĭlāt.
7.	Mafdūlŭ,	Fādĭlātŭ,	Măfādĭlun.	
8.	Mafdūlŭ,	Măfādīlŭ,	Fādĭlāt.	

IX.—BAHRI MUKTAZAB.

STANDARD.—*Mafdūlātŭ, Mustafdilun, Mustafdilun.*

137. Of this Metre there are only two Variations, both of them Octameter, viz.—

Var. 1.	Fādĭlātŭ,	Muftădĭlun,	Fādĭlātŭ,	Muftădĭlun.
2.	Fādĭlātŭ,	Mafdūlun,	Fādĭlātŭ,	Mafdūlun.

X.—BAHRI MUJTASS.

STANDARD.—*Mustafdilun, Fadilatun, Fadilatun.*

138. Of this Metre there are six Variations, all of them Octameter viz.—

Var. 1. Măfādĭlun, Fădĭlātun, Măfādĭlun, Fădĭlātun.
    2. Măfādĭlun, Fădĭlātun, Măfādĭlun, Fădĭliyān.
    3. Măfādĭlun, Fădĭlātun, Măfādĭlun, Fădĭlāt.
    4. Măfādĭlun, Fădĭlātun, Măfādĭlun, Fădĭlun.
    5. Măfādĭlun, Fădĭlātun, Măfādĭlun, Fadlun.
    6. Măfādĭlun, Fădĭlātun, Măfādĭlun, Fadlān.

XI.—BAHRI MUSHĀKIL.

STANDARD.—*Fādĭlātun, Mŭfādĭlun, Mŭfādĭlun.*

139. This Metre has only one Variation, a Hexameter, viz.—
    Fădĭlātŭ, Măfādĭl, Măfādĭl.

XII.—BAHRI SARĪ'.

STANDARD.—*Mustafdilun, Mustafdilun, Māfdŭlātŭ.*

140. This Metre has four Variations, all of them Hexameter, viz.—
    Var. 1. Muftădĭlun, Muftădĭlun, Fādĭlāt.
        2. Muftădĭlun, Muftădĭlun, Fădĭlan.
        3. Muftădĭlun, Muftădĭlun, Fād.
        4. Muftădĭlun, Muftădĭlun, Fădūlun.

XIII.—BAHRI JADĪD.

STANDARD.—*Fādĭlātun, Fādĭlātun, Mustafdilun.*

141. This Metre has only one Variation, a Hexameter, viz.—
    Fădĭlātun, Fădĭlātun, Măfādĭlun.

XIV.—BAHRI KARĪB.

STANDARD.—*Măfādĭlun, Mŭfādĭlun, Fādĭlātun.*

142. This Metre has two Variations, both of them Hexameter, viz.—
    Var. 1. Măfādĭlŭ, Măfādĭlŭ, Fădĭlātun.
        2. Mafdūlŭ, Măfādĭlu, Fădĭlātun.

(*a.*) The preceding fourteen Metres, together with their Variations, are all that I have been able to discover among native writers on the subject. It does not follow, however, that the list comprises all the Metres employed by the Persian Poets. In fact, a full and satisfactory work o Persian Prosody is at present a desideratum in our language.

POETIC LICENCE.

143. In Persian poetry the "Licentia Vatum" is somewhat more liberal than that which obtained among the ancient Greeks and Romans, or even than that which is allowed to us moderns. The Persian poetic licences of a general nature are the following:—In the first place, the vowel *kasra*, as well as its substitutes ى and ﹷ (*hamza*) representing the sign of the Genitive Case, or the concord of an Adjective, may be long or short at pleasure. Secondly, the vowel *fatḥa* preceding the "imperceptible ﺓ *h*," (§ 3) at the end of a word may be long or short at pleasure; in other words, the ﺓ may, in such cases, be reckoned as a final consonant, or as a mere *nothing*. Thirdly, the conjunction و "and," when sounded *as a vowel* (i.e. ŏ or o, vide § 52, *a*.) may be long or short at pleasure. Lastly, the initial ا *alif*, which is closely akin to the imperceptible ﺓ *h*, may be reckoned as a short vowel or a consonant at pleasure. Thus, in the expression بد ام "I am bad," if the *alif* be viewed as a consonant, the first syllable is long by position; if the *alif*, however, be viewed as a mere short vowel, the *a* of *bad* is short. In the former case, the two syllables make a Spondæus, in the latter an Iambus. The same rule, of course, applies to the initial آ *alif* with the *madda* (§ 19), which is always long, being equivalent to two *alifs*. The *alif* of the preposition از "from," "by," "than," &c., may be rejected, the ز made moveable by a short *kasra*; thus, for *az* the poet may use زِ *zi* should the metre require it. In some words when an initial short *alif* is followed by an inert consonant, the *alif* may be altogether omitted and its vowel transferred to the inert consonant; thus, *aknūn* may be written *kanūn*, and *uftada*, *fŭtāda*, if the metre demands it: this privilege, however, is not allowed in the case of words taken from the Arabic. Now when we consider the frequent occurrence of the above syllables, we may safely say that the Persian poets have had more licence allowed them, "quoad" quantity, than those of ancient Greece and Rome.

(*a*.) The following monosyllables, though written with a letter of prolongation, are generally short, viz. تو " thou ;" چو " when," " as ;" خود " self," " own ;" خوش " pleased ;" دو " two ;" but they may occasionally be lengthened. The words کِه and چِه, as Relative Pronouns or Conjunctions, together with their compounds, also the numeral سه " three," are, I think, generally short ; when, however, کِه and چِه are interrogatives they may occasionally be lengthened. Some few words are optionally written with or without a letter of prolongation, consequently they may form long or short syllables, as the metre requires ; thus, راه, شاه, and گاه may be written رَه, شَه, and گَه ; so دِگر or دیکر ,بِرُون or بیرُون ,خامُش or خامُوش ,بُد or بُود so

(*b*.) It is a rule in Persian verse that no word must be allowed to end with two inert consonants, except at the close of the hemistich. When such words, *in appearance*, do occur, the poet is privileged to add the short vowel *fatḥa*,* and occasionally a long vowel, to the last of the inert letters ; thus, گُفت is to be read *guftă*, and sometimes it is written گُفتا *guftā*. The same rule holds in the middle of

---

* I know not on what authority Dr. Lee, in his last edition of Jones's Persian Grammar, tells us that this supplementary vowel is a " short *kasra*." I object to the *kasra*, for the following reasons :—In the first place, I can find no native authority for it, the native writers merely saying that the letter " becomes moveable." Secondly, it is objectionable, as it interferes with the province of the *iẓāfat*, and is besides absolutely burlesque. Thirdly, analogy clearly points out to us that the supplementary vowel should be a *fatḥa* or short *ă*, for we occasionally meet with it as a long *ā*: thus, when the metre requires it, we meet with گُفتا ; hence we naturally infer the propriety of *guftă*, and not *guftĭ*, as Dr. Lee and his copyists have it. Lastly, Dr. Gilchrist, in his Hindūstānī Grammar, 4to. 1796, page 263, pointedly tells us that the " increment," as he calls it, *is a short ă*. Now Dr. Gilchrist, when composing his -section on Prosody, was attended by a staff of learned natives ; and it clearly follows that his authority on this point far outweighs that of Dr. Lee.

a word; thus, پرداختیم, which in prose is pronounced *pardākhtem*, must in verse be read *pardākhătem*; so کیستی must be read *kīsătī*.

(*c.*) When a word ends with the letter ن *nūn* preceded by any of the letters of prolongation (§ 12.), the *nūn* assumes the nasal sound, and does not count in scanning. I think, however, that this rule does not apply to Arabic words in which the final *nūn* is preceded by the diphthongs *ai* and *au*, as in the words عَین and عَون. If the Syntax requires that the final *nūn* should be followed by the *iẓāfat*, or should the Prosody require that it be followed by the *supplementary short ă* above mentioned, of course the *nūn* retains it natural sound. When a word, not at the close of a hemistich, ends, *in appearance*, with three inert consonants, such as گشتاسپ, the last consonant is entirely rejected in scanning, and the last but one assumes the supplementary short *ă*; thus the Dative Case of *Gushtāsp* is گشتاسپرا *Gushtāsp-rā*, which in scanning must be read *Gushtāsără*.

(*d.*) Two short syllables may be converted into one long syllable; thus بشنید *bishinīd* may be read *bishnīd*; so بگُذری becomes *bigzărī* or *bigzŭrī*, by withdrawing the vowel *pesh* from the second letter, and substituting it for the *fatḥa* of the third. The و and ي *ma'rūf* (i.e. *ū* and *ī*) at the end of a word not closing the hemistich, may be resolved into *ŭw* and *ĭy* respectively when the next word begins with ا *alif*; thus, هندُواش بخالِ *bă khāli Hindŭwash*; so بدلداري اش will be read *ba-dildārĭyash*. Finally, the letter ي at the end of a hemistich, if preceded by a long *ā* or *ū*, is not sounded or taken into account in scanning; thus in the following couplet from the *Gulistān*—

درختي که اکنُون گرفتست پاي   بنیرُوي مردي برآید زِ جاي

"The tree that has newly taken root may be plucked up by one man's strength." In these two hemistichs the final ي does not count.

SCANSION.

144. Let the reader bear in mind what we have just stated respecting the "Licentia Vatum," and he will find no difficulty in scanning any ordinary piece of Persian poetry. At first let him exercise himself on the easiest and most common metres, such as the *Baḥri Mutaḳārib*,

Var. 1st, in which the last mentioned couplet is composed, viz.
Fădŭlun Fădūlun Fădūlun Fădūl, or *Fădūlun Fădūlun Fădūlun
Fădal*. This couplet is to be scanned as follows, viz.—

Dĭra<u>kh</u>te | kĭ aknūṅ | gĭriftas | tă pā

Bănīrū | e mardē | băr āyad | zĭ jā.

Here we may notice a few of those peculiarities alluded to in our last
paragraph, viz. 1st., in the word *aknūṅ*, the final *ṅ* is nasal and does
not count; but had the metre required it the word might have been
written *kănūṅ*, and if a vowel followed the *n*, it would have retained
its natural sound, as in the expression كُنُونَت *kănūn-at*, "now to
thee." 2dly, the word گرفتست must be read *gĭriftastă*, as explained
in par. 143, *b*. 3rdly, in the expression بِنِیرُوي مَردِي, the final ي of
the first word, being the representative of the *izāfat*, is here short, but
it might be long if necessary. 4thly, in the expression بَرآیَد (for
بَرآیِد) the vowel of the prefix *băr* is here short; but had the metre
required, it might have been long, as stated in § 143. Lastly, the
final ي of either <u>h</u>emistich, as we have already noticed, goes for
nought in the scanning.

(*a*.) As a further exercise, the reader is requested to translate and
scan the following easy extract from the *Bostān of Sa'dī*. The metre
is the same as in the last couplet, and all the words will be found in
the Vocabulary. After the reader has made himself well versed in the
Ba<u>h</u>ri Muta<u>k</u>ārib, he may try his hand on the various specimens of
metre given in our " Extracts from the Poets," at the end of our
Selections.

شِنِیدم که در وقتِ نزعِ رَوان   بهرمُز چُنِین کفت نوشِیروان

که خاطرِ نِکهدارِ درویش باش   نه در بندِ آسایشِ خویش باش

نَیَاساید اندر دِیارِ تُو کس   چو آسایشِ خویش جوئي و بس

فراخِي دران مرزوکشور مخواه   که دِلتنگ بِیني رعیّت زِشاه

بِرو پاسِ درویشِ محتاج دار   که شاه از رعیّت بُود تاجدار

رعیّت چو بیخست وسلطان درخت   درخت اي پسر باشد ازبیخ سخت

(*b.*) I may here observe, that in all the manuscripts Persian poetry is to be read right across the page; and very frequently the space between the two hemistichs of a couplet (as well as the margin all around) is richly ruled with various coloured ink, and otherwise ornamented. In works of considerable extent, such as the *Shāhnāma*, and the *Khamsas* (§ 151 *a.*), the page generally contains four hemistichs, or two verses in width, which are, in like manner, to be read right across.

RHYME.

145. The Rhyme of the Persians resembles ours in all essential respects; the main principle of both is, that the last syllable of one hemistich must correspond in sound to the last syllable of that with which it is combined. It often happens, too, that the real rhyme in a Persian couplet may be the last syllable but one, as is often the case among ourselves; thus, in the following beautiful stanza by Burns:

> "Had we never loved so kindly,
> Had we never loved so blindly,
> Never met, or never parted,
> We had ne'er been broken-hearted."

Sometimes the three last syllables of each hemistich rhyme one with another respectively, as in the following distich:

همان به که لشکر بجان پروري   که سُلطان زِ لشکر کُند سَروَري

"It is proper that you should cherish the army with your life; for a king by his army attains superiority."

(*a.*) The Persians were allowed a more free scope than our moderns on the score of rhyme, for in Persian poetry the *same word* in the *same sense* may form the rhyme of each hemistich of a couplet; and not unfrequently does the same word, or succession of words, form the rhyme throughout a whole *Ghazal* or Ode.

OF THE VARIOUS KINDS OF POETIC COMPOSITION.

146. Of these the principal varieties are the *Rubā'ī*, the *Ghazal*, the *Kaṣīda*, the *Ḳiṭ'a*, the *Maṣnawī*, and the *Tarjī'*, each of which we shall now briefly describe. The elements from which all these are composed are, 1st, the *Miṣr'*, or "hemistich," consisting of three or four metrical feet; and, 2d, a combination of two *Miṣrā's*, which constitutes a *Bait* (§ 124 *a.*), literally "a house," which we may translate a "couplet" or "stanza." The second *Miṣrā'* of the *Bait* must have the same metre and rhyme as the first. When both have only the same metre, but not the same rhyme, the stanza is called *Fard*, or *Mufrad*, that is, "solitary."

OF THE RUBĀ'Ī, OR DUBAITĪ.

147. This is a short composition, in great favour among the Persian poets. It consists, as its name imports, of four hemistichs, or two stanzas, and bears some resemblance to the epigram of the ancients. The first, second, and fourth hemistichs must always have the same metre and rhyme: the third hemistich must also have the same metre, but not necessarily the same rhyme; however, there is no rule to the contrary. The *Rubā'ī* has twenty-four metres peculiar to itself, all of them derived from the *Baḥri Hazaj*, as we have shewn in the Tables, pages 134 and 135.

OF THE GHAZAL.

148. This kind of composition corresponds, upon the whole, with the Ode of the Greeks and Romans, or the Sonetta of the Italians. The most common subjects of which it treats are, the beauty of a mistress, and the sufferings of the despairing lover from her absence or indifference. Frequently it treats of other matters, such as the delights of the season of Spring, the beauties of the flowers of the garden, and the tuneful notes of the nightingales as they warble their melodies among the rosebushes; the joys resulting from wine and hilarity, are most particularly noticed at the same time; the whole interspersed with an occasional pithy allusion to the brevity of human life, and the vanity of sublunary matters in general. The more orthodox among the Musalmāns are rather scandalized at the eulogies bestowed upon the " juice of the grape" by their best poets, such as *Ḥāfiẓ* for example; and they endeavour to make out that the text is to be taken in a mystic or *spiritual* sense, such as we apply to the " Songs of Solomon." It appears to me, however, that *Ḥāfiẓ* writes upon this favourite theme just as naturally, and with as much gusto, as either Anacreon or Horace, who, in this respect, may be safely acquitted of the sins of mysticism. The first couplet of the *Ghazal* is called the *Maṭla'*, or " the place of rising"

(of a heavenly body), which we may translate the " Opening." It is a standard rule that both hemistichs of this couplet should have the same metre and rhyme. The remaining couplets must have the same metre, and the second hemistich of each (but not necessarily the first) must rhyme with the *Matla'*. The concluding couplet is called the *Makta'*, or "place of cutting short;" which we may translate the " Close;" hence the phrase, *Az matla' tā makta'*, " from beginning to end." In the *Makta'*, or close, the poet manages to introduce his own name, or rather his assumed or poetic name, called the *Takhallus*, though few of the older poets paid strict attention to this rule previous to the time of Hakīm Sanāyī, between A.D. 1150 and 1180. Anwarī occasionally introduces his own name in his *Ghazals*, but it is the exception and not the rule in his case. As a general law, the *Ghazal* must consist of at least five couplets, and not more than fifteen; but on this subject authors by no means agree, either with one another or with real facts. Hāfiz, for example, has several *Ghazals* consisting of sixteen, and even seventeen, couplets; and Hakīm Sanāyī has many that exceed the latter number.

OF THE KASĪDA.

149. This kind of poem resembles the Idyllium of the Greeks. Its subject · are generally praise of great personages, living or deceased; satire; elegy; and, sometimes, downright burlesque; also moral and religious reflections The opening and succeeding couplets of the *Kasīda* follow the same laws as those of the *Ghazal*. In the *Makta'*, or concluding couplet, the poet does not introduce his own *nom de plume*, as in the *Ghazal*; but when the subject is panegyric he generally finishes with a benediction or prayer for the health and prosperity of the person addressed, such as, " May thy life, health, and prosperity endure as long as the sun and moon revolve!" According to the author of the *Chār Gulzār*, the *Kasīda* must consist of not fewer than twenty-five couplets, nor must it extend to more than one hundred and seventy-five. With the Arabians the *Kasīda* seems to have been unlimited as to length, as they have sometimes made it exceed five hundred couplets. The Arabic root from which is derived the term *Kasīda* signifies " to exert one's self," and the composition so called is presumed to possess high literary merit. Of this description are the celebrated *Mu'allakāt*, or the seven Arabian prize poems, suspended of old in the temple of Mecca.

U

a. The work above alluded to, entitled *Chār Gulzār*, i.e. " The Four Rosebeds," was written early in the present century, at the suggestion of Sir Gore Ouseley, then a member of the Bengal Civil Service. The author's name is not given, he modestly styling himself the " meanest of God's creatures ;" but his third *Gulzār*, containing the prosody of the Persians, is particularly clear and to the purpose. I have therefore followed his authority, in preference to that of Gladwin and several others. The fact is, however, that none of them is quite correct as to the length of the *Ghazal* and *Kasida.* There are many Persian *Ghazals* consisting of only four couplets, and many more extending to twenty and upwards. On the other hand, there are many *Kasidas* of fewer than twenty-five couplets, and I have yet seen none extending to one hundred and seventy-five. Of this the reader may easily satisfy himself by consulting the Persian *Diwāns* composed from the time of *Anwari* to that of *Ahli* of Shīrāz, that is, from the middle of the twelfth to that of the sixteenth century of our æra, a period which may be justly considered as the *golden age* of Persian literature.

b. The term *Diwān* is applied to a collection of poetical pieces, consisting of *Kasidas, Ghazals,* and *Rubā'is,* occasionally concluding with a few *Mufrads* or couplets. The *Ghazals* form the greater portion of such collections, and are generally arranged alphabetically, in the order of their *Matla's ;* but this rule is not essential, nor was it observed by the older poets, such as *Abu-l-Faraj* of *Rona,* and *Anwari,* in whose *Diwāns* the *Kasidas* and *Ghazals* are intermixed, without the least attempt at alphabetical arrangement. When, however, we come down to the time of *Sa'dī,* in the thirteenth century of our æra, we find that the *Ghazals,* &c., are alphabetically arranged. All those whose rhymes terminate in *alif* come first, then those ending in *be,* and so on to *yā.* There have been at least a hundred Persian poets, old and recent, good, bad, and indifferent, who have composed *Diwāns.*

THE KIT'A.

150. This species of poetic composition consists of not fewer than two couplets, nor does it admit of more than one hundred and seventy-five, as in the case of the *Kasida.* The difference between the *Kit'a* and *Kasida* is merely this—that the two hemistichs of the first couplet do not rhyme in the *Kit'a,* but whatever may be the rhyme of the second hemistich

in the first couplet, the same must be continued in the second hemistich of every successive couplet. In conclusion, we may observe, that the *Ghazal*, the *Kaṣīda*, and the *Kit'a* may be composed in any metre which the poet may choose.

OF THE MAṢNAWĪ, OR MUZDAWAJ.

151. This is a class of poetic compositions of very extensive use among the Persians. It comprises what in our language are called the Heroic, the Didactic, the Satiric, and the Descriptive. The term *Maṣnawī* is generally applied to compositions of greater extent than those we have already described. It is quite unrestricted as to length—from three stanzas up to the verge of infinity, should the poet have sufficient matter to go on with, and life long enough to reach that goal. It consists of a succession of stanzas, all of the same metre, and the second hemistich of each stanza must rhyme with the first; but the stanzas themselves do not necessarily rhyme with one another, as in the *Ghazal*, &c. The metres assigned to the *Maṣnawī* are not numerous; the principal of them, so far as I know, are the following:—

I. Two modifications of the *Baḥri Mutaḳārib*, viz—

    1. *Fădū'un, Fădūlun, Fădūlun, Fădūl.*
    2. *Fădūlun, Fădūlun, Fădūlun, Fádal.*

These combined may be styled the Heroic Metre of the Persians. It holds the same rank in their versification as the Hexameter did in that of ancient Greece and Rome. The second modification differs from the first merely in the final syllable, and is optionally introduced in heroic poetry. In this metre are composed the *Shāhnāma* and the *Yūsuf o Zulaiḳhā*, by *Firdausī*; the *Khāwarnāma*, by *Ibn Ḥusain*; the *Sikandarnāma* and the *Khiradnāma*, by *Niẓāmī*, and also by *Jāmī*; the *Humā,i Humāyūn*, by *Khwāju Karmānī*; the *Nabīnāma* (author's name unknown to me); the *A,īna,e Sikandari*, by *Amīr Khusrū*, of *Dihlī*; the *Bostān* and *Pandnāma* of *Sa'dī*; the *Ḥamla,e Haidari*, by *Rafī' Khān*, and a great many others, which it were too tedious to enumerate.

II. Three modifications of the *Baḥri Hazaj*, viz.—

    1. *Măfādīlun, Măfādīlun, Măfādīl.*
    2. *Măfādīlun, Măfādīlun, Fădūlun.*
    3. *Măfdūlu, Măfādīlun, Fădūlun.*

In the first of these metres is composed a *Masnawī*, by *Amīr Khusrū*, the title of which I have been unable to ascertain. I think, however, it is the *Kissa,e Khizr Khān*. It stands first, but without any title, in a very fine copy of that poet's *Kulliyāt*, or whole works, in my possession, and thus commences—

سر نامه بنام آن خداوند   که دلهارا بخوبان کرده پیوند

In the second metre are composed the *Khusrū o Shīrīn*, by *Nizāmī*, and also by *Amīr Khusrū*; and the *Yūsuf o Zalaikhā*, by *Jāmī*, also by *Nāzim al Haruī*. In the third metre are composed the *Lailī o Majnūn*, by *Nizāmī*, and also by *Amīr Khusrū*, by *Jāmī*, and by *Hātifī*; the *Tuhfatu-l-'Irākain*, by *Khākānī*; and the *Subhatu-l'Abrār*, by *Jāmī*.

III. Two modifications of the *Bahri Ramal*, viz.—

      1. *Fādilātun, Fādilātun, Fādilāt.*
      2. *Fādilātun, Fādilātun, Fādilun.*

In these metres are composed the *Masnawī* of *Maulavī Rūmī*, with many imitations of the same by other poets; the *Mantiku-l Tair* and *Pandnāma* of *'Attār*, &c. It will be observed that the two metres here differ merely in the final syllable of each hemistich; hence the second may be optionally introduced in a stanza.

IV. Two modifications of the *Bahri Khafīf*, viz.—

      1. *Fādilātun, Mafādilun, Fādilāt.*
      2. *Fādilātun, Mafādilun, Fādilun.*

These two metres, differing only in the final syllable (as in the *Bahri Ramal*, No. III.), are so closely akin, that the second may be indifferently substituted in a stanza. In these metres are composed the *Hadīka* of *Hakīm Sanāyī*; the *Haft Paikar*, by *Nizāmī*; the *Hasht Bihisht*, by *Amīr Khusrū*; the *Silsilatu-z-Zahb*, by *Jāmī*, and numerous other poetic pieces of less note.

V. Two modifications of the *Bahri Sarī'*, viz.—

      1. *Muftadilun, Muftadilun, Fādilāt.*
      2. *Muftadilun, Muftadilun, Fādilun.*

These two metres, like those given in III. and IV., differ only in the final syllable, and may be substituted the one for the other. In these are composed the *Makhzanu-l-Asr r*, by *Niẓāmī*; the *Maṭla'u-l-Anwār* and *Ḳirānu-s-Sa'dain*, by *Amīr Khusrū*; the *Tuḥfatu-l-Aḥrār*, by *Jāmī*, &c.

a. A collection of Five distinct *Maṣnawīs*, each having generally a separate metre, is called a *Khamsa*, i.e. *The Five*, "par excellence." The most celebrated of these are by *Niẓāmī*, *Amīr Khusrū*, and *Jāmī*, all of which are alluded to in the foregoing description. In imitation of these, several poets of more recent date have composed *Khamsas* of considerable merit.

OF THE TARJĪ.

152. This species of poem resembles the *Ghazal*, with certain restrictions. It has a *Maṭla'*, like the *Ghazal*, and consists of from five to eleven couplets, and then a concluding couplet, which is in a metre and rhyme different from the others : in fact, it is what we call a "song with a burden." When several strophes in succession, each having the same metre but a different rhyme, conclude with the same "burden," it is called *Tarjī'-band*, of which specimens may be seen in the *Dīwāns* of *Sa'dī* and *Ḥāfiẓ*.

a. There are three other short strophes, scarcely worth noticing, but I here give the author of the *Chār Gulzūr's* definition of them. 1st, the *Murabba'*, consisting of four hemistichs, all having the same rhyme ; but the rhyming words must not be the same either in sense or spelling. In a poem consisting of a series of *Murabba's*, the last hemistich of each must rhyme with the opening stanza. 2nd, the *Mukhammas*, a stanza of five lines, regulated like the *Murabba'*. 3rd, the *Musaddas*, consisting of six hemistichs, or three couplets. The first four hemistichs are regulated like the *Murabba'*, and the last two hemistichs must have a different metre and rhyme from those of the first four.

153. I conclude this Section by a brief notice of the various metres employed in the last seven pages of the Selections appended to this work. It would have far exceeded our limited space to have given specimens of *all* the Persian metres which we have already detailed; but if the student will carefully peruse what is here laid before him, he will find himself fairly qualified to read with pleasure and profit the best works of the Persian poets.

(*a.*) *Extracts 1st and 6th.*—Both these are in the same metre, viz. *Baḥri Mutaḳārib*, Var. 1st and 2d (*v.* page 136). This, as we have already stated, is perhaps the most popular metre, as well as the easiest and most harmonious in the language. The only difference between Variations 1st and 2d is, that the last syllable of the former ends with two consonants, or with a double consonant; whereas that of the latter ends in a single consonant; but, in either case, the last *foot* is simply an Iambus.

(*b.*) *Extracts 2d and 5th.*—Both these are in the *Baḥri Khafif,* Variations 2d, 3d, and 4th (*vide* page 137). The difference between all three is very trifling. In Variations 2d and 3d the last foot is an *Anapæstus,* and in Variation 4th it is a Spondæus; and here we may notice, in passing, a general principle, which holds in Persian verse, as well as in the versification of the ancient Greeks and Romans, viz. that " *two short* syllables may be replaced by *one long*," and *vice versâ.* In the eighth and tenth lines, and also in the last line but one of Extract 2d, a poetic licence occurs which I overlooked in its proper place, viz. a *short vowel* may be occasionally *lengthened* by doubling the following consonant, and *vice versâ.* For instance, the beginning of line 8th must be read *dĭll ĭ ō,* instead of *dĭl ĭ ō.* The 10th line begins with *durr,* viz. *durr ŏ gōhar,* an " Epitritus secundus," where the *r* is doubled. Again, in the first hemistich of the last line but one, which runs thus—

ایلیْجِنین لفظ چُون دُرِ شِّهوار, the word دُر is spelt with a single ر, because the metre requires the vowel of *dŭr* to be short. In the sixth line we have an excellent instance illustrative of what I stated in my note, page 140, respecting the " supplementary short vowel;" the couplet runs thus :—

باز گُفتند حال مامُونرا   عرضه کردند حالِ محَزُونرا

In the first hemistich, the word حال requires the supplementary vowel; and if, with Dr. Lee and his *confrères,* we employ a short *i*, we absolutely pervert the meaning. In the second hemistich the word حال has the real *iẓāfat.* The couplet, then, is to be scanned thus :—

> " *Bāză guftan-dă ḥālă Mā-mūnrā,*
> *'Arẓă kardan-dă ḥūli maḥ-zūnrā.*"

Lastly, we have to notice a peculiarity in the orthography of this second extract. The student will observe that it contains an unusual sprinkling

of *ẕāls* (ذ), or *dotted dāls.*   In all MSS. written upwards of 400 years
ago, the rule was, that when in the middle of a word the letter *dāl* (د)
was both preceded and followed by a vowel, it assumed the soft sound
of our *th* in "mother," which in Persian was written ماذر *māthar.*   The
same rule held when د was the last letter of a word and preceded by a
vowel; thus, for the modern بِیاد and داد, they would write بِیاذ and داذ.
The extract is an exact transcript from a very fine MS. of the *Hadīḳa*
in my possession, written very nearly six hundred years ago.   This
peculiarity of the dotted *dāls* is a fair criterion of the age of a Persian
MS., as it shews that it must have been written previous to the middle
of our fifteenth century, or at least 400 years ago.

(*c.*) *Extract 3d.*—This spirited Ode, by *Khāḳānī,* is composed in the
Baḥri Rajaz, Var. 3d.   This, and another well known Ode by *Hāfiẓ,*
beginning " *Muṭrĭbi khush-nawā bigo*" (which is in the same metre),
are favourite songs with the Musalmāns of India.

(*d.*) *Extract 4th.*—This celebrated Ode, by *Hāfiẓ,* is distinguished
from most other poetic compositions by being written in one of the
so called *regular* metres, viz. the *Baḥri Hazaj.*   It is, in fact, a mere
repetition of the "Epitritus primus" from beginning to end.   This is
harping on one string with a vengeance—the same unvaried measure
seventy-two times over!

(*e.*) *Extract 7th.*—The first strophe of this *Tarjī'* is composed in the
Baḥri Hazaj, Var. 14.   The recurring couplet is in the *Baḥri Hazaj,*
Var. 15, and so is the second strophe, together with the same *burden.*

(*f.*) *Extract 8th.*—This beautiful fragment, expressive of the " Maladie du pays," is highly interesting, inasmuch as it is the oldest specimen
of Persian poetry that we possess.   It was composed by *Rūdaki,* some
900 years ago.   The metre is the *Baḥri Ramal,* Var. 12.

(*g.*) After the student has thoroughly studied this Grammar, together
with the Selections, from beginning to end, he is strongly recommended
to read the *Gulistān* of *Sa'dī,* as a further praxis in the language, both
in prose and verse.   At the same time, if he can bring to bear on the
task a moderate knowledge of Arabic, so much the better.   He had
better commence with the First Book of the work, leaving the Preface
to be read last.

APPENDIX.

CONSISTING OF TRANSLATIONS OF EXTRACTS FROM THE PERSIAN
POETS, WITH EXPLANATORY NOTES.

1. A TALE, FROM THE BOSTAN OF SA'DÍ.[a]

I have heard that once during a whole week no "son of the road"[b]
came to the hospitable dwelling of the Friend[c] [*of Omnipotence*]
From the benevolence of his disposition, he refrained from tasting his
morning meal, (saying,) "Perchance some hungry person may arrive
from his journey." He went out and looked in every direction; he
scanned the various quarters of the desert, and beheld, wending his
weary way, a solitary man, bent down like the willow, whose head and
beard were whitened with the hoar-frost of age. With kindness he
welcomed him, and, agreeably to the manners of the munificent, gave
him an invitation, saying, "Oh! apple of mine eye, perform an act
of courtesy by becoming my guest."[d] The old man advanced and readily
complied, for he knew the disposition of his host—on whom be peace!
The associates of Abraham's hospitable dwelling seated the old man
with respect. The table[e] was ordered to be spread, and the company
placed themselves around. When the assembly began to utter, "In

---

a. Sa'dí, one of the most esteemed writers of Persia, both in prose and verse, was born
at Shíráz about A.D. 1194. He was a man of great learning and genuine piety. He
passed much of his time in travelling; and at the advanced age of 116 solar years he
died, at his native place, where his tomb may still be seen, in an inclosure called the
Sa'díya, in the vicinity of the town.

b. The term "Son of the Road" (*ibnu-s-sabíl*) is an Arabian metaphor for a traveller.

c. The Arabs and Persians seldom speak of the patriarch Abraham by his Hebrew
name; he is uniformly styled *Khalíl Ulláh*, "The Friend of God;" or, simply, *Al Khalíl,*
"The Friend," as in the text.

d. Literally, "By partaking of my bread and salt."

e. The original term is *Khwán*. It literally signifies a "tray," containing a variety of
dishes, which is placed on a carpet spread on the floor, and around which the guests sit
cross-legged. Few of the Orientals, even to this day, make use of chairs and tables as
we do.

the name of God,"[a] (or to say grace,) not a word of Him was heard to proceed from the old man.

Then Abraham addressed him in such terms as these: "Oh! elder, stricken in years, thou appearest not to me in faith and zeal like other aged men. Is it not an obligatory law to invoke, at the time of eating thy daily bread, that Divine Providence from whence it is derived?" He replied, "I practise no rite which I have not heard from *my* priest, who worshippeth the fire." The good-omened prophet discovered that this old man of forlorn estate was a *Gabar*.[b] When he saw that he was an alien (*to the true faith*), he drove him away in miserable plight; the polluted being rejected by those who are pure.

A voice descended from the Most High God with this severe reproof: "O Abraham! for an hundred years have I given him food and preserved his life, and hast thou conceived an abhorrence for him in so brief a space! If a man pay adoration to fire, why shouldest thou therefore withhold the hand of charity?[c] Go, and call back the old man, stricken in years; from me do thou convey to him greeting. To me he (unconsciously) cries out, and weeps (at thy harsh treatment), his head and face and body all covered with dust."

Then Abraham[d] went after the aged man; with kindness he called him back from the wilderness. And when he came nigh, he thus addressed him: "May a hundred blessings rest on thy head! The True God hath given ear to thy complaints, and hath sent me after thee." When the old man, stricken in years, heard these words, he acknowledged the

---

a. The Arabic expression, *Bism Illāh*, "In God's name," is pronounced by the Musalmān people, not only when they sit down to their meals, but at the commencement of any important undertaking; also when they kill any animal for the purpose of food or sacrifice, otherwise the meat is deemed unlawful.

b. Gabar, commonly written *Gueber* or *Guebre*, is the term generally applied to the ancient fire-worshippers of Persia, of whom a very small remnant may be still met with in retired districts of the country.

c. In all manuscript, lithographed, and printed copies of the *Bostān* which I have yet seen, the tale finishes here at the word *charity*, with the exception of my own fine MS. of the work alluded to in p. 68 of my Grammar. I have here, for the first time, given the parable complete, both text and translation.

d. Literally, "The Prophet of his day." The Musalmāns reckon nine Great Prophets to whom written revelations were imparted, viz. Adam, Seth, Enoch, Noah, Abraham, Moses, David, Jesus, and Muhammad. The number of Minor Prophets, according to some, amounts to 124,000. *Vide* Binning's "Travels in Persia, &c.," 2 vols. 8vo. London, W. H. ALLEN & Co., 1857. A work that gives a true and satisfactory account of Persia as it *now* is.

Almighty Creator. · Through the grace of Him who is Adorable, that man became a convert to the true faith, and thus, though poor, he became more rich than any prince."

The above beautiful tale is highly interesting, inasmuch as it furnishes an instructive lesson, on the score of religious toleration, to men of *all creeds*. It is also remarkable as the production of a Musalmān who was sincerely attached to his own faith ; for, generally speaking, the followers of Muhammad are rather bigoted than otherwise towards those who do not believe like themselves. Lastly, the tale is the groundwork of Dr. Franklin's Parable, the true history of which I shall give hereafter.

2. A TALE FROM THE ḤADĪKA OF ḤAKĪM SANĀYĪ.[a]

"At one period of his sovereignty the Caliph Māmūn[b] became a persecutor, and shed the innocent blood of his people. To the race of Barmak he acted with such injustice, that no one remembers the like. After he had put to death the innocent Yahyā, fortune looked upon him sternly and harshly. The injured Yahyā had a mother, aged and frail, when thus deprived of the beloved of her heart She became the companion of sorrow in this world : consolation, which should be all sweetness, to her became poison. They told of this circumstance to Māmūn, and laid before him the pitiful case of the afflicted matron. They said, "She invokes evil upon thee, and prays for the downfall of thy sovereignty. Go, comfort her heart, and cease from thy hatred ; beg pardon of the aggrieved mother for thine injustice." At night Māmūn went, unattended by any of his people, (to her house), with the view of speaking in mitigation of his crime. Pearls and jewels he proffered to her in abundance ;—that, he considered as his best way of proceeding. He said to her, " O mother, all that has come to pass had

---

a. *Ḥakīm Sanāyī*, a distinguished Persian poet, of the Ṣūfī sect, was born at Ghazna, in the latter part of our eleventh century. He was for some time the court poet of the Ghaznavide sovereigns ; but afterwards, in the reign of Bahrām Shāh, he abandoned worldly objects, and devoted himself to a religious life. He died at an advanced age, in his native city, but I have not been able to ascertain the precise period.

b. The reign of Māmūn, the second son, and the second in succession from Harūn al-Rashīd, was distinguished as the most munificent in the annals of the Caliphate. At one period, however, that alluded to by the poet, the Caliph adopted some very heretical doctrines, which denied to the *Kurān* the authority of a divine revelation ; and for some years of his life he endeavoured to enforce on his subjects, by severe persecutions, the acknowledgment that the book, by them deemed sacred, was entirely of human origin, been predestined! Since destiny hath taken its course, of what avail is your sorrow? Henceforth be resigned, and forget your evil wishes towards me. Although Yaḥyā is no more, having undergone his doom, yet from this moment I will be your son: I will henceforth óccupy his place. Let your heart be comforted; abandon all hatred, malice, and evil-wishing."

The aged mother appropriately spoke out before him and said, "Tell me, O cruel prince! how can I help lamenting such a son? How can a king like *thee* be *his* substitute? How can thy jewels and offerings prove an equivalent? With all the grandeur that hath come to thee, canst thou ever occupy *his* place in my heart? When thou mentionest his name, is it possible for his mother to refrain from shedding tears? As for thee, with thy thousands of retinue, and all thy regal pomp, my heart will none of thee; canst *thou* fill the place of *him who is gone!"*

These few words, precious as royal pearls, remain as a memorial of that noble and injured woman. Māmūn felt humbled and abashed before her, and from that day forward he never allowed the blood ot any one of his people to be shed."

The above tale will prove interesting to the few good-natured people who advocate the *total* abolition of capital punishment, a measure to which I do not myself subscribe.

3. ODE FROM THE DĪWĀN OF KHĀḲĀNĪ.[a]

" O thou with cheeks like the tulip, and a bosom like the jasmine! O walking angel! who art thou?[b] O hard-hearted and cruel fair one, torment of my soul! who art thou? On the parterre, where thou flourishest, thou hast dazzled the eye of the rose; thou hast robbed the sugar-cane of its sweetness—O thou with rose-bud lips! who art thou? I have seen thy cypress-like form; I have heaved sighs innumerable; I have seen thy narcissus-like eyes—O moving cypress! who art thou? Flushed with the wine (of youth), thou roamest about, laying snares; at every one around thou aimest thy deadly shafts—O thou of the merciless

____

a. The time and place of *Khāḳānī's* birth are uncertain. He was the contemporary of *Ḥakīm Sanāyi,* and died at Tabrīz in A.D. 1186.

b. The expression, " Who art thou?" admits, throughout, of being translated, " Whose art thou?" as suggested to me by Moonshee Syed Owlād Allee, a learned gentleman from Oude. For reasons which it would be out of place here to discuss, I prefer my own version, as given above.

bow ! who art thou? Thy brow, fair as the new moon,[a] has deprived the luminary of its splendour—Oh, listen to my sighs and lamentations ! Thou disturber of my life—who art thou? Khākānī, thy slave, has become intoxicated from thy wine-cup; for thee will he lay down his life—O walking angel ! who art thou?"

The preceding Ode from _Khākānī_ is of that species of poetic composition called _Ghazal_, which is closely akin to the " Ode" of the Romans, or the " Sonetta" of the Italians. It is a fair specimen of a Persian " Love Song ;" and in India it is generally sung at entertainments by those fair songsters, commonly called Nautch Girls. _Hāfiz_ has a similar Ode, in the same metre, beginning " _Mutribi khush-nawā bigo_," which is also a great favourite on similar occasions.

4. ODE FROM THE DĪWĀN OF HĀFIZ.[b]

" If that lovely maid of Shīrāz would accept my heart, for the black mole[c] on her cheek I would give Samarkand and Bukhārā. Boy, bring me the wine that remains; for in Paradise thou wilt find neither the banks of the streamlet of Ruknābād,[d] nor the rosy bowers of Muṣallā. These wanton nymphs, these insidious fair ones, whose beauties raise a tumult in our city, have borne away the quiet of my heart, as Tartars their repast of plunder. Alas ! the charms of our darlings have no need of our imperfect love. What occasion has a face naturally lovely for perfumes, paint, moles, or ringlets? Talk to me of minstrels and

---

a. The moon, in all her phases, is a favourite simile, indicative of beauty, among Oriental poets. In order, however, to appreciate the propriety of the expression, the moon must be seen through the medium of a more southern atmosphere than that of London She must, for instance, be such as,

> " The moon whose orb,
> Through optic glass, the Tuscan artist views
> At evening, from the top of Fesolé,
> Or in Valdarno."

b. _Hāfiz_ was born at Shīrāz about A.D. 1300, and died at his native city in A.D. 1388. Of all the Persian poets, he is still the most admired by his countrymen. His works, like the _Kurān_, are often consulted for taking a _fāl_, or " omen," by those about to commence any important undertaking of uncertain issue. This was once the custom in Europe, when people consulted the works of Virgil, the _Sortes Virgilianæ_, or even the Bible itself, on similar occasions.

c. A mole on the cheek is esteemed an especial ornament in a Persian dame.

d. Ruknābād is a small streamlet, meandering through the plain, near Shīrāz: Muṣallā, with its shady bowers, roses, and nightingales, was one of the poet's favourite resorts in the suburbs.

of wine; and seek not to disclose the secrets[a] of futurity. No one, however wise, ever has, or ever will, discover this enigma.[b] I know well how, from that daily increasing beauty which Joseph possessed, a resistless love tore away from Zulaikhā[c] the veil of her chastity. Attend, O adorable object! to prudent counsels; for the young of a good disposition love the advice of the aged better than their own souls. Thou hast spoken ill of me, yet I am not offended : may God forgive thee!—Thou hast spoken well : but does a bitter answer become a lip like a ruby, that fe ds on nothing but sweetness? Thou hast composed thy <u>Gh</u>azal and strung thy pearls : come, sing them sweetly, O Ḥāfiẓ! for heaven doth sprinkle over thy poetry the sparkling brightness (shining circle) of the Pleïades."

The above Ode, from *Ḥāfiẓ*, is a fair specimen of this class of poetic compositions. It is discursive and flighty, touching on miscellaneous matters, grave and gay—a style in which Horace particularly delights.

5. ANOTHER ODE FROM THE DIWĀN OF ḤĀFIZ.

"O cupbearer, bring me a measure of wine; bring me one or two goblets of the pure liquor.[d] Bring me wine, which is the true medicine for the pangs of love, the grand panacea (for all the ills that affect) both old and young. I compare the wine to the sun, and the goblet to the moon : bring the sun to the bosom of the moon. Pour over me this liquid fire; that is, bring me the fire which is like water. If the rose has faded and gone, say to it, 'Go with a blessing :' fetch me, in its stead, the pure wine, fragrant as rose-water. If the cooing of the ringdove is no longer heard—what then? let us listen instead to the gurgling of the wine-flask. My wit has become altogether unruly; bring the fetters of the wine-cup to confine its exuberance. The drinking of wine is either a virtue or a vice; be it vice or virtue, bring

---

a. "Tu ne quæsïeris, scire nefas, quem mihi, quem tibi
Finem Di dederint, Leuconoë."
Horace, Carm. I. 11.

b. "Prudens futuri temporis exitum
Caliginosâ nocte premit Deus."
Ibid, III. 29.

c. The wife of Potiphar, so called by the Musalmāns.

d. "Deprome quadrimun Sabina,
O Thaliarche, merum diota."
Horace, I. 9.

the enlivening draught.   Grieve not at the frowns of fortune;[a]—what has past, let it go; call for the melody of the harp and lute.[b]   I cannot behold my beloved one, except in the midst of my dreams; therefore bring me wine, the medicine that procures sleep.   Although I am already intoxicated, let me have two goblets more, so that my senses may be completely drowned.[c]   Give to *Ḥāfiẓ* one or two goblets, full measure; bring the wine, whether perdition or salvation be the consequence."

This Ode from *Ḥāfiẓ* has a decided leaning towards the Anacreontic or Bacchanalian class of poetry.   I have mentioned, in another place, that the more orthodox Muslims are sadly scandalized at the freedom and palpable gusto with which their favourite poet revels in praise of the "juice of the grape," which, according to their prophet, Muhammad, is "one of the abominations of Satan."   They therefore give out, that the whole of such effusions are to be taken in a mystic, Ṣūfī, or spiritual sense.   On this point we shall say more by and bye: in the meantime, it appears to me, that, here at least, *Ḥāfiẓ means what he says*, just as much as ever did Anacreon, Horace, Robert Burns, or Thomas Moore, gentlemen who had no pretensions to *spiritualism*, always excepting the spirit of Bacchus.

---

a.   " Fortuna sævo laeta negotio, et
        Ludum insolentem ludere pertinax,
           Transmutat incertos honores,
              Nunc mihi, nunc alii benigna."

Horace, III. 29.

b.   ''Bring us down the mellowed wine,
        Rich with years that equal mine;—
        I pray thee, talk no more of sorrow;
        To the gods belong to-morrow.
        And, perhaps, with gracious power,
        They may change the gloomy hour.
        Let the richest essence shed
        Eastern odours on your head,
        While the soft Cyllenian lyre
        Shall your labouring breast inspire."

Horace, V. 13.   Translated by FRANCIS.

c.   " I pray thee, by the gods above,
        Give me the mighty bowl I love; ·
        And let me sing, in wild delight;—
        I will—I will be mad to-night!"

Anacreon, IX.   Translated by MOORE.

6. ODE, FROM THE MYSTICAL DĪWĀN OF MAULĀNĀ JALĀLU-D-DĪN RŪMĪ.[a]

" I WAS,[b] ere a name had been named upon earth ;
 Ere one trace yet existed of aught that has birth :
 When the locks of the LOVED ONE[c] streamed forth for a sign,
 And Being was none, save the Presence Divine!
 Named and name were alike emanations from Me,
 Ere aught that was " I" yet existed, or " We ;"
 Ere the veil of the flesh for Messiah was wrought,
 To the Godhead I bowed in prostration of thought!
 I measured intently—I pondered with heed,
 (But, ah, fruitless my labour !) the Cross and its Creed.
 To the Pagod[d] I rushed, and the Magian's shrine ;
 But my eye caught no glimpse of a glory divine!
 The reins of research to the Ka'ba[e] I bent,
 Whither, hopefully thronging, the old and young went ;
 Ḳandahár and Herát searched I wistfully through ;
 Nor above, nor beneath, came the LOVED ONE to view.
 I toiled to the summit, wild, pathless, and lone,
 Of the globe-girding Ḳáf,[f]—but the 'Anḳā had flown !

---

a. Maulānā Jalālu-d-Dīn's family belonged to Balkh, in Transoxiana, where he was born towards the end of our twelfth century. In the course of time he settled in Rūm, or Asia Minor, where he died in A.D. 1262; hence his surname, Rūmī. He is considered to be of the greatest authority among the numerous sect called Ṣūfīs, of whom more hereafter.

b. The poet here speaks of himself as an embodied spirit. His soul is understood to have existed from all eternity, as an infinitely small emanation of the Deity.

c. The LOVED ONE, here and elsewhere, in Ṣūfī phraseology, denotes God the Eternal without Beginning and without End. The poet here describes the struggles of the human soul, while confined in its tenement of clay, in search of Divine knowledge.

d. The Pagod denotes the Brahminical faith ; and the Magian, that of the ancient Persians and Chaldeans, who adored the fire, and the hosts of heaven.

e. The *Ka'ba* is the " sanctum sanctorum" of the Temple of Mecca.

f. The good old-fashioned notion of this inhabitable earth of ours was, that it was a mere flat surface, like a round table, the outer rim of which was encompassed all around by a chain of impassable mountains, named Ḳáf, inhabited by the Jinns, and also by a gigantic bird, called by the Arabs *'Anḳā*, and by the Persians *Simurgh*. The *'Anḳā*, the *Simurgh*, the *Rukh*, the *Phœnix*, and the *Griffin* appear to have been all " birds of a feather," i.e. " *raræ aves in terris.*"

The sev'nth earth I travers'd—the sev'nth heaven explor'd,
But in neither discern'd I the Court of the Lord!
I question'd the Pen and the Tablet of Fate,
But they whisper'd not where He pavilions his state:
My vision I strain'd; but my God-scanning eye
No trace, that to Godhead belongs, could descry.
My glance I bent inward: within my own breast,[a]
Lo, the vainly sought elsewhere! the GODHEAD confess'd!
In the whirl of its transport my spirit was toss'd,
Till each atom of separate being I lost;
And the bright Sun of Tauriz[b]—a madder[c] than he,
Or a wilder, the world hath not seen, nor shall see!"

The above translation was made by my late friend, Professor F. Falconer, of University College, and appeared in the *Asiatic Journal* about twenty years ago. It is a *genuine* Ṣūfī Ode; and Mr. Falconer has admirably succeeded in seizing and transfusing the spirit and sublimity of the original into his English version. Generally speaking, metrical versions from Eastern poets are too much diluted by a superfluous verbiage, consisting merely of high-sounding epithets, no-ways belonging to the original. Such is not here the case; Sir William Jones himself could not have done it in more excellent taste.

7. TARJĪ'-BAND, FROM THE DĪWĀN OF ḤĀFIZ.

"O silver-bosomed cypress! a form delicate as the rose, the beauty of whose cheeks surpasseth that of the moon at eve! Return! for your absence hath melted my soul, and deprived my heart of ease and rest. From the allurement of the mole on your cheek, and from the snares of your waving ringlets, the bird of my heart hath fallen into your net. Since my wish of a meeting with you is unattainable, I must content myself in bemoaning your absence. Here I am at present lamenting our separation: under such circumstances, what must be the result? You would

---

a. "Ego erravi querens te exterius, qui es interius; et multum laboravi querens te extra me, et tu habitas in me."—*St. Augustine*, Solil.

b. In his *Dīwān, Maulānā Rūmī* assumes the poetic name of *Shams,* "the Sun," out of compliment to his spiritual guide and preceptor *Shamsu-d-Dīn Tabrīzī,* i.e. "Tabrīzī, the Sun of Religion."

c The *madness* and *wildness* here alluded to denote, in Ṣūfī phraseology, religious ardour, and abstraction from all sublunary objects.

say that, excepting grief and pain, destiny had bereft me of every thing in your absence.   O Ḥāfiẓ! what constitutes fortune or wealth, except the society of thy fair one, and the wine, and the goblet?   Seeing that I cannot now realize from you the wishes of my heart, O solace of my life!—*It is best not to turn away my face from patience; perhaps I may yet obtain my heart's desire.*

" Were I to die under the pangs of love, nevertheless my heart should not cease to grieve for you.   Your eyebrow,[a] like a bow, smiteth incessantly with the arrows of amorous glances.   The pen could not describe my longing desire, even although old Saturn were to be my secretary. I am old in the sufferings of love, although but an infant—an infant in the paths of love, yet old in years; seeing that during your absence, tyrannic fortune holds me in the fetters of sorrow.—*It is best not to turn away my face from patience; perhaps I may yet obtain my heart's desire.*"

The species of poem called by the Persians *Tarjī'-band* consists of a series of strophes, each differing in metre and rhyme, varying in length from eight to five couplets, each strophe ending with the same chorus or burden, like the words in italics in the preceding specimen.   In the original there are eight strophes, all ending, as above, with the words, " *It is best,*" &c.   The reader will, I venture to say, excuse me for having omitted six strophes out of the eight, as too much swe.tmeat is very apt to cloy on the mental, as well as on the carnal appetite.

8. FRAGMENT OF AN IDYLL, BY RŪDAKĪ.[b]

"The remembrance of the *Jū,e Mūliyān*[c] is ever present in our minds; the memory of the kind friends we have left ever occupies our thoughts.

---

a.   " Let her eyebrows sweetly rise
In jetty arches o'er her eyes,
Gently in a crescent gliding,
Just commingling, just dividing."
Anacreon, XVI., by MOORE.

b. *Rūdakī*, the father of Persian poetry, was born in or near Bukhārā, towards the close of the ninth century of our era.   The place and period of his death are uncertain. His works, which we are told were very numerous, are in all probability for ever lost to us, with the exception of a few fragments quoted by later writers.

c. The *Jū,e Mūliyān*, literally, " Robbers' Streamlet," is, or was, a small river in the neighbourhood of Bukhārā.

The sandy desert of Āmū,[a] with all its hardships, will feel soft as silk under our feet, in the moment of our return. The stream of the Jaiḥūn, joyful at seeing our faces, will sparkle up to the breasts of our steeds in its eagerness to embrace us. Rejoice, O Bukhārā! mayest thou long flourish; thy prince, with his happy train, is coming to visit thee. The prince is the cypress, and Bukhārā the garden; towards the garden the cypress is now on its way. The prince is the moon, and Bukhārā the sky; into the sky the moon is now about to ascend."

The preceding fragment, by the poet *Rūdakī*, is interesting, inasmuch as it is the oldest specimen of modern Persian poetry that has been handed down to us. The author of a Persian historical work, entitled *Tarīkhi Guzīda*, or "Select History," states, that the occasion of composing the Idyll was this:—*Naṣr*, the prince of Bukhārā, who was *Rūdakī's* patron, having removed with his court to Herāt, about A.D. 935, became so attached to the pleasures of the latter city, that he never could be brought to return to his own capital. The courtiers, however, were all seized with a fit of the "maladie du pays," or home-sickness, and prevailed upon *Rūdakī* to try his eloquence upon their master. Accordingly, our bard, seizing a favourable opportunity, addressed to *Naṣr* the above eulogium on Bukhārā, accompanied by a suitable melody upon the harp. The effect is said to have been electric: the prince immediately started from his seat, and, without the least preparation, set out with his followers towards the capital of his dominions.

Daulat Shāh observes on this Idyll, in his "Lives of the Persian Poets," written somewhat more than five centuries after *Rūdakī* :—"The learned are astonished that a composition, distinguished by nothing but its simplicity, and totally destitute of the graces and ornaments of poetry, should have produced such an extraordinary effect; for there is certainly no court of the present time that would not reject such verses with disgust!!!" Now all this is mere matter of taste and feeling. The words, simple as they are, probably accompanied with some favourite

---

a. Āmū, name of a town situated on the banks of the Jaiḥūn (which we call the Oxus), a river that rises in the mountains of Badakhshān, and flows westerly into the sea of Aral. Between the right bank of the river and Bukhārā there lies a sandy desert, of some forty miles broad, occupied, on some green spots here and there, by wandering Uzbeks and Turkomans, gentlemen who seldom trouble their heads about any nice distinctions between the terms *meum* and *tuum*; and these constitute the "hardships" to which the poet here alludes. The appellation *Āmū* is also applied to a branch of the Jaiḥūn, above the town so named.

local tune, sufficed to rouse the natural attachment of the man to his native soil, and to his friends and relations at a distance. The words are not more simple than those of " Lochaber no more," or those of the " Ranz des Vaches;" and we know the effect these have, when heard in far remote lands, upon natives of the Grampian glens and Alpine valleys.

9. FROM THE AKHLĀKI MUHSINĪ.[a]

" I steadily tread in the path of exertion, for man can expect that only for which he labours. If I get the mantle of my desire into my hand, then am I relieved from sorrow and regret. If, with all my efforts, my undertakings should not succeed, I may, nevertheless, be excused;—so, good-bye."

10. KIT'AE TĀRĪKH, OR ETEOSTICHON.

My friend, Moonshee Syed Owlād Allee, has just favoured me with a very neat *Kit'a*, or strophe, consisting of four hemistichs, in the last of which the sum of the numerical values of all the letters amounts to 1861, the *date* of this work. Its appropriate place would be at the end of the Persian text, only it came too late to be there inserted.

۱۰ ــ قِطعهٔ تاریخ

شُد از طبعِ جنابِ ڈاکتّر فوربس   بماهِ جنّوری این نسخه مطبوع

در عقلِ این کتابِ ڈاکتّر فوربس   خردْ گُفتا پیِ تاریخِ سالش

" In the month of January, this work was impressed by the seal of the honourable Dr. Forbes. Intelligence has proclaimed the period of its date, viz. 'The pearl of wisdom is this bo·k by Dr. Forbes.' "[b]

---

a. A work on Ethics, written some four centuries ago by *Husain Vā'iz al Kāshifi.* It is divided into forty chapters, each treating of some distinct moral subject. The above stanzas, which I have adopted as a motto for the Title-page of my Persian Grammar, are from chap. xiii., which treats of " Exertion and Perseverance."

b. In Europe, during the middle ages, when Latin was the language of literature, such memorial verses as the above were common. The Latin, however, laboured under this disadvantage, that its alphabet contained only seven numerical letters, viz. I, V, X, L, C, D, and M; whereas every one of the letters in Arabic and Persian counts for something. A curious coincidence of this kind is to be found in a line from Ovid, written more than fifteen centuries before the event to which it is applied, viz.—

'F I L I V s ante DIeM patrIos, InquIrIt In annos."

" The son prematurely makes inquiry into the years of his father."

It will be found that the sum of the numerical letters of the above line amount to 1568, the year in which Prince Charles of Spain was put to death, by the command of his stern father, Philip II., for plotting treason and rebellion.

Of this ingenious *morceau*, I have only to say, that I disclaim the complimentary part, which, the reader must bear in mind, is Oriental. I may further mention, that the word denoting *pearl* may also be read *gate*, according as we pronounce it *dur* or *dar*: this, of course, is an additional merit in the effusion, as it kills two *fat* birds with one stone.

DR. FRANKLIN'S IMAGINARY CHAPTER OF GENESIS.

1 " And it came to pass, after these things, that Abraham sat in the door
2 of his tent, about the going down of the sun. And, behold, a man, bent with age, was coming from the way of the wilderness, leaning on a
3 staff. And Abraham arose and met him, and said unto him, 'Turn in, I pray thee, and wash thy feet, and tarry all night; and thou
4 shalt arise early in the morning and go on thy way.' And the
5 man said, ' Nay; for I will abide under this tree.' But Abraham pressed him greatly: so he turned, and they went in unto the tent;
6 and Abraham baked unleavened bread, and they did eat. And when Abraham saw that the man blessed not God, he said unto him, 'Wherefore dost thou not worship the Most High God,
7 Creator of heaven and earth?' And the man answered and said, 'I do not worship thy God, neither do I call upon his name; for I have made unto myself a God, which abideth always in mine
8 house, and provideth me with all things.' And Abraham's zeal was kindled against the man; and he arose, and fell upon him, and
9 drove him forth with blows into the wilderness. And God called
10 unto Abraham, saying, ' Abraham, where is the stranger?' And Abraham answered and said, ' Lord, he would not worship thee, neither would he call upon thy name; therefore have I driven him
11 from before my face into the wilderness.' And God said, ' I have borne with him these hundred and ninety and eight years, and nourished him, and clothed him, notwithstanding his rebellion against me; and couldst not thou, who art thyself a sinner, bear
12 with him one night?' And Abraham said, ' Let not the anger of my Lord wax hot against his servant: Lo, I have sinned; forgive
13 me, I pray thee.' And he arose, and went forth into the wilderness,
14 and sought diligently for the man, and found him: And returned with him to his tent; and when he had entreated him kirdly, he
15 sent him away on the morrow with gifts. And God spake unto

Abraham, saying, ' For this thy sin shall thy seed be afflicted four hun-
16 dred years in a strange land.   But, for thy repentance, will I deliver
them; and they shall come forth with great power, and with
gladness of heart, and with much substance.' "

The above-version of " The Chapter" appeared in print, for the first
time in this country, in April 1764, not long after it had been *extem-
porized* by Dr. Franklin at a social party, when residing in London, as
agent for the colony of Pennsylvania, about a century ago.   Some ten
years later, Dr. Franklin communicated a copy of it to Lord Kaimes,
which appeared in the latter's " Sketches of the History of Man," 1774.
In this last version, the five concluding verses are omitted, most probably
by the Doctor himself.   Lord Kaimes says, " The following parable
against persecution was communicated to me by Dr. Franklin, of Phila-
delphia, a man who makes a figure in the learned world."   Then follows
the parable as above, concluding at the end of the eleventh verse ; after
which, his Lordship appropriately remarks :—" The historical style of
the Old Testament is here finely imitated ; and the moral must strike
every one who is not sunk in stupidity and superstition.   Were it really
a chapter of Genesis, one is apt to think that persecution could never
have shewn a bare face among Jews or Christians.   But, alas ! that is
a vain thought.   Such a passage in the Old Testament would avail as
little against the rancorous passions of men, as the following passages in
the New Testament, though persecution cannot be condemned in terms
more explicit.[a]   ' Him that is weak in the faith, receive you, but not to
doubtful disputations.   For one believeth that he may eat all things :
another, who is weak, eateth herbs.' &c.

" Our Saviour himself declared against persecution in the most express
terms.   The Jews and Samaritans were of the same religion ; but some
trivial differences in the ceremonial part of worship, rendered them
odious to each other.   Our Saviour being refused lodging in a village
of Samaria, because he was travelling to Jerusalem, his disciples, James
and John, said, ' Lord, wilt thou that we command fire to come down
from heaven, and consume them, even as Elias did ?'   But he rebuked
them, and said, ' The Son of Man is not come to destroy men's lives,
but to save them.' "[b]

---

a. Epistle of St. Paul to the Romans, chap. xiv   *b.* Gospel of St. Luke, ix. 54.

I shall now briefly state what I believe to be the true history of Dr. Franklin's celebrated "Chapter," about which there has been a good deal of discussion. The original, so far as we yet know, is *Sa'dī's* tale of "Abraham and the Gabar," the Persian text and literal translation of which I have here given. A free and abridged translation of this tale into Latin was made by Gentius, a learned Orientalist of Holland, about the middle of the seventeenth century, and published at Amsterdam in 1651, in the Preface to a work entitled "Historia Judaica," &c. Some years later, Bishop Jeremy Taylor translated into English the Latin version of Gentius, still further abridged, and inserted the same at the conclusion of his "Discourse of the Liberty of Prophesying," saying, "I end with a story which I find in the Jews' books."[a] Some fifteen years after Bishop Taylor's death, Dr. Franklin's father emigrated to New England, and carried with him a select library of theological works, among which, we may rest pretty confident, was the "Discourse of the Liberty of Prophesying." Dr. Franklin tells us, in his Autobiography, that, at the age of twelve or thirteen, he read most of his father's stock of Theology, simply because he had no access to books of any other description. The "Jewish story concerning Abraham" naturally made a deep impression on his youthful mind; so that, more than forty years after, when residing in London, he jocosely, (if it be not profane to say so), passed it off in a select company as a "Chapter of Genesis."

Let us now examine our proofs of what we have just stated. Of Gentius's version, which is in the British Museum, I have only to

---

a. Bishop Taylor has been censured for giving out that he found the parable in the "Jews' books," in which, to be sure, nobody else has yet found it. I think, however, I can easily account for the mistake, which originated in the vague manner in which Gentius mentions his authority—*Sa'dī*, of Shīrāz, whom he designates simply as *Sa'dus*, without any hint of his nationality. Now, Taylor was no Persian scholar; and, as he found the parable in the Preface to a "History of the Jews," he naturally concluded that *Sa'dus* was a Rabbinical writer. But the most curious circumstance is, that there really existed a very learned Hebrew Theologist and Grammarian, named *Sa'dia* (Ben Joseph), who was born in Egypt towards the close of our ninth century. Now, the name of the Hebrew sage is identical with that of the poet of Shīrāz, both being derived from one and the same root, the latter being written *Sa'dī*, and the former *Sa'dia*, with the addition of a Chaldee termination. Hence Taylor concluded that the author of the tale must have been the Hebrew Rabbi *Sa'dia*; though, it must be confessed, that the good Bishop did stretch it a trifle too far, when he loosely stated that he "*found* it in the Jews' books."

remark that it concludes thus :—" Qua Divinâ voce monitus Abrahamus, senem ex itinere revocatum domum reducit; tantis officiis pietate et ratione colet, ut suo exemplo, ad veri Numinis cultum eum perduxerit." This paragraph is interesting, inasmuch as it proves that the manuscript of the *Bostān*, used by Gentius, *had* the last seven verses of the tale alluded to in page 153, note *c*, which are so seldom to be met with in any copy of the work.[a]

Bishop Taylor's version runs thus :—" When Abraham sat at his tent door, according to his custom, waiting to entertain strangers, he espied an old man, stooping, and leaning on his staff, weary with age and travel, coming towards him, who was a hundred years of age. He received him kindly, washed his feet, provided supper, caused him to sit down; but observing that the old man ate, and prayed not, nor begged for a blessing on his meat, he asked him why he did not worship the God of heaven. The old man told him that he worshipped the fire only, and acknowledged no other God; at which answer Abraham grew so zealously angry, that he thrust the old man out of his tent, and exposed him to all the evils of the night and an unguarded condition. When the old man was gone, God called to Abraham, and asked him where the stranger was: he replied, ' I thrust him away, because he did not worship thee.' God answered him : ' I have suffered him these hundred years, although he dishonoured me, and couldst not thou endure him one night, when he gave thee no trouble ?' ' Upon this,' saith the story, ' Abraham fetched him back again, and gave him hospitable entertainment and wise instruction.' Go thou and do likewise, and *y* charity will be rewarded by the God of Abraham."

They say that " a tale *loses nothing* in the telling or carrying of it," but such is not the case here; for, in the first place, Gentius takes great liberties with his text, chiefly in the way of abridgment; in the second

---

a. This version of the story I remember perfectly having read at school, in an English class-book, entitled " Barrie's Collection," then much used in Scotland. Several years after I left school I fell in with Dr. Franklin's " Chapter," and had no difficulty whatever in determining the source from which it must have been derived. The wonder is, however, that Bishop Heber endeavours to prove Franklin guilty of plagiarism, for which there is not a shadow of ground. Franklin simply gave Taylor's version a scriptural form of *chapter and verse*—nothing more; for he possessed too much mental capital of his own to be guilty of appropriating any thing of the sort belonging to others.

place, Bishop Taylor makes equally free with Gentius ; and, thirdly, Franklin deviates considerably from Taylor.

I extract the following valuable contribution from the " Notes and Queries" of July 29th, 1854. It was communicated by a gentleman who signs himself " M.," and states, that it is a cutting from some periodical of the last century, found by him among the papers of a friend.

> " *A supposed Chapter in the Bible, in favour of Religious Toleration.*
>
> " Some time ago, being in company with a friend from North America, as well known throughout Europe for his ingenious discoveries in natural philosophy, as to his countrymen for his sagacity, his usefulness, and activity, in every public-spirited measure, and to his acquaintance for all the social virtues; the conversation happened to turn on the subject of Persecution. My friend, whose understanding is as enlarged as his heart is benevolent, did not fail to urge many unanswerable arguments against a practice so obviously repugnant to every dictate of humanity. At length, in support of what he had advanced, he called for a Bible, and, turning to the Book of Genesis, read as follows :—' And it came to pass, after those things,' &c.
>
> " I own I was struck with the aptness of the passage to the subject, and did not fail to express my surprise, that in all the discourses I had read against a practice so diametri cally opposite to the genuine spirit of our holy religion, 1 did not remember to have seen this chapter quoted; nor did I recollect my having ever read it, though no stranger to my Bible. Next morning, turning to the Book of Genesis, I found there was no such chapter, and that the whole was a well-meant invention of my friend, whose sallies of humour, in which he is a great master, have always an useful and benevolent tendency.
>
> " With some difficulty I procured a copy of what he pretended to read, which I now send you, for the entertainment of your readers ; and you will perhaps think it not un-reasonable at a time when our church more particularly calls upon us to commemorate the amazing love of Him, who, possessing the divine virtue of charity in the most supreme degree, laid down his life *even for his enemies.a*
>
> " I am, &c.,
>
> " *April* 16, 1764. " W. S."

The foregoing communication is what we call highly suggestive. In the first place, we see that the " Chapter" was given out by Franklin, when residing in this country, *some* time before April 1764, that is, between 1757 and 1762. Secondly, so far as we can here infer, the " Chapter" was recited extempore; though it is not improbable that the Doctor had previously arranged the verses in his own mind, from his recollection of what he had read in his early days. It is highly probable,

---

a. I regret that I have not sufficient leisure and opportunity for consulting the various Magazines and other periodicals that appeared in London in 1764, for the months of April and May. We have no reason whatever to doubt the truth of the fulness communication, only it would be satisfactory to get at the real name of the periodical out of which the cutting was made.

too, that, after forty years and more, Dr. Franklin had completely forgotten the name of the author in whose works he had read the story. Lastly, is it not very likely that the initials " W. S.," at the end of *the cutting*, are those of William Strahan, the King's Printer, afterwards M.P., between whom and Franklin there existed the most intimate friendship ever after the latter's arrival in England for the second time, in 1757 ?

I have only to add one extract more, with a few notes of my own, from the Introduction to Jeremy Taylor's Works, 3d Edition, by Bishop Heber, who says (vol. I. p. ccix.) :—

" He (Taylor) concludes his treatise (on Prophecy) with the celebrated story of Abraham and the idolatrous traveller, which Franklin, with some little variation, gave to Lord Kaimes as a ' Jewish Parable on Persecution,' and which this last-named author published in his ' Sketches of the History of Man.' A charge of plagiarism has, on this account, been raised against Franklin ; though he cannot be proved to have given it to Lord Kaimes as his own composition, or under any other character than that in which Taylor had previously published it ; that, namely, of an elegant fable by an uncertain author, which had accidentally fallen under his notice. It is even possible,[1] as has been observed by a writer in the *Edinburgh Review* (Sept. 1816), that he may have met with it in some magazine without Taylor's name. But it has been unfortunate for him that his correspondent evidently appears to have regarded it as his composition ;[2] that it has been published as such in all the editions of Franklin's collected works; and that, with all Franklin's abilities and amiable qualities, there was a degree of quackery in his character, which, in this instance as well as in that of his professional epitaph on himself, has made the imputation of such a theft[3] more readily received against him, than it would have been against most men of equal eminence,

" Whether Taylor himself found this story where he professes to have done, it has long been a matter of suspicion. Contrary to his general custom, he gives no reference to his authority in the margin ; and, as the works of the most celebrated Rabbins had been searched for the passage in vain, it has been supposed that he had ascribed to these authors a story of his own invention, in order to introduce with a better grace an apt

---

[1] It is much more probable that Franklin read it, when twelve years of age, in his father's library, as may be inferred from the following paragraph in his Autobiography :— " My father's little library was principally made up of books of practical and polemical theology. I read the greatest part of them. I have since often regretted, that, at a time when I had so great a thirst for knowledge, more eligible books had not fallen into my hands." It is highly probable, then, that here Franklin fell in with the story, and that it formed the only portion of his theological reading that he afterwards remembered.

[2] This is very incorrect. I have already quoted all that Lord Kaimes says about the parable ; and there is no evidence whatever that his Lordship regarded it as Franklin's composition. There is also an inconsistency in the Bishop's assertion ; for he has already stated that it was given by Dr. Franklin as " a Jewish parable on Persecution :" if so, how could Lord Kaimes have regarded it as Franklin's?

[3] These remarks on Franklin are harsh, inaccurate, and uncharitable ; and the Doctor's whole life and works furnish the best refutation of them.

illustration of his moral. My learned friend Mr. Oxlee, whose intimate and extensive acquaintance with Talmudic and Cabalistic learning is inferior to few of the most renowned Jewish Doctors themselves, has at length discovered the probable source from which Taylor may have taken this beautiful apologue, in the epistle dedicatory prefixed to the translation of a Jewish work, by George Gentius, who quotes it, however, not from a Hebrew writer, but from the Persian poet *Sa'dī*. The story is, in fact, found, *word for word*,[1] in the *Bostān* of this last writer, as appears by a literal translation which I have received, from the kindness of Lord Teignmouth. The work of Gentius appeared in 1651, a circumstance which accounts for the fact that the parable is introduced in the second, not in the first, edition of the *Liberty of Prophesying*. That Taylor ascribes it to ' the Jews' books' may be accounted for from his quoting at second-hand, and from the nature of the work where he found it."

I have thus endeavoured to lay in the clearest light the history of the " Chapter," about which there has been hitherto so much controversy. I think I have investigated the matter more thoroughly than has yet been done; and I take my leave of the reader, in the words of Horace—

> " Vive, vale ; si quid novisti rectius istis,
> Candidus imperti, si non, his utere mecum."

THE ṢŪFĪ DOCTRINES.

The educated and reflecting portion of the people of Persia, though conforming outwardly with the ceremonies of the Muḥammadan religion, have, within the last seven or eight centuries, revived among themselves a much purer creed, or, at least, one that savours less of materialism. The doctrine of the Ṣūfī sect may be briefly described as a pure Theism, or rather a Pantheism. It inculcates a belief in one Great God, who is Eternal, without beginning and without end. The human soul, also, is considered to be eternal in the same sense, inasmuch as it is an infinitely small emanation of the Deity, whose Spirit pervades all space.

This doctrine is very ancient; it prevailed among the most eminent of the Hindū philosophers, viz. those of the Vedānta school. We also find it fully expounded in the works of Plato, especially in the Phædon. Without some acquaintance with it, the student will be unable to understand the finest productions of the Persian poets, who are generally of the Ṣūfī sect. Hence, I cannot better conclude this work than by subjoining the best account extant of this curious subject. It is from the

---

[1] This is very far from being *a fact*, as the reader may at once see, by comparing the Persian text, or my translation of the same, with the versions by Taylor and Franklin.

pen of Sir William Jones, and will be found at greater length in the
hird volume of the " Asiatic Researches," 8vo. edition, London, 1799.

"A figurative mode of expressing the fervour of devotion, or the
ardent love of created spirits toward their beneficent Creator, has prevailed from time immemorial in Asia, particularly among the Persian
Theists, both ancient Hūshangīs and modern Sūfīs, who seem to have
borrowed it from the Indian philosophers of the Vedānta school; and
their doctrines are also believed to be the source of that sublime, but
poetical Theology, which glows and sparkles in the writings of the old
Academics. 'Plato travelled into Italy and Egypt,' says Claude Fleury,
'to learn the Theology of the Pagans at its fountain head.' Its true
fountain, however, was neither in Italy nor in Egypt (though considerable
streams of it had been conducted thither by Pythagoras, and by the
family of Misra), but in Persia or India, which the founder of the Italic
sect had visited with a similar design. What the Grecian travellers
learned among the sages of the East, may perhaps be fully explained, at
a season of leisure, in another dissertation; but we confine this essay to
a singular species of poetry, which consists almost wholly of a mystical
religious allegory, though it seems, on a transient view, to contain only
the sentiments of a wild and voluptuous libertinism. Now, admitting
the danger of a poetical style, in which the limits between vice and
enthusiasm are. so minute as to be hardly distinguishable, we must
beware of censuring it severely, and must allow it to be natural, though
a warm imagination may carry it to a culpable excess; for an ardently
grateful piety is congenial to the undepraved nature of man, whose
mind, sinking under the magnitude of the subject, and struggling to
express its emotions, has recourse to metaphors and allegories, which it
sometimes extends beyond the bounds of cool reason, and often to the
brink of absurdity.

" The Vedāntīs and Ṣūfīs concur in believing that the souls of men
differ infinitely in *degree*, but not at all in *kind*, from the Divine Spirit,
oʾ which they are *particles*, and in which they will ultimately be ab-
sorbed; that the Spirit of God pervades the universe, always immediately
present to his work, and, consequently, always in substance; that He
alone is perfect benevolence, perfect truth, perfect beauty; that the love
of Him alone is *real* and genuine love, while that of all other objects is
absurd and illusory; that the beauties of nature are faint resemblances,
like images in a mirror, of the Divine charms; that, from eternity without

beginning, to eternity without end, the Supreme Benevolence is occupied in bestowing happiness, or the means of attaining it; that men can only attain it by performing their part of the primal covenant between them and the Creator; that nothing has a pure, absolute existence but mind or spirit; that material substances, as the ignorant call them, are no more than gay pictures presented continually to our minds by the sempiternal artist; that we must beware of attachment to such phantoms, and attach ourselves exclusively to God, who truly exists in us, as we exist solely in Him; that we retain, even in this forlorn state of separation from our beloved, the idea of heavenly beauty, and the remembrance or our primeval vows; that sweet music, gentle breezes, fragrant flowers, perpetually renew the primary idea, refresh our fading memory, and melt us with tender affections; that we must cherish those affections, and, by abstracting our souls from vanity, that is, from all but God, approximate to his essence, in our final union with which will consist our supreme beatitude. From these principles flow a thousand meta_ phors and other poetical figures, which abound in the sacred poems of the Persians and Hindūs, who seem to mean the same thing in substance, and differ only in expression, as their languages differ in idiom. The modern Ṣūfīs, who profess a belief in the Ḳurān, suppose, with great sublimity both of thought and of diction, an *express contract*, on the day of eternity without beginning, between the assemblage of created spirits and the supreme soul, from which they were detached, when a celestial voice pronounced these words, addressed to each spirit separately, ' Art thou not with thy Lord?' that is, art thou not bound by a solemn contract with him? and all the spirits answered with one voice, ' Yes.' The Hindūs describe the same covenant under the figurative notion, so finely expressed by Isaiah, of a *nuptial contract*; for, considering God in the three characters of Creator, Regenerator, and Preserver, and supposing the power of preservation and benevolence to have become incarnate in the person of *Krishna*, they represent him as married to *Rādhā*, a word signifying ' atonement,' ' pacification,' or ' satisfaction,' but applied allegorically to the soul of man, or rather, to the whole assemblage of created souls, between whom and the benevolent Creator they suppose that reciprocal love, which Barrow describes with a glow of expression perfectly Oriental, and which our most orthodox Theologians believe to have been mystically shadowed in the Song of Solomon, while they admit that, in a literal sense, it is an epithalamium on the marriage of the sapient king with the princess of Egypt. The very learned author of the 'Prelections on Sacred Poetry' declared his opinion that the Canticles were founded on historical truth, but involved an allegory of that sort, which he named mystical; and the beautiful poem on the loves of *Lailī* and *Majnūn,* by the inimitable *Niẓāmī* (to say nothing of other poems on the same subject), is indisputably built on true history, yet avowedly allegorical and mysterious; for the introduction to it is a continued rapture on divine love; and the name of *Lailī* seems to be used in the *Maṣnavī* and the odes of *Ḥāfiẓ* for the omnipresent Spirit of God.

"It has been made a question, whether the poems of *Ḥāfiẓ* must be taken in a literal or in a figurative sense; but the question, does not admit of a general.and direct answer; for even the most enthusiastic of his commentators allow that some of them are to be taken literally, and his editors ought to have distinguished them, as our Spencer has distinguished his four odes on 'Love and Beauty,' instead of mixing the profane with the divine, by a childish arrangement, according to the alphabetical order of the rhymes. *Ḥāfiẓ* never pretended to more than human virtues, and it is known he had human propensities; for, in his youth, he was passionately in love with a girl, surnamed *Shākhi Nibāt,* or, 'The Branch of Sugarcane,' and the Prince of Shīrāz was his rival. Since there is an agreeable wildness in the story, and since the poet himself alludes to it in one of his odes, I give it you at length, from the commentary:—There is a place called Pīri sabz, or, 'The Green Old Man,' about four Persian leagues from the city; and a popular opinion had long prevailed, that a youth, who should pass forty successive nights in Pīri sabz without sleep, would infallibly become an excellent poet. Young *Ḥāfiẓ* had accordingly made a vow that he would serve that apprenticeship with the utmost exactness; and for thirty-nine days he rigorously discharged his duty, walking every morning before the house of his coy mistress, taking some refreshment and rest at noon, and passing the night awake at his poetical station; but, on the fortieth morning, he was transported with joy on seeing the girl beckon to him through the lattices, and invite him to enter. She received him with rapture, declared her preference of a bright genius to the son of a king; and would have detained him all night, if he had not recollected his vow, and, resolving to keep it inviolate, returned to his post. The people of Shīrāz add (and the fiction is grounded on a couplet of *Ḥāfiẓ*), that, early next morning, an 'old man in a green mantle,' who was no less a personage than _Khiẓr_ himself, approached him at Pīri sabz, with a cup brimful of nectar, which the Greeks would have called 'The water of Aganippe,' and rewarded his perseverance with an inspiring draught of it. After his juvenile passions had subsided, we may suppose that his mind took that religious bent which appears in most of his compositions; for there can be no doubt that the following distichs, collected from different odes, relate to the mystical Theology of the Ṣūfis:—

" ' In eternity, without beginning, a ray of thy beauty began to gleam; when love sprang into being, and cast flames over all nature;—on that day thy cheek sparkled even under thy veil, and all this beautiful imagery appeared on the mirror of our fancies.—Rise, my soul; that I may pour thee forth on the pencil of that supreme artist, who comprised in a turn of his compasses all this wonderful scenery!—From the moment when I heard the divine sentence, _I have breathed into man a portion of my spirit_, I was assured that we were His, and He ours.—Where are the glad tidings of union with Thee, that I may abandon all desire of life! I am a bird of holiness, and would fain escape from the net of this world.—Shed, O Lord, from the cloud of heavenly guidance, one cheering shower, before the moment when I must rise up like a particle of dry dust!—The sum of our transactions, in this universe, is nothing: bring us the wine of devotion;· for the possessions of this world vanish.— The true object of heart and soul is the glory of union with our beloved; that object really exists, but without it both heart and soul would have no existence!—Oh, the bliss of that day, when I shall depart from this desolate mansion; shall seek rest for my soul, and shall follow the traces of my beloved!—Dancing with love of his beauty, like a mote in a sunbeam, till I reach the spring and fountain of light, whence ,yon sun derives all his lustre !'

" The couplets which follow relate as indubitably to human love and sensual gratifications:—

" ' May the hand never shake which gathered the grapes! may the foot never slip which pressed them!—That poignant liquor, which the zealot calls the mother of sins, is pleasanter and sweeter to me than the kisses of a maiden.—How delightful is dancing to lively notes and the cheerful melody of the flute, especially when we ·touch the hand of a beautiful maiden.—_Call for wine, and scatter flowers around: what more_ *canst thou ask from fate?* Thus spoke the nightingale this morning : what sayest thou, sweet rose, to his precepts ?—Bring thy couch to the garden of roses, that thou mayest kiss the cheeks and lips of lovely damsels, quaff rich wine, and smell odoriferous blossoms.—O' branch of an exquisite rose-plant! for whose sake dost thou grow ? Ah! on whom will that smiling rosebud confer delight ?—The rose would have discoursed on the beauties of my charmer, but the gale was jealous, and stole her breath before she spoke.—In this age, the only friends who are free from blemish are a flask of pure wine and a volume of elegant love songs.—Oh, the joy of that moment, when the self-sufficiency of inebriation rendered me independent of the prince and of his minister !'

" Many zealous admirers of *Ḥāfiẓ* insist, that by wine he invariably means devotion ; and they have gone so far as to compose a dictionary of words in the language, as they call it, of the Ṣūfīs. In that vocabulary sleep is explained by meditation on the divine perfections, and perfume by hope of the Divine favour; gales are illapses of grace ; kisses and embraces, the raptures of piety ; idolaters, infidels, and libertines are men of the purest religion, and their idol is the Creator himself; the tavern is a retired oratory, and its keeper a sage instructor : beauty denotes the perfection of the Supreme Being ; tresses are the expansion of his glory ; lips, the hidden mysteries of his essence ; down on the cheek, the world of spirits, who encircle his throne ; and a black mole, the point of indivisible unity : lastly, wantonness, mirth, and inebriety, mean religious ardour and abstraction from all terrestrial thoughts. The poet himself gives a colour, in many passages, to such an interpretation ; and, without it, we can hardly conceive that his poems, or those of his numerous imitators, would be tolerated in a Musalmān country, especially at Constantinople, where they are venerated as divine compositions. It must be admitted, that the sublimity of the mystical allegory, which, like metaphors and comparisons, should be general only, not minutely exact, is diminished, if not destroyed, by an attempt at particular and distinct resemblances ; and that the style is open to dangerous misinterpretation, while it supplies real infidels with a pretext for laughing at religion itself.

On this occasion I cannot refrain from producing a most extraordinary ode, by a Ṣūfī of Bukhārā, who assumed the poetical surname of 'Iṣmat :—

" ' Yesterday, half inebriated, I passed by the quarter where the vintners dwell, to seek the daughter of an infidel who sells wine.—At the end of the street, there advanced before me a damsel, with a fairy's cheeks, who, in the manner of a pagan, wore her tresses dishevelled over her shoulders like the sacerdotal thread. I said, " O thou, to the arch of whose eyebrow the new moon is a slave, what quarter is this, and where is thy mansion?"—She answered, " Cast thy rosary on the ground; bind on thy shoulder the thread of paganism; throw stones at the glass of piety, and quaff wine from a full goblet:—After that, come before me, that I may whisper a word in thine ear: thou wilt accomplish thy journey if thou listen to my discourse."—Abandoning my heart, and rapt in extacy, I ran after her, till I came to a place in which religion and reason forsook me.—At a distance I beheld a company, all insane and inebriated, who came boiling and roaring with ardour from the wine of love;—without cymbals, or lutes, or viols, yet all full of mirth or melody ; without wine, or goblet, or flask, yet all incessantly drinking.—When the cord of restraint slipped from my hand, I desired to ask her one question, but she said, " Silence !—This is no square temple, to the gate of which thou canst arrive precipitately ; this is no mosque to which thou canst come with tumult, but without knowledge. This is the banquet-house of infidels, and within it all are intoxicated; all, from the dawn of eternity to the day of resurrection, lost in astonishment.—Depart, then, from the cloister, and take the way to the tavern ; cast off the cloak of a dervise, and wear the robe of a libertine."—I obeyed : and, if thou desirest the same strain and colour with '*Ismat*, imitate him, and sell this world and the next for one drop of pure wine.'

" Such is the strange religion, and stranger language of the Ṣūfis ; but most of the Asiatic poets are of that religion, and if we think it worth while to read their poems, we must think it worth while to understand them. Their great *Maulavi* assures us, that ' they profess eager desire, but with no carnal affection, and circulate the cup, but no materi goblet ; since all things are spiritual in their sect, all is mystery within mystery.' "

THE END.

LEWIS AND SON, PRINTERS, SWAN BUILDINGS, MOORGATE STREET.

VOCABULARY.

PERSIAN AND ENGLISH.

N.B.—In order that the Student may not waste time in useless search, he must be careful to reduce each word to its simple form, by stripping it of such prefixes and additions as it may happen to have, before he looks for it in the Vocabulary. The prefixes are, 1st, بِ, used as a preposition before a noun, and, in verbs, prefixed, as بِ or بِیِ, to the Future, and, redundantly, to the Preterite. 2dly, نَ or نِی and مَ or مِی, prefixed to verbs to denote negation (Gram. § 49). 3dly, مِی or هِمِی prefixed to verbs, to denote the Present and Imperfect Tenses. The ordinary affixes are, 1st, the ي, denoting unity, &c. (Gram. § 35); as, شَخْصِي "a certain person" (in the Vocabulary, look for شخص). 2dly, The plural terminations, ان, گان, یان, ریان and ها (Gram. § 27), together with the termination را. 3dly, The terminations added to form the various persons of the verb; and, lastly, pronominal affixes, مَ—, تَ—, شَ—. (Vide Gram. § 39 and § 64, &c., and more fully in the Syntax.) By attending to these few hints, the learner will be spared some trouble, and the Vocabulary will incur less censure on the score of deficiency.

اب

آبْ *āb,* water, splendour.

ابراهیم ادهم *Ibrāhīm Adham,* name of a pious sovereign of Balkh.

آبرو *ābrū,* honour, reputation.

ابله *ablah,* foolish, *s.* a fool.

آتش *ātish,* or *ātash,* fire; anger.

اتفاقا *ittifākan,* accidentally, by chance.

آثار *āsār,* pl. traces; a pound weight.

اثبات *isbāt,* confirmation, proof.

اثرٔ *asar,* mark, sign, vestige, effect.

اثنا *asnā,* middle; *dar asnā-e ān,* or *dar īn asnā;* in the mean while.

احتراز *ihtirāz,* taking care of one's self.

احمق *ahmak,* foolish, a fool.

ارز

احوال *ahwāl,* pl. circumstances, affairs; state, condition.

اختیار *ikhtiyār,* choice, power, control.

آخر *ākhir,* the end, at last; *ākhir ul amr,* in short, finally.

ادا *adā,* payment, fulfilment; *adā kardan* or *sākhtan,* to pay, fulfil.

ادب *adab,* politeness, courtesy.

آدم *Ādam,* the first man; hence آدمي a man, one of the human race.

آر *ār,* bring thou (from آوردن).

ارادت *irādat,* or اراده *irāda,* will, inclination, intention, design.

ارزان *arzān,* cheap, worthy.

آرزو ārzū, desire; ārzū-mand, desirous, longing for.

اركان arkān, pillars, feet in prosody; arkān-i daulat, pillars of state, nobles, courtiers.

آري ārī, yea, yes, yea verily.

از az, from, by, with, than.

آزاد āzād, free, emancipated; a hermit.

آزار āzār, affliction, vexation.

ازان azān, thence, therefore.

آزمودن āzmūdan, to try, test.

اسامي asāmī, names, or a list of names.

آسايش āsāyish, ease, indulgence.

اسباب asbāb, means; goods and chattels.

اسب or اسپ asp, a horse.

استاد ustād, master, preceptor.

استادن istādan, to stand, persist.

استخوان ustukhwān, a bone.

استماع istimā', hearing.

اسكندر Iskandar, Alexander the Great.

اسفار asfār, travels: plur. of سفر.

اسم ism, a name, noun in Grammar.

اسمار asmār, stories, conversations.

آسمان āsmān, the sky, the heavens.

آسودن āsūdan, to repose, be at ease.

آسيب āsīb, trouble, annoyance.

اسير asīr, a prisoner, captive.

اصطبل istabal, a stable.

اصلا aslan, at all, in the least.

اطلاع itlā', information, notice; 'ittilā', investigating, searching for.

اظهار izhār, manifestation, pointing out.

اعتماد i'timād, confidence, reliance.

اعراب A'rāb, an Arab of the desert, or an uncivilized wandering Arab.

آغاز āghāz, a beginning.

افتادن uftādan, to fall, to happen.

افترا iftira, calumny, slander.

آفريدن āfrīdan, to create root (آفرين).

آفرين āfrīn, creating; applause; bravo!

افگندن afgandan, to cast, throw.

افلاس iflās, poverty, destitution.

افلاطون Aflātūn, Plato, the Grecian sage.

اقارب akārib, relatives, relations.

اقرار ikrār, confirmation, confession.

اكثر aksar, most, frequently.

اكنون aknūn, now, at present.

آگاه āgāh, aware of, informed.

اگر agar, if; اگرچہ agarchi, though.

ال al, the Arabic article "the," prefixed to Arabic nouns. (Gr. § 22.)

البتہ albatta, in truth, assuredly.

التفات iltifāt, notice, attention.

الحاد ilḥād, idolatry, infidelity.

الحال al-ḥāl, at present, now.

الحاصل al-ḥāṣil, in short, finally.

الزام ilzām, conviction.

القصہ al-kiṣṣa, in short, finally.

الله Allāh, God.

الهي ilāhī, Divine; the Deity.

اما ammā, but, nevertheless.

امان amān, protection, safety.

امانت amānat, a deposit, a thing en-trusted, or consigned to one.

امتحان imtiḥān, trial, examination.

آمدن āmadan, to come, to be (r. آي).

امر amr, matter, affair, subject.

امروز imroz, to-day (for īn-roz, this day).

آموختن āmokhtan, to learn, to teach.

اميد ummed, hope, expectation.

اميدوار ummedvār, hopeful.

امير amīr, a commander; a grandee.

آن ān, that, it, he, she.

انبار ambār, a store, quantity.

انبان *ambān*, a leathern bag.

آنجا *ānjā*, there, in that place.

آنچنان *ānchunān*, such as that, so.

آنچه *ānchi*, that which, whatsoever.

انداختن *andākhtan*, to throw.

اندام *andām*, body, person.

اندر *andar*, or اندرون *andarūn*, within.

اندك *andak*, a little, a few.

اندكي *andakī*, a small portion.

انسان *insān*, man, the human race.

انصاف *inṣāf*, justice, one's right.

انعام *in'ām*, a gratuity or present.

انكار *inkār*, denial, refusal.

انگشت *angusht*, the finger.

انگشتري *angushtarī*, a ring.

انگور *angūr*, a grape, raisin.

انواع *anwā'*, various sorts or kinds.

آنه *āna*, (in India) a nominal coin, the sixteenth part of a rupee.

او *ō*, 3d pers. pron., he, she, or it.

آواز *āwāz*, sound, noise, voice.

آوردن *āwardan* (r. آور or آر), to bring, to relate; *āwarda and*, they have related (Lat. "ferunt," they say.)

اول *awwal*, the first; at first.

اولاد *aulād*, family, offspring.

آویختن *āwekhtan*, to cling to, lay hold of.

اهل *ahl*, people, men, persons.

آهنگ *āhang*, design, intention.

آهنگر *āhan-gar*, a worker in iron, a blacksmith, an armourer.

اي *ai*, interject. O!

آیا *āyā*, sign of interrogation.

ایاز *Aiyāz*, a man's name.

ایشان *eshān*, plur. of او, they.

ایفا *īfā* payment, fulfilment.

ایمان *īmān*, faith, conscience.

این *in*, pron., he, she, it, or this.

اینجا *īnjā*, here, in this place.

اینچنین *īnchunīn*, such as this, thus.

اینقدر *īnkadar*, to this extent, so much.

اینكه *īnki*, he who, that which.

آئنه *ā,īna*, a mirror; times; *har,ā,īna*, always, at all events, assuredly.

ب

ب *ba* (in Arabic, *bi*), a preposition, by, with, in, to; *bi*, verbal prefix.

با *bā*, in company with, possessed of.

باد *bād*, the wind; *bar bād dādan*, to give to the wind, to cast away.

بادشاه *bādshāh*, a king.

بار *bār*, a burden; time, as in the phrase *yak-bār*, once; *dū-bār*, twice.

باره *bāra*, behalf; *dar bārā e kase*, in behalf of any one.

باز *bāz*, a hawk: as an adverb, this word signifies iteration or repetition; as, *bāz-raftan*, to go back; *bāz-kardan*, to put back, or open (a door, &c.); *bāz-namūdan*, to declare, shew forth.

بازار *bāzār*, a market-place, market.

بازي *bāzī*, a game, play; *bāzī yāftan*, to win the game.

بازیدن *bāzīdan*, to play, to gamble.

باش *bāsh*, be thou, wait, remain.

باعث *bā'is*, cause, reason, motive.

باغ *bāgh*, a garden, an orchard.

باغبان *bāghbān*, a gardener.

باقي *bāḳī*, remainder, remaining.

باك *bāk*, fear, hesitation.

بالا *bālā*, above, on the top.

يالكل *bilkull*, entirely, "in toto."

بام ا *bām*, roof of a house.

بامداد *bāmdād*, in the morning.

بانگ *bāng*, a voice, sound, cry; *bāng-zadan*, to call out.

باور *bāwar*, true, creditable; *bāwar-kardan* or *dāshtan*, to believe.

باورچيخانه *bāwarchī-khāna*, literally, cook-house; a kitchen.

باهم *bāham*, together, united.

بايستن *bāyistan*, to be proper, necessary: generally used impersonally; as بايد *bāyad*, it is necessary, &c.

بچه *bachcha*, the young of any animal.

بخشيدن *bakhshīdan*, to bestow, to forgive, to spare.

بخيل *bakhīl*, a miser; adj., stingy.

بد *bad*, evil, bad: much used in composition; as, بدخوي *bad-khū,e*, of ill-temper; بد روي *bud-rū,e*, ill favoured, of an ugly face.

بدنام *badnām*, a bad name, reproach.

بدنهاد *badnihād*, depraved, perfidious.

بدانجا *badānjā*, (بهآنجا) in that place.

بدر *ba-dar*, out, to the door.

بدين *badīn*, for بهاين, in this; hereby, in this.

بر *bar*, on *or* upon, for, at.

برابر *barābar*, breast to breast; like, equal, on a level with.

برادر *barādar* and *birādar*, brother.

برادرانه *birādarāna*, worthy of a brother.

برآمدن *bar-āmadan*, to come up, come to pass, to rise (as the sun).

برآوردن *bar-āwardan*, to bring up, prolong, to bring about.

براي *barā,e*, for the sake of; *barā,e khudā*, for God's sake.

باخاستن *bar-khāstan*, to rise up, to depart, to cease.

بردار *bar-dār kashīdan* or *-kardan*, to hang, to crucify.

برداشتن *bar-dāshtan*, to hold up, to sustain, to carry off.

بردن *burdan* (root, *bar*), to bear, to carry away, bring.

بركندن *bar kandan*, to pluck out, to eradicate, to exterminate.

برکه *birka*, a pond, pool.

برگشتن *bar-gashtan*, to return.

برگماشتن *bar-gumāshtan*, to send forth.

برج *biranj*, rice.

برو *bar-o*, on him, her, &c.; *biraw*, imperative of *raftan*, go thou.

برهم *barham*, confused, offended, enraged.

برهنه *barahna*, naked, bare.

بريان *biryān* or *buryān*, baked, fried.

بزرجمهر *Buzurjmihr*, a man's name.

بزرگ *buzurg*, great: applied to age, it means old, reverential.

بس *bas*, enough; *bas-kardan*, to have done, to leave off.

بساط *bisāt*, a bed, carpet, covering.

بستر *bistar*, a bed, couch.

بستن *bastan* (root, *band*), to bind.

بسيار *bisyār*, much, many, very.

بعد *ba'd*, at the end, after: generally applied to time.

بقال *bakkāl*, a grocer, an oil-merchant.

بلا *balā*, evil, misfortune, calamity.

بلخ *Balkh*, name of a city.

بلدان *buldān*, cities, regions.

بلع bala', swallowing, devouring.

بلکه balki, but, rather, on the contrary.

بلند buland, tall, high, great.

بلي balā (also balī), yea, verily, indeed.

بنابرين bina-bar-īn, on this account.

بند band, fetter; dar band, desirous.

بندگي bandagī, servitude, submission.

بنده banda, a slave, servant.

بوي bū or bū͵e, fragrance, smell.

بودن būdan, to be, exist (r. بُو or باش).

به ba, by, with, in.

به bih, good; (also) better.

بهانه bahāna, pretence or pretext.

بهتر bihtar, better; bihtarīn, best.

بهره bahra, a share, portion; utility.

بي be, without, deprived of.

بيار biyār, imper. of āwardan, to bring.

بيان bayān, explanation, narration.

بيبي bībī, a lady, mistress.

بيعانه bai'āna, earnest-money.

بيجا bejā, out of place, improper.

بيجگري be-jigarī, timidity, cowardice.

بيچاره be-chāra, helpless, forlorn.

بيچيزي be-chīzī, destitution.

بيحيا be-ḥayā, shameless, impudent.

بيخ bekh, root of a tree; origin.

بي خرجي be-kharjī (also be-kharchī),
  non-expenditure, economy.

بيدار be-dār, watchful, awake.

بيرون berūn, out, outside.

بيست bīst, twenty.

بيعقل be-'akl, insane, stupid.

بيکبار ba-yak-bār, all at once.

بيگانه begāna, a stranger.

بيمار bīmār, sick, unhealthy.

بيماري bīmārī, sickness.

بين bīn, see thou (r. of ديدن).

بيني bīnī, the nose.

بيوفا be-wafā, faithless, false.

بيهوده behūda, foolish, vain.

پ

پا pā, the foot.

پاپوش pā-posh, foot-covering, slipper.

پادشاه pādshāh, a king.

پارچه pārcha, a garment.

پارسي Pārsī or Pārasī, Persian.

پاره pāra, a bit, fragment; pāra-kar-
  dan, to break to pieces.

پاس pās, a watch of the day or night;
  pās-bān, a sentinel; pās-dāshtan, to
  keep watch, to mount guard.

پاسباني pāsbānī, keeping watch.

پاک pāk, clean; pāk-kardan, to wipe.

پاکيزه pākīza, pure, clean.

پانصد pānṣad, five hundred.

پختن pukhtan, to cook.

پدر padar or pidar, father.

پذيرفتن pazīraftan (r. pazīr), to sustain, receive.

پر pur, full; par, a wing or feather.

پرتاب partāb, aim; partāb-hardan,
  to aim or take aim.

پرداختن pardākhtan, to accomplish.

پرده parda, a veil, screen.

پرسيدن pursīdan, to ask, interrogate.

پرواز parwāz, flight, on the wing.

پروردن parwardan, to cherish, to rear.

پرهيزگار parhezgār, temperate, pure.

پريدن parīdan, to soar, to fly.

پس pas, then, after, finally; pas o pesh
  kardan, to demur, make evasion.

پسر *pisar*, a son, a boy.

پسند *pasand*, agreeable; *pasand-āma-dan*, to be agreeable.

پسندیدن *pasandīdan*, to approve of.

پشت *pusht*, the back.

پشیمان *pashemān*, penitent, regretful.

پشه *pasha*, a gnat, a mosquito.

پناه *panāh*, aid, shelter, asylum.

پنبه *pumba*, cotton; *pumba-farosh*, cotton-seller.

پنج *panj*, five; *panjum*, fifth.

پنجاه *panjāh*, fifty.

پنداشتن *pindāshtan*, to consider, imagine, believe, think.

پوست *post*, skin, hide.

پوشیدن *poshīdan*, to put on (a garment), to cover, conceal; *poshānīdan*, to cause to be clothed, covered, &c.

پیاده *piyāda*, a pedestrian; a pawn.

پیدا *paidā*, manifest, born, created.

پیر *pīr*, old, aged, an old man, an elder.

پیراهن *pīrāhan*, a garment.

پیش *pesh*, before, in front.

پیشینه *peshīna*, former, past.

پیشه *pesha*, a trade, profession.

پیك *paik*, a runner *or* courier.

پیل *pīl*, an elephant; also فیل *fīl*.

ت

تا *tā*, that, so that, until.

تابع *tābi'*, subjected, subdued.

تاجدار *tājdār*, crown-holder, a king.

تار *tār*, dark; also *tārīk*.

تازیانه *tāziyāna*, a scourge, whip; *tāziyāna-zadan*, to flog.

تافتن *tāftan*, to turn, twist, revolve, shine.

تامل *ta,ammul*, meditation, consideration.

تبسم *tabassum*, a smile.

تجارت *tijārat*, traffic, merchandise.

تجاهل *tajāhul*, pretending ignorance.

تجسس *tajassus*, search, inquiry.

تجویز *tajwīz*, leave, permission.

تحسین *tahsīn*, praise, commendation.

تحیر *tahayyur*, astonishment.

تخت *takht*, a throne.

تخم *tukhm*, grain, seed-stone.

تدبیر *tadbīr*, arrangement, contrivance.

تراشیدن *tarāshīdan*, to cut off, cut away.

تردد *taraddud*, perplexity, dismay.

ترسانیدن *tarsānīdan*, to terrify: causal of *tarsīdan*, from the root *tars*, fear.

ترسیدن *tarsīdan*, to be afraid.

ترش *tursh*, sad, stern, morose.

ترك *tark*, abandonment, forsaking.

ترك *Turk*, a Turk or Turkomān.

تست *tust*, for *tū-ast*, *azāni tust*, it is of thee, *or* it is thine.

تشریف *tashrīf*, ennobling; *tashrif burdan*, to honour an inferior with a visit; to condescend.

تشویش *tashwīsh*, disturbance, trouble.

تصدیق *tasdīk*, verifying, confirmation.

تصویر *taswīr*, a picture, a portrait,

تعاقب *ta'āḵub*, pursuit, following.

تعالی *ta'ālā*, He is exalted; God.

تعب *ta'b*, labour, fatigue.

تعبیر *ta'bīr*, interpretation, explanation.

تعزیت *ta'ziyat*, condolence.

تعظیم *ta'ẓīm*, magnifying, revering.

تفاوت *tafāwut*, distance, difference.

تفرج *tafarruj*, enjoying or viewing.

تفکر *tafakkur*, thought, contemplation.

تقاضا *takāzā*, dunning, demanding.

تقریب *takrīb*, proximity, presence.

تقصیر *taksīr*, delinquency, crime.

تکذیب *takzīb*, accusation of falsehood; giving one the lie direct.

تگ *tag*, bottom, depth; *dar tag*, underneath, subjected to.

تلاش *talāsh*, search, investigation.

تماشا *tamāsha*, a spectacle, show.

تمام *tamām*, all, entire, the whole.

تنبیه *tambīh*, admonition, reproof.

تنها *tanhā*, alone, solitary.

توانستن *tawānistan*, to be able.

تو *tū*, 2d pers. pron. thou.

توبیخ *taubīkh*, blaming, chiding.

توله *tūla*, name of a certain weight.

توقف *tawakkuf*, delay, putting off.

تونگر *tawangar*, powerful, rich.

تهمت *tuhmat*, accusation, calumny.

تهنیت *tahniyat*, congratulation.

تهی *tahī*, or *tihī*, empty; *tahī-dast*, empty-handed, destitute.

تیار *taiyār*, ready, prepared.

تیر *tīr*, an arrow; *tīr-andāz*, an archer; *tīr-andāzī*, archery.

تیز *tez*, sharp, swift, violent, keen.

تیمور *Tīmūr* and *Taimūr*, the far-famed conqueror, commonly called Tamerlane; properly *Taimūr-lang*, i. e. Taimur the Lame.

ث

ثبت *sabat*, proof, confirmation.

ثواب *sawāb*, reward, retribution (in a future state).

ج

جا *jā*, place; *jā-kardan*, to occupy a place, to settle.

جاسوس *jāsūs*, a scout *or* spy.

جامه *jāma*, a garment.

جان *jān*, soul, life; a beloved one.

جانب *jānib*, side, direction.

جای *jā,e*, anywhere, in some place.

جبرا *jabran*, forcibly.

جد *jadd*, grandfather, ancestor.

جدا *judā*, separate, apart.

جرمانه *jurmāna*, a fine *or* penalty.

جریده *jarīda*, a memorandum-book.

جستن *justan* (root جو), to seek.

جگر *jigar*, the liver; courage.

جلاد *jallād*, an executioner.

جلد *jald*, quick, swift; quickly.

جماعت *jamā'at*, a number, crowd.

جمع *jam'*, an assembly; *jam'-shudan*, to assemble, *or* be assembled.

جمیع *jamī'*, all, the whole.

جنبیدن *jumbīdan*, to shake, move (intransitively); hence, *jumbanīdan*, to shake, move (actively).

جنگ *jang*, war, battle.

جنگل *jangal*, a forest of thickets.

جنگلی *janglī*, wild, untamed.

جواب *jawāb*, an answer.

جوان *jawān*, a young man, *juvenis*.

جواهر *jawāhir*, jewels; *jawāhir-khāna*, the jewel-house, treasury.

جوشن *jaushan*, a cuirass, coat of mail

جوع *jū'*, hunger, appetite.

جهاز *jahāz*, a ship, boat.

جهان *jahān*, the world, an age; *jahān-*

panāh, Asylum of the world, a mode of addressing an Oriental sovereign.

جيب *jaib* or *jeb*, a pocket, purse; also, a mantle.

چ

چادر *chādar* or *chādir*, a mantle, sheet.

چاره *chāra*, resource, remedy.

چاشت *chāsht*, the mid-day meal.

چاه *chāh*, a pit, well.

چرا *chirā*, why? wherefore? *chirā-ki*, because, since, *or* since that.

چراغ *chirāgh*, a lanthorn, lamp.

چريدن *charīdan*, to graze, feed.

چشم *chashm*, the eye; hope.

چقدر *chi-kadar*, how much?

چكيدن *chakīdan*, to drop, to fall by drops.

چگونه *chigūna*, what sort? how? why?

چنان *chunān*, like that, such as that.

چند *chand*, some, several.

چندبار *chand-bār*, several times, often.

چندين *chandīn*, so much, so much as this.

چنگل *changul*, a hook, a claw.

چنين *chunīn*, such as this, so much.

چون *chūn*, like, when? how? why?

چوب *chob* or *chūb*, a stick, piece of wood.

چه *chi*, that, that which; what?

چهار *chahār*, four; *chahārum*, fourth.

چيدن *chīdan* (root چين), to gather, collect, to cull (flowers, &c.)

چيز *chīz*, a thing, an affair.

چيست *chīst*, What is it? for *chi* and *ast* or *hast*.

ح

حاذق *hāzik*, skilful, expert.

حاصل *hāsil*, result; *hāsil-kardan*, to acquire; *hāsil shudan*, to be acquired, to be attained.

حاضر *hāzir*, present, in attendance; *hāziran*, those attending. 42

حال *hāl*, condition; *dar hāl* or *fi-l-hāl*, immediately, forthwith.

حالا *hālan*, now, presently.

حالت *hālat*, condition, state.

حامل *hāmil*, bearer, carrier.

حبشي *habshī*, an Abyssinian *or* Negro.

حبه *habba*, a particle, a grain.

حرام زاده *harām-zāda*, unlawful-born, a reprobate, rogue, scamp.

حرمان *hirmān*, disappointment.

حريف *harīf*, a rival, companion.

حسد *hasad*, envy, malice.

حشمت *hashmat*, pomp, retinue.

حصه *hissa*, a share, portion.

حضرت *hazrat*, (literally) presence; Your Majesty, Highness, &c.

حضور *huzūr*, presence, the royal presence, the King's Court.

حق *hakk*, truth, right; *hakk ta'ālā*, God, the Most High.

حقيقه *hakīka* or *hakīkat*, truth, circumstance, real state.

حكايات *hikāyāt*, stories, tales: plur. of

حكايت *hikāyat*, a story, narrative.

حكم *hukm*, order, sentence (of a Judge)

حكما *hukamā*, sages, learned men.

حكمت *hikmat*, sagacity, contrivance

حكيم *hakīm*, a sage, a doctor.

حماقت *himākat* (also *humk*), folly.

حمل *haml*, a burden; *haml kardan*, to impose a burden, to assail.

حوا *Hānā*, Eve, the first woman.

حواله كردن *hawāla kardan*, to give in charge, to consign, entrust.

حوض *hawẓ*, a pond, tank for bathing.

حيا *hayā*, shame, modesty.

حيات *hayāt*, life, lifetime.

حيران *hairān*, astonished, bewildered.

حيرت *hairat*, astonishment.

حيله *hīla*, trick, stratagem.

خ

خادم *khādim*, an attendant, a slave.

خاستن *khāstan* (r. *khez*), to stand up.

خاطر *khāṭir*, the heart, soul; *khāṭir jam' dāshtan*, to be of good cheer; *khāṭir nigāh dāshtan*, to cherish, to win *or* possess the heart.

خاك *khāk*, the earth, dust.

خالي *khālī*, bare, empty, void of.

خاموش *khāmosh*, silent. 30

خاموشي *khāmoshī*, silence.

خان *khān*, an inn; also a Tartar title, lord, ruler; vulgarly, the *Cham*.

خانه *khāna*, a house, mansion.

خانه خرابي *khāna-kharābī*, ruin of one's house, destruction.

خائن *khā,in*, a deceiver, treacherous.

خبر *khabar* or *khabr*, news, information.

خبردار *khabar-dār*, attentive, aware.

خجل *khajal*, ashamed, abashed.

خجلت *khajlat*, shame, bashfulness.

خدا *khudā*, God; a master, lord. 42

خداوند *khudāwand*, a lord, master.

خدمت *khidmat*, service, presence.

خر *khar*, an ass; *khar-gosh*, a hare.

خراب *kharāb*, destruction, evil, bad.

خراساني *khurāsānī*, a native of Khurāsān, a Bactrian.

خراندن *khurāndan*, to cause to eat; to give food, to treat.

خرد *khurd*, small, little; *khirad*, wisdom; *khiradmand*, wise, sensible.

خرما *khurmā*, the fruit of the date-tree.

خروس *khuros*, á cock.

خريدن *kharīdan*, to buy, to purchase.

خريطه *kharīṭa*, a purse.

خزانه *khizāna*, a treasury, store.

خسارت *khasārat*, loss, damage.

خسپيدن *khuspīdan*, to sleep.

خشم *khishm* or *khashm*, anger.

خشنود *khushnūd*, content, joyful.

خصي *khaṣī*, a goat.

خط *khatt*, a letter, an epistle.

خطا *khaṭā*, an error, failure, missing.

خطيب *khaṭīb*, a preacher.

خلاص *khalāṣ*, liberation, freedom.

خلاف *khilāf*, the contrary, opposite.

خلعت *khil'at*, a dress of honour.

خلوت *khalwat*, privacy, retirement.

خليدن *khalīdan*, to pierce into the flesh (as a thorn), to prick.

خفتن *khuftan*, to sleep (r. خسپ *khusp*).

خنثي *khunṣa*, a hermaphrodite.

خنده *khanda*, smile, laughter.

خنديدن *khandīdan*, to smile, laugh.

خو *khū* or خوي *khū,e*, temper, disposition.

خواب *khwāb*, sleep, dream (v. Gr. § 13, *b*).

خوابيدن *khwābīdan*, to sleep.

خواجه *khwāja*, a master, merchant.

خوار *khwār*, devouring: used in composition; as, *bisyār-khwār*, a glutton.

خواستن *khwāstan*, to wish, will, desire.

خواندن _khwāndan_, to read, to call.

خواهر _khwāhar_, a sister.

خوب _khūb_, good, beautiful.

خوبي _khūbī_, goodness, beauty, virtue.

خود _khud_, (pron.) self; (subst.) a friend.

خور _khur_, food.

خورد _khurd_, small, little.

خوردن _khurdan_, to eat; to suffer.

خوش _khush_, pleasant, good; _khush āmadan_, to be agreeable, to be welcome.

خوشي _khushī_, joy, pleasure.

خوشدامن _khushdāman_, a mother-in-law, a wife's mother.

خوشنود _khushnūd_, pleased, satisfied.

خوشه _khūsha_, a bunch of grapes.

خويش _khwesh_, self. (Vide Gr. § 39.)

خيانت _khiyānat_, treachery, dishonesty.

خيريت _khairīyat_, welfare, safety.

د

دادن _dādan_, to give, pay (r. دِه _dih_).

دار _dār_, the gallows, a gibbet: in composition it means possession.

داروغه _dārogha_, the head man of an office.

داشتن _dāshtan_, to possess, hold, have.

دامن _dāman_, skirt of a garment.

دانا _dānā_, wise, prudent.

دانستن _dānistan_, to know, to think.

دانشمند _dānishmand_, wise, learned.

دانه _dāna_, a grain, seed.

دائم _dā,im_, always, perpetual.

دختر _dukhtar_, a daughter, a damsel.

دخل _dakhl_, entrance.

در _dar_, a door; prepos. in, into, at; _ba-dar_, out, to the door.

دراز _darāz_, long, distant; also _dirāz_.

درامدن _dar-āmadan_, to enter.

دراويختن _dar-āwekhtan_, to contend, grapple with.

دربان _darbān_ (also _darwān_), a door-keeper, a porter.

درخت _dirakht_, a tree, a stalk.

درد _dard_, pain (bodily or mental).

در رسيدن _dar-rasīdan_, to arrive, enter.

درست _durust_, right, true.

درم _diram_, money, a small silver coin.

در ماندن _dar-māndan_, to be destitute, to be "in a fix," to be weary.

دروازه _darwāza_, a door, a gate. _13_

دروغ _durogh_, a lie, falsehood; _durogh-go_, a liar. _18_

درون _darūn_, in, inside, within.

درويش _darwesh_, poor, a mendicant.

درهم _dar-ham_, together, contracted; _rū,e dar-ham kashīdan_, to be offended, to frown.

دريا _daryā_, the sea, a river.

دريافت _daryāft_, discovery.

دريافتن _dar-yāftan_, to discover.

دريچه _daricha_, a window.

درين _dar-īn_, in this, herein.

دزد _duzd_, a thief, a robber.

دزدي _duzdī_, theft; _ba-duzdī raftan_, to be stolen, to go by theft.

دزديدن _duzdīdan_, to steal. _49_

دست _dast_, the hand; _dast-burd_, assault, victory (in play, &c.).

دستار _dastār_, a turban.

دستور _dastūr_, rule, custom.

دشمن _dushman_, an enemy.

دشمني _dushmanī_, enmity, hostility.

دشنام *dushnām*, abuse.

دعا *du'ā*, prayer, supplication.

دعوي or دعوا *da'wā*, a claim, request.

دفتر *daftar*, a volume, a book.

دفع *daf'*, repelling, warding off. 27

دفن *dafn*, burying, hiding underground.

دل *dil*, the heart, mind; *dil-tāng*, distressed in heart; *dil-jū,ī*, seeking the heart; kindness, courtesy.

دلق *dalk*, a dress worn by mendicants.

دم *dam*, a breath, a moment; *dum*, the tail.

دندان *dandān*, a tooth.

دمّل *dummal*, also دنبل *dumbal*, a tumour, a sore.

دنبال *dumbāl*, stern, rear, behind.

دنيا *dunyā*, the world, the present life.

دو *dū*, two; *dū-pahr*, mid-day.

دوا *dawā*, medicine, cure.

دور *dūr*, distance, far, remote.

دوزخ *dozakh*, hell.

دوست *dost*, a friend, companion.

دوستي *dostī*, friendship.

دوش *dosh*, the shoulder; last night.

دوشينه *doshīna*, of or during last night.

دوكان *dūkān*, a shop, office.

دولت *daulat*, wealth, fortune.

دوم *duwum*, the second, secondly.

دويدن *dawīdan*, to run.

دويم *dūyum*, the same as *duwum*.

ده *dah*, ten: *dih*, a village; also, give, root of *dādan*, to give.

دهانيدن *dihānīdan*, to cause to give.

دهقان *dihkān*, a villager, a peasant.

دي *dī*, yesterday, yesternight.

ديار *diyār*, a country, kingdom.

ديانت *diyānat*, probity, honesty; *diyānat-dār*, honest, conscientious.

ديدار *dīdār*, a sight, an interview.

ديدن *dīdan* (root بين *bīn*), to see, to experience, to suffer.

ديروز *dīroz*, yesterday.

ديشب *dī-shab*, yesternight.

ديگر *dīgar*, another, again.

دينار *dīnār*, name of a coin, a denarius.

ديوار *dīwār*, the wall of a house, &c.

ديوانه *dīwāna* or *devāna*, mad. II

ذ

ذائقه *zā,iḳa*, the palate, taste.

ذو القرنين *zū-l-ḳarnain*, two-horned, an epithet applied by the Arabs to Alexander the Great.

ر

راحت *rāḥat*, tranquillity, enjoyment.

راز *rāz*, a secret, a mystery.

راست *rāst*, straight, right, true.

راندن *rāndan*, to drive away, send.

راوي *rāwī*, a narrator, historian.

راه *rāh*, road, path.

رحم *ruḥm* or *ruḥum*, mercy, pity.

رحمن *raḥmān*, merciful, compassionate.

رحيم *raḥīm*, gracious, forgiving.

رخ *rukh*, the cheek; the castle at chess.

رخصت *rukhṣat*, dismissal, leave.

رزاق *razzāḳ*, the Bestower; God.

رسانيدن *rasānīdan*, to send, convey.

رسن *rasan*, a rope, string.

رسيدن *rasīdan*, to arrive, reach.

رشيد *rashīd*, wise, upright.

رضا *riẓā*, satisfaction, consent.

رعایت ri'āyat, observance ; ri'āyat-kardan, to observe, maintain.

رعیت ra'iyat, subjects, the people.

رفتن raftan (root رو raw), to go, move.

رفو rafū, repair, mending.

رفوگر rafūgar, a repairer, mender.

رنج ranj, sorrow, vexation, pain.

رنجیدن ranjidan, to grieve, vex.

رو rū or روی rū,e, the face ; rū ba-rū, in presence, face to face.

روان rawān, going ; the soul, spirit.

روباه robāh, a fox ; robāh-bacha, a fox-cub.

روپه rūpa, silver ; a rupee.

روپیه rūpiya, a rupee, a silver coin value about two shillings.

روز roz, a day, time in general.

روزگار rozgār, lifetime, the world, fortune.

ره rah, a road, path ; rahguzarī, a highway ; rahzan, a highwayman.

رهانیدن rahānīdan, to release, rescue ; causal of رستن rastan (root ره rah).

ریختن rekhtan, to spill, destroy.

ریز rez, a crumb, particle.

ریسمان rismān, a rope, chord.

ریش rīsh, the beard ; a suit of clothes for festive occasions : resh, a sore, a wound.

ز

زاده zāda, born, a descendant ; used in comp., as, shāh-zāda, born of a king.

زاغ zāgh, a crow, a raven.

زاهد zāhid, a holy man, a hermit.

زائیدن zā,idan, to bear, bring forth.

زبان zabān, the tongue, a language.

زبون zabūn, a captive, a dupe.

زجر zijr, hindering, force, threat.

زدن zadan (r. زن zan), to strike, inflict.

زر zar, gold, money, wealth.

زراعت zarā'at, cultivated ground.

زشت zisht, hideous, ugly, improper ; zisht-rū,e, of an ugly face ; zisht-khū,e, of a vile temper.

زمان zamān, time, season, an age.

زمین zamīn, earth, land, region.

زن zan, a wife, a woman.

زنا zinā, fornication, rape.

زندان zindān, a prison, a jail.

زندقه zindaka, idolatry, impiety.

زندگي zindagī, existence, life.

زنده zinda, alive.

زنهار zinhār, take care ! beware !

زوجه zauja, a wife.

زود zūd, soon, quick, speedily.

زور zor, force, violence.

زیاده ziyāda, more, increase.

زیان ziyān, loss, damage.

زیر zer, beneath, below.

زیرا zīrā or zīrā-ki, because, since.

زیستن zīstan, to live, exist.

زین zīn, a saddle.

س

ساختن sākhtan, to make, frame, form.

ساعت sā'at, an hour, an instant.

سال sāl, a year.

سان sān, mode, manner ; chi-sān, how ?

سانحه sāniḥa, a marvellous event.

سائس sā,is, a groom, a manager.

سایه sāya, shade, shelter.

سبب sabab, cause, reason.

سبو sabū, a cup, jar, pot, pitcher.

سپر *sipar*, a shield, a target.

سپردن *supurdan* or *sipurdan* (r. سپار *sipār*), to entrust, consign.

ستودن *sitūdan*, to praise.

ستون *sutūn*, a pillar, prop.

سخاوت *sakhāwat*, liberality, munificence.

سخت *sakht*, hard, strong, violent.

سخن *sukhan* or *sukhun*, a word, a matter, a thing in general.

سر *sar*, the head, top; a design: *sirr*, a secret.

سرا or سراي *sarā* or *sarā,e*, an inn.

سراپا *sar-ā-pā*, from head to foot.

سراسيمه *sarāsīma*, disturbed, delirious.

سراع *surāgh*, a sign, mark, trace.

سر بمهر *sar bamuhr*, sealed up at the top.

سر راة *sar-i-rāh*, a road, highway.

سرشت *sirisht*, nature, constitution.

سركار *sarkār*, a headman; the Court, the Government.

سرود *surod*, a song, a melody.

سزا *sazā*, desert, punishment.

سفر *safar*, a journey, voyage.

سكندر *sikandar*, Alexander the Great.

سگ *sag*, a dog.

سلام *salām*, salutation, peace, safety.

سلطان *sultān*, an emperor, king.

سليس *salīs*, easy, familiar, not abstruse.

سمت *samt*, direction, side, quarter.

سمع *sam'*, hearing, the ear.

سنگ *sang*, a stone, a weight.

سو *sū*, side, direction.

سوار *sawār*, a horseman, a trooper; *sawār shudan*, to be mounted.

سوال *su,āl*, asking, begging, a question.

سواي *siwā,e*, except, besides.

سوختن *sokhtan*, to burn, to be inflamed.

سوداگر *saudāgar*, a merchant.

سوگند *saugand*, an oath.

سوم *sivum*, the third, thirdly.

سويت *sawiyat*, equality, fairness.

سه *sih*, three.

سياست *siyāsat*, punishment.

سياة *siyāh*, black, dark.

سيخ *sīkh*, a spit.

سير *sair*, a walk, a journey.

سيله *sīla* (also *sīlī*), a blow, a slap.

سيم *sīm*, silver, silver metal.

سينه *sīna*, the bosom, breast.

سيوم *sīvum*, the third, thirdly.

ش

شادي *shādī*, marriage, rejoicing.

شاعر *shā'ir*, a poet.

شام *shām*, evening.

شاة *shāh*, a king, monarch.

شاهد *shāhid*, a witness, a bystander.

شاةزاده *shāh-zāda*, a king's son, prince.

شايستن *shāyistan*, to be fit, proper.

شب *shab*, night, evening.

شتاب *shitāb*, haste, speed.

شتر *shutur*, a camel.

شجاعت *shajā'at*, valour, prowess.

شخص *shakhs*, a person.

شدن *shudan*, to be, become.

شرح *sharḥ*, interpretation, commentary.

شرط *shart*, stipulation, wager.

شرم *sharm*, shame, bashfulness.

شرمنده *sharmanda*, ashamed, confounded, abashed.

شروع *shurū'*, beginning, attack.

شريف *sharīf*, noble, eminent, holy.

شریك sharīk, a partner, companion.

ششتن shustan (r. shū), to wash.

شش shash, six.

شطرنج shatranj, the game of chess.

شعله shu'la, a flame.

شفاعت shifā'at, intercession.

شفقت shafkat, pity, affection.

شك shakk, doubt.

شکار shikār, hunting, prey, game.

شکایت shikāyat, complaint.

شکر shukr, thanks; shakar, sugar.

شکست shikast, defeat, disaster.

شکستن shikastan, to break, defeat.

شکم shikam, the belly.

شگون shugūn, an omen of good.

شما shumā, you: plur. of تو, thou

شمشیر shamshīr, a sword, scimitar.

شناختن shinākhtan (r. شناس shinās), to know, recognise.

شنیدن shinīdan, to hear; also shunī-dan, shanīdan.

شور shor, noise, tumult, uproar.

شوهر shohar and shauhar, a husband.

شهد shahd, honey, sugar.

شهر shahr, a city; a lunar month.

شهمات shah-māt, checkmate.

شیر sher, a lion; (in India) a tiger.

شیشه shīsha, a phial, a glass.

شیطان Shaitān, Satan, the devil.

ص

صاحب sāhib, a companion, a lord, master: in composition, it means endowed with; as, sāhib-kamāl, possessed of perfection (vide § 29 b.).

صاف sāf, pure, clear, evident.

صالح sālih, honest, sincere, wise.

صباح sabāh, morning, dawn of day; 'ala-s-sabāh or صباحا sabāhan, early in the morning.

صبح subh, the morning, dawn, Aurora.

صحرا sahrā, a desert, a plain.

صد sad, a hundred.

صراف sarrāf, a money-changer.

صرف sarf, changing, turning; sirf, pure, merely, simply.

صعوه sa'wa, a kind of sparrow.

صف saff, drawing up (men) in ranks; saff-zada, mustered, arrayed.

صلاح salāh, advice, counsel.

صلح sulh, peace, concord.

صندوق sandūk, a chest, box, trunk sandūkcha, a small box.

صورت sūrat, form, figure, face.

صید said, hunting, prey, game.

ض

ضامن zāmin, a surety, sponsor.

ضعیف za'īf, infirm, weak, poor.

ضیافت ziyāfat, a feast, invitation.

ط

طاق tāk, a shelf, recess in a wall; copula.

طالب tālib, asking, studious.

طبابت tibābat, the medical art.

طبیب tabīb, a doctor, physician.

طرف taraf, extremity, direction, side.

طعام ta'ām, food, eating.

طعمه tu'ma, food, dinner.

طفل tifl, an infant, a child.

طلا tilā, gold, gold fringe.

طلاق talāk, divorce, dismissal.

طلب *talab*, petition, demand, wages; *talab-dāshtan*, to search.

طلبیدن *talubīdan*, to seek for, call.

طمع *tama'*, avidity, desire.

طور *taur*, mode, manner, condition.

طوطی *tūtī*, a parrot.

طول *taul* or *tūl*, length, duration.

طی *tayy*, traversing, travelling; *tayy-kardan*, to traverse, pass over.

طیب *tayyib*, good, agreeable.

ظ

ظالم *zālim*, tyrannical, oppressive.

ظاهر *zāhir*, clear, evident, certain.

ظرف *zarf*, a vessel, a vase, bottle.

ظریف *zarīf*, witty, learned, graceful.

ع

عادل *'ādil*, upright, just.

عاری *'ārī*, naked, destitute, bare.

عاشق *'āshik*, a lover, loving.

عاقل *'ākil*, wise, intelligent.

عالم *'ālam*, the world, time, state; *'ālim*, learned, wise.

عبادت *'ibādat*, worship, adoration.

عبارت *'ibārat*, style (in writing), sense.

عتاب *'itāb*, reproof, anger.

عجائب *'ajā,ib*, marvels, wonders.

عجب *'ajab* or عجوبه *'ajūba*, a wonder, strange, marvellous.

عجیب *'ajīb*, rare, wonderful.

عدالت *'adālat*, justice, equity; *'Adālat-panāh*, Asylum of Justice.

عدل *'adl*, justice, integrity.

عذر *uzr*, excuse, apology.

عرب *'Arab*, an Arab, applied to those who dwell in towns.

عرض *'arz*, a representation, speech.

عز و جل *'Azza wa jalla*, May He be honoured and glorified! *i.e.* God.

عزیز *'azīz*, dear, precious.

عصا *'asā*, a staff, a bludgeon.

عطار *'attār*, a druggist, a perfumer.

عطر *'itr*, odour, perfume.

عفو *'afū*, forgiveness, indulgence.

عقد *'akd*, an agreement, alliance.

عقل *'akl*, reason, sense, wisdom.

عقوبت *'akūbat*, punishment, torture.

علامت *'alāmat*, a sign, mark, token.

علم *'ilm*, knowledge, science.

علوم *'ulūm*, sciences (plur. of last word).

علما *'ulamā*, (plur.) the learned.

علی *'Alī*, a man's name.

علی *'ala*, on *or* at, upon.

عمر *'umr*, lifetime, age.

عمل *'amal*, action, conduct, rule.

عنان *'inān*, a bridle, the reins.

عنایت *'ināyat*, a favour, bounty.

غ

غالب *ghālib*, prevailing, victorious.

غایت *ghāyat*, the extreme, extremely.

غرض *gharaz*, wish, design; *al-gharaz*, in short, finally.

غرفه *ghurfa*, or *gharfa*, a window.

غرور *ghurūr*, pride, haughtiness.

غریب *gharīb*, poor, strange, rare.

غصه *ghussa*, grief, anger.

غضب *ghazab*, anger, vengeance.

غلام *ghulām*, a slave, a boy.

غله *ghalla*, corn, grain.

غلیظ *ghalīz*, coarse, rude, sordid.

غم *gham*, grief, care, anxiety.

غمگين *ghamgīn*, sorrowful.

غيب *ghaib*, secrecy, invisibility.

ف

فارسي *Fārsī*, also پارسي *Pārsī*, Persian.

فايدة *fā-ida*, profit, benefit.

فتح *fath*, an opening, a victory.

فجر *fajr*, the dawn, morning.

فراخور *farākhur*, suitable to, proportional, in accordance with.

فراخي *arākhī*, extension, abundance.

فراش *farrāsh*, a chamberlain.

فراغ *farāgh*, leisure, cessation.

فراموش *farāmosh*, forgetfulness.

فراوان *farāwān*, great, important.

فربه *farbih*, fat, flourishing.

فردا *fardā*, to-morrow.

فرزند *farzand*, a son, a child.

فرستادن *firistādan*, to send.

فرصت *fursat*, opportunity, leisure.

فرمان *farmān*, a command, edict.

فرمودن *farmūdan*, to order: it is used in the sense of "to speak, say," on the part of a superior; also, to do.

فرو *faro* (before a vowel, فرود *farod*), down, below, underneath.

فروختن *farokhtan* (r. فروش), to sell.

فروش *farosh* (in composition), a seller.

فرياد *faryād*, a complaint, a cry for aid.

فريادي *faryādī*, a complainant, plaintiff.

فريب *firīb* or *fareb*, deception; *fareb-dādan*, to impose on, to deceive.

فريفتن *fireftan*, to deceive, to mistake.

فصل *fasl*, season; a section, chapter.

فقرا *fukarā*, poor people: plur. of

فقير *fakīr*, a poor person, a mendicant.

فكر *fikr*, thought, anxiety.

فلاطون *Falātūn*, the same as *Aflātūn*.

فلان *fulān*, some one, such a one

فلوس *fulūs*, coins of small value, cowries, dibs; money in general.

فوج *fauj*, an army, troops.

فورا *fauran*, instantly, forthwith.

فهميدن *fahmīdan*, to understand.

في *fī*, in: used only in Arabic phrases.

فيل *fīl*, an elephant (also پيل *pīl*).

ق

قابو *ḳābū*, means, opportunity.

قاضي *ḳāzī*, a Muhammadan Judge.

قبول *ḳabūl*, consent, agreement.

قتل *ḳatl*, killing, execution.

قد *ḳad*, length, stature, figure (also *ḳadd*).

قدر *ḳadar*, measure, quantity, extent.

قدرت *ḳudrat*, power, daring.

قديم *ḳadīm*, old, ancient.

قرار *ḳarār*, settlement, agreeing.

قرض *ḳarz* or *ḳirz*, a loan, a debt.

قرضدار *ḳarz-dār*, a debtor.

قسم *ḳasam*, an oath; *ḳasam-khurdan*, to swear; literally, to eat an oath.

قسمت *ḳismat*, division, partition.

قصد *ḳasd*, purpose, design.

قصدا *ḳasdan*, purposely, intentionally.

قصر *ḳasr*, a citadel, a palace.

قضا *ḳazā*, fate; office of *ḳāzī*.

قطعه *ḳiṭ'a*, a section, part, stanza.

قلاده *ḳilāda*, a collar for the neck.

قمار *ḳimār*, dice or any game of hazard.

قوت or قوة *ḳūwat*, strength, firmness.

قوي *ḳawīy*, strong, powerful.

قهرا *ḳahran*, by force, on compulsion.

قيد355 *ḳaid*, thraldom, imprisonment.

قيمت *ḳimat*, price, value.

ك

كار *kār*, business, use, affair.

كاغذ *kāghaz* or *kāghiz*, paper, a letter.

كامل *kāmil*, perfect, entire, accomplished.

كام *kām*, desire, intention ; *kām nā-kām*, willingly *or* unwillingly.

كاه *kāh*, straw, hay, grass.

كباب *kabāb*, meat, fried or roasted.

كتاب *kitāb*, a book, an epistle.

كثيف *kaṣif*, coarse, thick.

كجا *kujā*, where? what place? how?

كج مج *kaj-maj*, crooked, cross purposes.

كدام *kudām*, what one? which?

كرايه *kirāya*, hire, fare, rent.

كردن *kardan* (r. كن *kun*), to do, to make.

كس *kas*, a person, any, some one.

كسب *kasb*, gain, art, trade.

كشادن *kushādan*, to open, disclose.

كشاكش *kashākash*, contention, battle.

كشت *kisht*, check, a term at chess.

كشتزار *kishtzār*, a corn-field.

كشتن *kushtan*, to slay, kill, extinguish.

كشودن *kushūdan*, to open, to subdue.

كشيدن *kashīdan*, to pull, draw, delineate.

كفر *kufr*, impiety, infidelity.

كفن *kafan*, a winding-sheet, a shroud.

كلان *kalān*, great, aged, elder.

كلمات *kalimāt*, words, sayings.

كلوخ *kulūkh*, a clod, brick.

كلي *kullī*, all, the whole.

كليد *kalīd*, a key.

كم *kam*, little, few, scarce.

كمال *kamāl*, perfection, accomplishment

كمان *kamān*, a bow.

كنار *kinār*, side, bosom, margin.

كناره *kināra* or *kanāra*, side, brink, shore of the sea or river.

كندن *kandan*, to dig, extract, tear up.

كنيز *kanīz*, a maiden, a maid-servant

كوتاه *kotāh*, short, small.

كوتوال *kotwāl*, a magistrate, judge.

كور *kor* or *kūr*, blind.

كوز *kūz*, hump-backed, crooked.

كه *ki*, who? that, used as a conjunctive particle, like the Greek ὅτι, after verbs signifying to think, speak, tell, &c.

كهن *kuhan*, also كهنه *kuhna*, old, worn

كيست *kist*, for كه, and هست or است, who is?

كيسه *kīsa* or *kesa*, a purse, a bag.

گ

گاه *gāh*, time, also place (in composition).

گاهي *gāhe*, one time, sometime.

گدا *gadā*, poor, a beggar, mendicant.

گذاشتن *guzāshtan*, to quit, forsake, leave.

گذر *guzar*, a pass, passing.

گذشتن *guzashtan* (r. گذر *guzar*), to pass, pass by.

گر *gar*, if: contraction of اگر.

گران *girān*, heavy, important, valuable.

گربه *gurba*, a cat.

گرد *gird*, around ; *gard*, dust.

گردانيدن *gardanīdan*, to circulate, to effect, cause to become.

گردن *gardan*, the neck.

گرديدن *gardīdan*, to turn round, to be, to become.

گرسنه *gursina*, hungry, famished.

گرسنگي *gursinagi*, hunger, starvation.

گرفتار *giriftār*, caught, involved, a capture.

گرفتن *giriftan*, to catch, seize, to begin: so in German, *fangen*, to catch; *anfangen*, to begin.

گرم *garm*, warm, hot, passionate.

گرما *garmā*, heat, the hot season.

گرو *giraw*, a pawn, pledge, wager.

گروه *guroh*, a troop, band, company.

گريختن *gurekhtan, girekhtan*, to flee, run away, to escape.

گريستن *girīstan*, to weep, bewail; so *giriyān-shudan*, to be weeping.

گستردن *gustardan*, to spread, arrange.

گشتن *gashtan*, (r: *gard*), to be, to become.

گفتن *guftan* (r. گو *gū*), to say, speak.

گفت‌وگو *guft-ō-gū* or *guftgū*, conversation, chit-chat.

گله *gala* or *galla*, a flock, herd.

گم *gum*, lost, missing.

گماشتن *gumāshtan*, to consign, to send forth, to depute.

گناه *gunāh*, fault, crime, sin.

گنج *ganj*, a treasure, a store.

گندم *gandum*, wheat.

گواه *gawāh*, a witness, an evidence.

گواهي *gawāhī*, testimony, evidence.

گورستان *goristān*, a burying-ground.

گوسپند *gospand*, also گوسفند *gosfand*, a sheep, a ram, a goat.

گوش *gosh*, the ear.

گوشت *gosht*, flesh, meat.

گونه *gūna*, mode, manner, form.

ل

لا *lā*, (a negative particle, Arab), no, not: used as a prefix, as in لاجواب *lā-jawāb*, without an answer, silenced.

لائق *lā,ik*, worthy, proper, fit for.

لبادة *labāda* or *lubāda*, a thick outer garment, a boat-cloak.

لت *lat*, a thump, a blow.

لجام *lijām* or *lajām*, a bridle, the reins.

لذيذ *laz̄iz*, sweet, pleasant.

لرزة *larza*, a shaking, trembling, tremor.

لطيف *latīf*, good, pleasant, kind.

لطيفه *latīfa*, a witty saying, pleasantry.

لعل *la'l*, a ruby, a gem.

لفظ *lafz*, a word, a vocable.

لقمه *lukma*, a morsel, a mouthful.

لك *lak*, a numeral expressive of 100,000.

لگام *ligām* or *lagām*, a bridle.

لنگ *lang*, lame, an epithet, applied to the celebrated Tīmūr.

ليكن *lekin*, but, yet, nevertheless.

م

ما *mā*, we: plur. of the 1st person.

مات شدن *māt-shudan*, to be check-mated; *māt-kardan*, to give check-mate, to overcome.

ماجرا *mā-jarā*, an accident, event, what has passed or occurred.

مادر *mādar*, a mother.

مادة *māda*, a female.

ماديان *mādiyān*, a mare.

مال *māl*, wealth, treasure, property.

مالك *mālik*, a master, possessor.

ماليدن *mālīdan*, to rub, to anoint.

ماندن *māndan*, to remain, continue.

ماه *māh*, the moon, a month.

ماهي *māhī*, a fish ; *māhī-gīr*, a fisher-man, a fish-catcher.

مبادا *ma-bādā*, May it not be! God forbid !

مبالغه *mubālagha*, a strenuous effort, urgency, hyperbole.

مبلغ *mablagh*, a sum (of money), price.

متأمل *muta-ammil*, thoughtful, contemplative, pondering.

متدين *mutadayyin*, orthodox, religious.

متعجب *muta'ajjib*, astonished, wondering.

متفكر *mutafakkir*, meditating, thoughtful.

متقي *mutaki*, sober, pious, temperate.

مثل *misl*, similitude, like, likeness.

مجذوب *majzūb*, abstracted, absent.

مجرد *mujarrad*, solitary, alone.

مجلس *majlis*, an assembly, company.

محبوبه *mahbūba*, loved, esteemed.

محتاج *muhtāj*, in want of, destitute.

محروم *mahrūm*, excluded, disappointed.

محظوظ *mahzūz*, pleased, delighted.

محقر *muhakkar*, vile, trifling, contemptible, worthless.

محكم *muhkam*, strong, firm, firmly.

محمد *Muhammad*, a man's name, the celebrated prophet of the Muslims.

محمود *Mahmūd*, a man's name, a king of Ghizni, about A.D. 1000.

محو كردن *mahw-kardan*, to wipe out.

مختار *mukhtār*, absolute, a free agent.

مختلف *mukhtalif*, diverse, various.

مدت *muddat*, a space of time.

مدح *madh*, praise, eulogy, encomium.

مدرسه *madrasa*, a college, school.

مدعي *mudda'ī*, plaintiff, accuser.

مذكور *mazkūr*, mentioned, aforesaid.

مرا *marā*, me, to me.

مرافعه *murāfa'a*, a law-suit.

مرتبه *martaba*, step, dignity, a time.

مرثيه *marsiya*, an elegy, a funeral oration.

مرد *mard*, a man, a hero.

مردم *mardum*, a person, man.

مردن *murdan*, (root مير *mīr*), to die.

مرده *murda*, plur. *murdagān*, dead.

مرز و كشور *marz o kishwar*, empire, kingdom, territories.

مرغ *murgh*, a fowl, a bird.

مسافر *musāfir*, a traveller, a stranger.

مساكن *masākin*, habitations, dwellings.

مست *mast*, intoxicated, wanton, furious

مستي *mastī*, intoxication, lust.

مسجد *masjid*, a mosque, *or* any place of worship.

مسخره *maskhara*, a jester, a buffoon.

مسكين *maskīn*, humble, poor, wretched.

مسلوب *maslūb*, seized, stripped, erred.

مسند *masnad*, a throne, a prop.

مشت *musht*, the fist, a blow.

مشغول *mashghūl*, occupied, engaged in.

مشهور *mashhūr*, celebrated, notorious.

مصاحب *musāhib*, a companion, a friend ; courtier (Latin, *comes*.)

مصلحت *maslahat*, good counsel, good policy, the best course to adopt *or* the best thing to be done.

مصور *musawwir*, a painter.

مطبخ *matbakh*, the kitchen.

مطرب *mutrib*, a musician, a minstrel.

مطلع *muttali'*, inspecting, seeing.

مع *ma'*, with, in the company of.

معاف *mu'āf*, forgiven, spared, free.

معامله mu'āmala, transaction, affair.

معاينه mu'āyana, seeing clearly.

معذور ma'zūr, excused, excusable.

معروف ma'rūf, celebrated, well known.

معلم mu'allim, a doctor, teacher, sage.

معلوم ma'lūm, known, evident.

معنی ma'nā, or ma'nī, sense, meaning, fact, a sacred record.

مغل Mughal, name of a Tartar or Scythian tribe, vulgarly Mogul.

مفقود mafḳūd, missing, not to be found.

مفلس muflis, poor, indigent.

مفلسي muflisī, poverty, destitution.

مفيد mufīd, useful, salutary.

مقام maḳām, place, residence.

مقدار miḳdar, quantity, space, measure.

مقراض miḳrāz, shears, scissors.

مقفل muḳfal, locked, bolted; stingy.

مگر magar, but, unless, only.

مکس magas, a fly.

ملاقات mulāḳāt, meeting, interview.

ملعون mal'ūn, accursed, the Evil One.

مارل mā'ūl, wearied, vexed.

ملک milk, property: mulk, a country, kingdom; malik, a king; malak, an angel.

ممکن mumkin, possible, practicable.

من man, the 1st pers. pronoun, I.

منادي manādi, a proclamation.

منازعت munāza'at, contention, litigation.

مناقشه munāḳasha, quarrel, dispute.

منتخب muntakhab, a selection.

منجم munajjim, an astrologer.

منزل manzil, an abode, a stage, an inn.

منصب manṣab, a high station, dignity.

منع man', prohibition, prevention.

منقار minḳār, a beak, a bill.

منكر munkir, one who denies, refuses.

مواخذة mu-ākhaza, taking satisfaction, calling to account.

موافق muwāfiḳ, conformable to, like.

موت maut, death.

موجب mūjib, cause, motive, reason.

موجود maujūd, existing, found, ready.

موصوف mauṣūf, praised; described.

مولوي maulawī, a doctor, lawyer.

موم mūm or mom, wax, a wax candle.

موهوم mawhūm, imaginary, fancied.

موي mū,e, hair, wool, fur.

مهر muhr, a seal, a signet ring; mihr, friendship, love.

مهربان mihr-bān, kind, beneficent.

مهلت mihlat, delay, space of time.

مهمان mihmān, a guest, a stranger.

مي mai, wine, spirituous liquor.

ميان miyān, middle, interval, space,

ميخ mekh, a peg, a tent pin or pole.

ن

نا nā, a negative particle, when placed before adjectives, &c.

نابينا nābīnā, not seeing, blind.

ناچار nāchār, helpless, without remedy.

ناحق nāḥaḳḳ, unjust, untrue.

ناخوش nākhush, displeased.

ناقل nāḳil, a narrator, historian.

ناگاه nā-gāh, suddenly, unexpectedly.

نالش nālish, lamentation, complaint.

نالشي nālishī, a complainant, plaintiff.

نام nām, name, renown.

نامردي nā-mardī, unmanliness, cowardice.

نان nān, a loaf, bread in general.

نائب nā,ib, a lieutenant, deputy.

نجات *najāt*, freedom, salvation, escape.

نديم *nadīm*, a companion, a courtier.

نذر *nazr*, a present *or* offering.

نر *nar*, a male.

نزد *nazd*, near, about, in the possession of.

نزديك *nazdīk*, near, close to.

نزع *naz'*, removal; *naz'i rawān*, the last breath, the soul's departure.

نسبت *nisbat*, affinity, connection.

نشان *nishān*, a trace, mark.

نشانيدن *nishānīdan*, to place, cause to sit down; also نشاندن.

نشستن *nishastan* or *nishistan* (r. نشين *nishīn*), to sit, stop, settle.

نصف *nisf*, the half, middle.

نصيحت *nasīhat*, advice, sermon.

نظر *nazar*, the sight, the eye.

نعم *nu'm*, prosperity, good fortune.

نعمت *ni'mat*, a blessing, favour, prosperity, good fortune.

نفع *naf'*, gain, profit, advantage.

نفقه *nafaka*, maintenance, salary.

نقاش *nakkāsh*, a painter. مصور

نقد *nakd*, ready money, cash.

نقش *naksh*, a painting, a picture.

نقصان *nuksān*, damage, deficiency, loss.

نكته *nukta*, a point, a quaint saying.

نگاه *nigāh*, a look, observation; *nigāh-dāshtan*, to watch over, preserve; *nigāh-dār*, a preserver: also used as an interjection, beware! have a care!

نماز *namāz*, prayer, worship.

نمود *namūd*, an appearance, index.

نمودن *namūdan*, to appear, to shew, to make.

نو *nau*, new, fresh, young.

نوبت *naubat*, time, turn, opportunity.

نوشتن *navishtan* (r. of نويس *navīs*), to write; also نبشتن *nabishtan*.

نوشيروان *Naushīrawān*, name of a Persian king, famed for equity.

نوكر *naukar*, a servant, slave.

نوبسنده *navīsanda*, a writer.

نه the negative particle, not; *nuh*, nine.

نهادن *nihādan*, to place, put, apply.

نيابت *niyābat*, the office of a deputy.

نيز *nīz*, also, even, likewise.

نيست *nīst*, he, she, it, is not.

نيك *nek*, good, beautiful, right.

نيكنامي *nek-nāmī*, fame, renown.

نيكو *neko*, good, excellent.

نيم *nayam*, I am not.

نيم *nīm*, the half, the middle.

و

و *wa* (sometimes *o*), and, but.

وا *wā*, back, reverse.

واپس *wāpas*, back, returned.

واردات *wāridāt*, events, occurrences.

وجب *wajab*, a span, about nine inches.

وجه *wajh*, face, mode, manner.

وزارت *wazārat*, the office of a *wazīr*.

وزير *wazīr*, a minister, king's vicegerent.

وصف *wasf*, description, quality.

وطن *watn* or *watan*, one's native country, home, birthplace.

وعده *wa'da*, a promise, a vow, a pledge.

وعظ *wa'z*, a sermon, admonition, lecture.

وفا *wafā*, fidelity, sincerity.

وفات *wafāt*, death, decease.

وقت *wakt*, time, hour, season

وكيل *wakīl*, an agent, deputy, factor.
وي *wai*, 3d pers. pron. he, she, it.

ه

هارون *Hārūn*, a man's name; *Hārūn-ar-rashīd*, "Hārūn the Wise," one of the *Khalīfas*, of Baghdād.
هجو *hajw*, ridicule, satire, lampoon.
هر *har*, every, each.
هرچند *harchand*, although, notwithstanding.
هرچه *harchi*, whatsoever.
هركه *harki*, every one who, whosoever.
هرگاه *hargāh*, every time, whenever.
هرگز *hargiz*, ever, at all, on any account.
هرمز *Hurmuz*, name of a Persian king.
هزار *hazār*, a thousand.
هزيمت *hazīmat*, flight, defeat.
هستن *hastan*, to be, to exist; a defective verb (vide § 48, *b*.).
هشت *hasht*, eight.
هم *ham*, even, also; together.
همان *ham-ān*, that very, even that; *ham-ān-dam*, that very instant.
همچو *hamchū*, even as, like; *hamchunān*, such as that, even so.
همراه *ham-rāh*, a companion, along with.
همسايه *ham-sāya*, a neighbour.
همه *hama*, all, every one.

هميشه *hamesha*, always.
همين *ham-īn*, even this, this very.
هندو *Hindū*, an Indian, a Hindū.
هندوستان *Hindūstān*, India.
هنوز *hanoz*, yet, still, at present.
هنگام *hangām*, time, season.
هوا *hawā*, the air, the sky.
هيچ *hech*, any, at all, in the least.

ي

يا *yā*, either, or.
ياد *yād*, memory, remembrance.
يادگار *yādgār*, a memorial.
يار *yār*, a friend.
يافتن *yāftan*, to find, obtain.
يعني *ya'nī*, that is to say, namely.
يقين *yakīn*, certainty, for certain.
يك *yak*, one, a *or* an : sometimes joined to the following word; as,
يكجا *yak-jā*, in one place, together.
يكدرم *yak-diram*, a *diram*, a small coin.
يكديگر *yak-dīgar*, one another.
يكسال *yak-sāl*, one year, a twelvemonth.
يكسان *yaksān*, equal, similar, identical.
يكهزار *yak-hazār*, a thousand.
يكيك *yak-yak* or يكبيك *yak-ba-yak*, one by one, individually, one after another.

LEWIS AND SON, PRINTERS, SWAN BUILDINGS, MOORGATE STREET.

حِکایاتِ لطِیف در عِبارتِ سلیس

۱ شخصی از افلاطُون پُرسِید ـــ که سالهای بِسیار در جهاز بُودِی و سفرِ دریا کردی ـــ در دریا چه عجائِب دِیدِی؟ گُفت ـــ عجب همِین بُود ـــ که از دریا بکنارهٔ سلامت رسِیدم *

۲ گدائی بر درِ وازهٔ تَوَنگری رفت و سُوال کرد * از اندرُونِ خانه جواب آمد که بِی بِی در خانه نِیست * گدا گُفت پارهٔ نان سُوال کرده بُودم ـــ بِی بِی را نخواستم که چُنین جواب یافتم *

۳ مسخرهٔ با زنی شادِی کرد * بعد از چهار ماه زنِ او پسر زائِید * شوهر را گُفت ـــ اِین پِسر را چه نام خواهِی داشت؟ گُفت پِیک ـــ چِرا که راه نُه ماه در چهار ماه طَی کرد *

۴ طبِیبی هرگاه بگورِستان رفتِی ـــ چادر بر سر و رُوی خُود کردِی * مردُمان پُرسِیدند که سبب اِین چِیست؟ گُفت از مُردگانِ اِین گورِستان شرم مِیکُنم ـــ زِیرا که از دوای من مُرده اند *

۵ روزی پادشاهی مع شاهزاده بشِکار رفت * چُون هوا گرم شُد پادشاه و شاهزاده لبادهٔ خُود را بر دوشِ مسخرهٔ نهادند * پادشاه تبسُّم

کُرد و گُفت — اَی مسخره — برِ تُو بارِ یك خر اسْت * گُفت بلکِه بارِ دو خر *

۶ کُوزی را گُفتند میخواهي كِه پُشتِ تُو راسْت شَوَد یا پُشتِ دیگر مردُمان همچو پُشتِ تُو كُوز گردد؟ گُفت میخواهم كِه پُشتِ دیگر مردُمان كُوز گردد — تا از آن چشْم كِه دیگران مرا می بینند — من انها را به بینم *

۷ روزی پادشاهي از شاعِری رنجید * جلّاد را فرمُود كِه رُوبرُوی من بِكُش * جلّاد برای شمشیر آوردن رفْت * شاعِر حاضراَنِ گُفت — تا شمشیر آورده شَوَد مرا سیلهای بزنید كِه پادشاه خُوش شَوَد * پادشاه تبسُّم نمُود ُ تقْصیرِ او بخْشید *

۸ شخْصي مرتبهٔ بزرگ یافْت * دوستي برای تهنِیت پیشِ او رفْت * آن شخْص پُرسید كِیسْتي — و چرا آمده؟ دوسْتِ او شرمنْده گردید و گُفت — مرا نِي شناسي؟ دوستِ قدیم تُو ام — برای تعزِیَت نزدِ تُو آمده ام — شُنیده ام كِه كُور شُدهٔ *

۹ شخْصي دسْتارِ درُویشي گِرفْت و گُریخْت * درُویش بگورسْتان رفْت و نِشسْت * مردُمان اورا گُفتند كِه آن شخْص دسْتارِ تُرا بطرفِ باغ بُرد — در گورِسْتان چرا نِشسْته و چِه میكُني؟ گُفت — او نِیز آخِر اینْجا خواهد آمد — ازِین سبب اینْجا نِشسْته ام *

۱۰ نقّاشي در شهْري رفْت و آنجا پیشهٔ طبابت آغاز كُرد * بعد

چنْد روز شخْصي از وطنِ او درآن شهْر رسید و اورا دید و پُرسید که حالاً چه پیشه میکُني؟ گُفت طبابت ٭ پُرسید چرا؟ گُفت از براي آنکه اگر درین پیشه تقْصیري میکُنم ـــ خاك آنرا مي پوشد ٭

۱۱ سُلْطان سکنْدرِ ذُو الْقَرنَین روزي بر دِیوانه‌ء گُذر کرْد و گُفت ـــ اَي دِیوانه از من چیزي بخواه ٭ گُفت مگسان تشْویشم میدهنْد بِگو که ندهنْد ـــ سُلْطان گُفت ـــ اَي دِیوانه چیزي طلب کن که در حُکْمِ ما باشد ٭ دِیوانه گُفت هرگاه مگسي در اِخْتیارِ تُو نیسْت از تُو چه خواهم طلب کرد؟

۱۲ روزي شخْصي با خُود میگُفت که هرچه در زمین و آسْمان اسْت همه براي من اسْت ٭ مرا بِسْیار بُزُرگ خُدا آفْرید ٭ درآن اثْنا پشه‌ء بر بینيِ او نِشسْت و گُفت ـــ تُرا چُنین غُرور نشایَد ـــ زیرا که هرچه در زمین و آسْمان اسْت خُدا براي تُو آفْرید ـــ بلْکه تُرا براي من ٭ ندانَي که از تُو بُزُرگترم؟

۱۳ شاعِري تَونْگري را مَدْح کرْد ـــ هیچ نَیافْت ٭ پس هجْو کرْد ـــ تَونْگر اورا هیچ نگُفت ٭ روزِ دیگر شاعِر بر درْوازه‌ء او رفْت و نِشسْت ٭ تَونْگر گُفت اَي شاعِر ـــ مَدْح کرْدي ـــ هیچ تُرا ندادم ـــ هجْو کرْدي هیچ نگُفْتم ـــ حالاً چِرا اِینْجا نِشسْته‌ء؟ گُفت حالاً میخواهم که اگر بمیري مرْثیه‌ء تُو بِگویم ٭

۱۴ نابِینائي در شبِ تار چِراغ در دسْت و سبُو بر دوش گِرفْته در

بازار میرفت * شخصی از وي پُرسید کِه اَي احمق روز و شب در چشم تُو یکسان اَست * از چِراغ تُرا فائده چیست؟ نابینا خندید و گُفت — این چِراغ براي من نیست — بلکِه براي تُست — تا در شبِ تار سبُوي مرا نشِکنی *

۱۵ شاعري مِسکین پیشِ تونگري رفت و چُنان نزدیکِ او نشِست کِه میانِ شاعر و تونگر از یك وجب زیاده تفاوُت نبُود * تونگر ازین سبب برهم شُد و روي تُرش کُرد و پُرسید — کِه در میانِ تُو و خرچِه تفاوُت اَست؟ گُفت بقدرِ یك وجب * تونگر ازین بسیار خجِل شُد و عُذر نمُود *

۱۶ شخصي با بخیلي دوستي داشت * روزي بخیلرا گُفت کِه حالّا بسفر میروم — انگُشتري خُود بمن بِده — آنرا با خُود خواهم داشت — هرگاه آنرا خواهم دید تُرا یاد خواهم کُرد * جَواب داد کِه اگر مرا یاد داشتن میخواهي — هرگاه انگُشت خُود خالي بِبیي مرا یاد کُن — کِه انگُشتري از فلان خواسته بُودم — نداد *

۱۷ شخصي در خواب با شیطان مُلاقات کُرد * یك سیلي بر روي او زد و ریشِ اورا گِرفت و گُفت * اَي ملَعُون دُشمنِ ما هستي — و براي فریب دادنِ ما مرُئمان ریشِ دراز میداري * چُون سیلي دیگر بر روي او زد — بیدار شُد — و ریشِ خُودرا در دستِ خُود دید * شرمنده گردید — و بر خُود خندید *

۱۸ پادشاهي دانِشمَنديرا طلبيد و گُفت ـــ ميخواهم كِه تُرا قاضيِ ايِن شهر كُنم * دانِشمَند گُفت لايِقِ اينكار نيم * پادشاه پُرسيد چرا * جَواب داد كِه اگر راسْت گُفتم ـــ مرا معذُور داريد * و اگر دُروغ گُفتم ـــ پس دُروغگورا قاضي كردن مصْلِحت نيسْت پادشاه عُذرِ دانِشمَند پسنْديد ـــ و اورا معذُور داشْت *

۱۹ درويشي تقْصيرِ بُزرگ كرد * پيشِ حبَشيِ كوتْوال بُردَند * كوتْوال حُكم كرد كِه تمام رويِ درويش سِياه كُنيد ـــ و درتمام شهر گردانيد * درويش گُفت ـــ اَي كوتْوال نُصفِ رُويِ من سِياه كُن ـــ و گرنه همه مردُمانِ شهر خواهند دانِسْت كِه حبَشيِ كوتْوال هسْتم * كوتْوال ازيِن سُخن خنْديد ـــ و تقْصيرِ درويش مُعاف كرد *

۲۰ شخْصي را به تُهمتِ زندْقة و اِلْحاد نزْدِ هارون اَلرَّشيد آورْدَند ـــ و او اِنكاري نمُود * هارون اَلرَّشيد گُفت ـــ هرآيِنه ميزنم تا اِقْرار كُني * آن مرْد گُفت اِين خِلافِ حُكمِ خُداسْت * حق تعالىٰ فرمُوده اسْت كِه تُو مردُمان را بِزَني تا اِقْرار بايِمان كُنَند ـــ و تُو مرا ميزَني كِه اِقْرار بكُفْر بِنُمايِم * هارون بخنْديد و اورا بخْشيد *

۲۱ روزي شاعري تقْصيري كرد * پادشاه جلّاد را فرمُود كِه رو بِرويِ من اورا بِكُش * لرزهٔ در انْدام شاعر اُفتاد * نديمي اورا گُفت ـــ اِين چِه نامرْدي و بيچِگريسْت؟ مرْدان گاهي اينْچِنين نميترسند * شاعر گُفت ـــ اَي نديم اگر تُو مرْدي بِيا ـــ بجايِ من بِنْشين تا من

حِکایاتِ لطیف

بر خیزم * پادشاه این لطیفه پسندید ـــ و خندید ـــ و تقصیرِ او معاف فرمود *

۲۲ شخصی پیشِ یك نویسنده رفت و گفت ـــ خطّی برای من بنویس * گفت پای من درد میکند * آن شخص گفت تُرا جائی فرستادن نمیخواهم ـــ که چنین عذر میکنی * جواب داد که این سخن تُو راست است ـــ لیکن هرگاه که برای کسی خط می نویسم ـــ طلبیده می شوم برای خواندنِ آن ـــ زیرا که دیگر شخص خطِّ من خواندن نمیتواند *

۲۳ شخصی نزدِ طبیب رفت و گفت ـــ شِکمِ من درد میکند ـــ دوا کن * طبیب پرسید ـــ امروز چه خورده‌ء؟ گفت نانِ سوخته * طبیب دوا در چشمِ او کردن خواست * آن شخص گفت اَی طبیب دردِ شِکمرا با چشم چه نِسبت؟ حکیم گفت اول تُرا دوایِ چشم می باید کرد ـــ زیرا که اگر چشمت درُست بودی ـــ نانِ سوخته نمیخوردی *

۲۴ اعرابی شُتُر گُم کرده بود * سوگند خورد که چون بیابم ـــ بیکدِرم بفروشم * چون شُتُر یافت ـــ از سوگندِ خود پشیمان شُد * گُربه‌ء در گردنِ شُتُر آویخت * و بانگ زد ـــ که شُتُر را بیکدِرم میفروشم ـــ وگُربه بصد دِرم ـــ امّا از یکدیگر جُدا نمی کنم ونمی فروشم * شخصی در آنجا رسید وگفت چه ارزان بُود این شُتُرا اگر این قِلاده در گردن نبُودی؟

پادْشاه بِسْیار خُوش شُد * بعداز دو روز خبرِ شِکسْت آمد * پادْشاه
بر آن شَخْص سِیاسْت کرْدن خواسْت * عرْض کرْد که اَي خُداونْد
لایقِ سِیاسْت نَیم — زیرا که دو روز شُمارا خُشْنُود کرْدم * چرا مرا نا
خُوش مِيکُنید * پادْشاهِ اِین لطِیفها را پسنْدید و اورا اِنْعام فرمُود *

۳۲ امِیرِ تَیمُورِ لنْگ چُون بِهِنْدُوسْتان رِسِید و مُطرِبان طلبِید و
گُفْت — شُنِیده ام که دراِین شهرِ مُطرِبانِ کامِل اند * مُطرِبي نابِینا
پِیشِ پادْشاه حاضِر شُد و سُرود آغاز کرْد * پادْشاه بِسْیار خُوش
گرْدِید و نامِ او پُرسِید * گُفْت نامِ من دَولت اسْت * پادْشاه گُفْت
دَولت هم کور مِيشَوَد * او جَواب داد که اگر دَولت کور نبُودي —
بهانهِ لنْگ نه آمدي * پادْشاهِ اِین جَواب پسنْدید و اِنْعامِ بِسْیار
باو داد *

۳۳ شَخْصِي بِسْیار مُفْلِس بُود — اسْپي داشْت — آنْرا در اِصْطبل
بسْت — لیکِن طرفي که سرِ اسْپان مِيشَوَد دُمِ او کرْد — و منادِي
درداد که — اَي مرْدُمان تماشاي عجب به بِینید که سرِ اسْپ بجاي
دُم اسْت * همه مرْدُمانِ شهر جمْع شُدنْد * هر شَخْصِي که درُونِ
اِصْطبل براي تماشا رفْتن مِيخواسْت از او انْدکِي نقْد مِيگِرفْت و اورا
راهِ مِيداد * هرکِه در آن اِصْطبل مِيرفْت شرْمنْده از آنْجا بازِي آمد —
و هِیچ نِمي گُفْت *

۳۴ پادْشاهي از مُنَجِمي پُرسِید که چنْد سال از عُمرِ من باقِي

اِست؟ گُفت دَه سال * پادْشاه بِسیار مُتفکِّر گَردید و همچو بِیمار بر
بِستر اُفتاد * وزِیر بِسیار عاقِل بود مُنَجِّمرا رُو بروی پادْشاه طلبید و
پُرسید ــ که چَند سالِ عُمرِ تُو باقِي اِست؟ گُفت بِیسْت سال * وزِیر
همان وقْت از شمْشیر مُنَجِّم را رُو بروی پادْشاه بقتْل رِسانید * پادْشاه
خُوشنُود گَردید و حِکمَتِ وزِیر پسنْدید و باز سُخنِ هِیچ مُنَجِّم نشُنید *

۳۵ شاعِري پیشِ تُونْگري رفْت و بِسیار اورا سِتُود * تُونْگر خُوشنُود
شُد و گُفْت ــ نزدِ من نقْد نِیسْت ــ لیکِن غلّهٔ بِسیار اسْت ــ
اگر فرْدا بِیائي بِدِهم * شاعِر بحانهٔ خُود رفْت و وقْتِ فجْر نزْدِ تُونْگر
باز آمد * تُونْگر پُرسید چِرا آمدي؟ گُفْت دِیروز وعْدهٔ دادِنِ غلّه
کَردید ــ ازِین سبب آمدهام * تُونْگر گُفت ــ عجب احمق هسْتي
ــ تُو از سُخن مرا خُوش کردِي ــ من نِیز تُرا خُوش نمُودم ــ حالاً
غلّه چِرا دِهم؟ شاعِر شرْمنْده شُده باز رفْت *

۳۶ زنِي مِیرفْت ــ مرْدي اورا دید و دُنْبالِ او رَوان شُد * زن
ورُسید که چِرا پسِ من مِي آئي؟ گُفْت بر تُو عاشِق شُده ام * زن
گُفْت بر من بِچِه عاشِق شُدهٔ؟ خواهرِ من از من خُوبْتر اسْت ــ
پسِ من مِي آید ــ بِرَو و بر او عاشِق شَو * مرْد از آنْجا بر گشْت و
زنِي بدصُورت دِید ــ بِسیار ناخُوش گَردید و باز نزْدِ او رفْت و گُفْت
ــ چِرا دُروغ گُفْي؟ زن گُفْت تُو نِیز راسْت نگُفْي ــ اگر عاشِقِ من
مِي بُودي پیشِ دِیکری چِرا مِیرفْي؟ مرْد شرْمنْده شُد *

۲۵ پادشاهي در خواب دید که تمامِ دندانهاي او اُفتاده اند * از منجّمي تعبیرِ آن پُرسید * گفت که اَولاد و اقاربِ پادشاه همه رو بِروي پادشاه خواهند مُرد — پادشاه در خشم شُد — و منجّم را قید کرد — و منجّمِ دیگري را طلبید و تعبیرِ آن خواب پُرسید * عرض کرد که از همه اَولاد و اقاربِ پادشاه زیاده‌تر خواهد زیست * پادشاه این نُکته پسندید و اِنعام داد *

۲۶ دُزدي در مقامِ شخصي براي دُزدیدنِ اسپ رفت * اِتّفاقاً گرفتار شُد * صاحبِ اسپ دُزد را گفت — اگر حکمتِ دُزدي اسپ مرا بِنمائي — تُرا آزاد بِکُنم * دُزد قبول کرد — و نزدِ اسپ رفت — و رسنِ پاي او کُشاد * بعد از آن لگام داد — پس بر اسپ سوار شُد — وتیز راند — و گفت — بِبین این طورِ دُزدي میکُنند * مردُمان هرچند که تعاقُبِ او کردند — نیافتند *

۲۷ روزي مُرغي بر درختي نِشسته بود * پادشاه اورا دید — و با حاضران گفت که این را به تیر خواهم کُشت * تیر و کمان را گرفت — و تیر بر مُرغ انداخت — و خطا کرد * مُرغ پرید * پادشاه بِسیار خجل گردید * شخصي براي دفعِ خجلت گفتن گرفت — که پادشاه اگر اوّل مُرغ را کُشتن خواست — کُشتن مي تَوانِست — لیکن بر جانِ او رحم کرد — و قصداً خطا نمُود *

۲۸ شخصي با یکي شرط کرد که اگر بازي نیابم یک اثارِ گوشت از

اَنْدامِ من بِتراش * چُون بازيِ نَيافت مُدّعي اِيفايِ شَرْطِ خواسْت * او قبُول نکَرْد * هر دو پیشِ قاضي رفْتَنْد ـــ قاضي مُدّعي‌را گُفْت ـــ مُعاف کُن * قبُول نکَرْد * قاضي برهم شُد و فرمُود کِه بِتراش ـــ لیکِن اگر اَنْدك زِیاده از اَثار خواهي تراشِید ـــ تُرا سِیاست خواهم نمُود * مُدّعي نتوانسْت * ناچار شُده مُعاف کرْد *

۲۹ شخْصي خطّي مي نوِشْت * مرْدي بیگانه نزْدِ او نِشْسْت و طرفِ خطّ مِیدِید * آن شخْص در خطّ نوِشْت کِه مرْدي بیگانه و احْمق نزْدِ من نِشِسْته اسْت ـــ و خطّرا مِیخوانْد ـــ از این سبب هِیچ راز نِمي نوِیسم * آن مرْد گُفْت مرا احْمق مي پِنْداري ـــ چرا راز نِمي نوِیسي ؟   خطِّ تُو نَخوانْده ام * نوِیسنْده گُفْت اگر خطِّ من نَخوانْدي ـــ چِگُونه معْلُوم کرْدي کِه چُنین نوِشْته ام *

۳۰ درْویشي نزْدِ خواجهٴ بخیلي آمد وگُفْت ـــ پدرِ من وتُو آدم اسْت و مادرحَوّاسْت ـــ پس ما و شُما برِدار باشیم * و تُرا این همه مال اسْت ـــ اگر مرا قِسْمتِ برادرانه دِهي چِه شَوَد * خواجه غُلامِ خودرا گُفْت کِه یك فُلوسِ سِیاه وِیرا دِه * گُفْت اَي خواجه چِرا قِسْمتِ سَوِیَت رِعایت نِمیکُني * گُفْت خاموش باش ـــ اگر برادرانِ دِیگر شِنِنَوْند ـــ این نِیزبتُو نِمي رسد *

۳۱ پادْشاهي بر دُشْمني فَوج فِرِسْتاد * آن فَوج شِکسْت یافت * شخْصي جلْد نزْدِ پادْشاه آمد و خبْر رسانِید کِه فَوجِ شُما فتْح یافت *

٣٧ روزي پادشاهي ظالم تنها از شهر بیرون رفت — شخصي‌را زیرِ درختي نشسته دید — پُرسید که پادشاهِ این مُلك چگونه است — ظالم یا عادل؟   گُفت بسیار ظالم است پادشاه گفت مرا مي شناسي؟   گُفت نه * پادشاه گفت منم سلطانِ این مُلك * آن مرد ترسید و پُرسید — مرا میداني؟ پادشاه گفت نه * گفت پسرِ فُلان سوداگر ام * هر ماه سه روز دیوانه میشَوَم * امروز یکي از آن سه روز است * پادشاه خندید و اورا هیچ نگُفت *

٣٨ شخصي هر روز شش نان میخرید * روزي دوستي از وي پُرسید — شش نان‌را هر روز چه مي کُني؟   گُفت ناني‌را نگاه میدارم و یك نان‌را مي اندازم و دُو نان‌را واپس میکُنم و دُو نان‌را قرض میدهم * آن دوست گفت سُخنِ تو هیچ نمي فهمم صاف بگو * گفت یك نان که میدارم میخورم — و ناني که مي اندازم خوشدامن را میدهم — و دُو نان که واپس میکُنم مادر و پدر را میدهم — و دُو نان که قرض میکُنم پسرانِ خود را میدهم *

٣٩ دُو زن در طفلي مُنازعت میکردند و گَواه نداشتند * هردُو پیشِ قاضي رفتند وانصافت خواستند قاضي جلّاد‌را طلبید و فرمود که این طفل‌را دُو پاره کُن و بهرِ دُو زن بده * زني چون این سُخن شنید خاموش ماند — و زنِ دیگر شور و فریاد آغاز کرد — که برايِ خُدا طفل مرا دُو نیم مكن — اگر چُنین انصاف است طفل‌را نمي خواهم *

قاضي بیَقین پِنداشت کِه مادرِ طِفل همین اسْت * طِفل با و سِپُرد ـــ
وزنِ دیگر را تازیانه زده راند *

۴۰ شخْصي را یك کیسهٔ دینار در خانه گُم شُد * او بِقاضي خبر
کرد * قاضي همه مردُمانِ خانه را طلبید و بهر کس یکٔیك چوب داد ـــ
که همه آن در طُولُ برابر بود ـــ و گُفت هر کِه دُزْد اسْت چوبِ
او بقدرِ یك انگُشْت دراز خواهد شُد * چون همه را رُخْصت کرد
شخْصي کِه دُزْدیده بُود ترسید و چوبِ خُود را بقدرِ یك انگُشْت تراشید
* روزِ دیگر چُون قاضي همه را طلبید و چوبها دید معلُوم کرد که دُزْد
کیسْت * کیسهٔ دینار از او گرِفت و سیاست نمُود *

۴۱ شبي قاضي ء در کِتابي دید کِه هر کِه سرِ خُوْد میدارد و ریشِ
دراز احْمق میشوَد * قاضي سرِ خُوْد داشْت و ریشِ بِسْیار دراز * با
خُود گُفت کِه سر را بزرُگ کردن نمیتوَاّم ـــ لیکن ریشْ را کوتاه خواهم
کرد * مقْراض تلاش کرد نیَافْت ـــ ناچار نیم ریشْ را در دسْت گرِفت
و نیم نزدِ چِراغ بُرد * چُون مُوی را آتش گرِفت شُعله بردسْتِ او رسید
ریشْ را گُذاشْت * همه ریشِ او سوخْته شُد * قاضي بِسْیار شرْمنْده
گرْدید به سببِ اینْ کِه هرچِه در کِتاب بُود با اثْباتِ رسید *

۴۲ روزي سِکنْدر با حاضِران گُفت کِه گاهي کسي را محْرُوم نکرْنَم
هر کس هرچِه از من خواسْت بخْشیدم * شخْصي آن وقْت عرْض کرد کِه
خُداونْد مرا یکْدِرم در کار اسْت بخْشِ * سِکنْدر فرمُود که از بادْشاهان

چیز مُحَقَّر خواستَن بی‌ادبی است * آن شخص گُفت که اگر پادشاه‌را از یکدِرم دادن شرم می‌آید مُلکی مرا بخشد * سکندر گُفت اول سُوال کردی کم از مرتبهٔ من — و دیگر سُوال کردی زیاده از مرتبهٔ خود * هر دو سُوال بیجا کردی * آن شخص لا جَواب و شَرمَنده گردید *

۴۳ شخصی نوکرِ خودرا گُفت که علی الصّباح اگر دو زاغ‌را یکجا نِشِسته بینی مرا خبر کُن که آنهارا خواهم دید و شُگونِ نیک خواهم یافت * تمام روز مرا بخوشی خواهد گذشت القِصّه نوکرِ او دو زاغ‌را یکجا دید * صاحِبِ خودرا خبر داد * صاحِبِ او چون بیرون آمد یک زاغ‌را دید — دیگر زاغ پریده بُود * بسیار بر نوکر غُصّه شُد و تازیانه زدن گرفت * همان وقت دوستی برای او طعام فِرِستاد * نوکر عرض کرد که اَی خُداوند — یک زاغ‌را دیدی طعام یافتی — اگر دو زاغ‌را میدیدی می یافتی آنچه من یافتم *

۴۴ دو مُصَوِّر باهم گُفتند که ما هر دو کسان تصویر بکشیم به بینیم کُدام خوب میکشد * یک مُصَوِّر خوشهٔ انگُور نقش نمود و آنرا بر درِوازه آویخت * مُرغان آمدند و بر آن مِنقار زدند * مردُمان آن تصویررا بسیار پسندیدند و در خانهٔ مُصَوِّرِ دیگر رفتند و پُرسیدند که کُجا تصویر کشیده‌؟ — گُفت در پسِ این پرده * مُصَوِّرِ اول خواست که پرده بردارد چون دست بر پرده نهاد معلُوم کرد که پرده نیست — بلکه دیوار است که بر آن تصویر کشیده است * مُصَوِّر

ثانِی گُفت که تو چُنان تصویر کشیدی که مُرغان فریفتَند — و من
چُنان تصویر کشیدَم که مُصوّر فریفت *

۴۵ شخصی یك طُوطی پَرورد — و اورا زبانِ پارسی آموخت *
طوطی درجوابِ هر سُخن می گُفت — دراین چه شك * روزی آن
شخص طُوطی را در بازار برای فروختن بُرد و صد رُوپیه قیمتِ آن ظاهِر
کرد * مُغلی از طُوطی پُرسید که لائقِ صد رُوپیه هستی؟ گُفت — در
این چه شك * مُغل خوشنُود شُد و طُوطی را خرِید وبهانهٔ خُود بُرد *
هر سُخن که با طُوطی میگُفت جوابِ آن — دراین چه شك —
مییافت * در دِلِ خُود شرمِنده و پشیمان گردِید و گُفت حماقت کردم
که چُنین طُوطی خرِیدم * گُفت — دراین چه شك * مُغل را تبسّم
آمد و طُوطی را آزاد کرد *

۴۶ دانِشمندی در مسجد می نِشِست و با مردُمان وعظ می گُفت
* شخصی در آن مجلِس هر روز می گِریِست * روزی دانِشمند گُفت که
سُخنِ من در دِلِ این شخص بسیار اثر میکُند ازین سبب میگرِید *
دیگران آن شخص را گُفتَند که در دِلِ ما سُخنِ دانِشمند هیچ اثر نمیکُند
چِگُونهٔ دِل داری که میگرِیی؟ گُفت بر سُخنِ دانِشمند نمیگرِیم —
بلکه یك خصی پرورده بُودم و اورا بِسیار دوسّت داشتم — چون
خصی پیر شُد مُرد * هرگاه دانِشمند سُخن میگوید و رِیشِ او می
جُنبد خصی مرا یاد می آید — زیرا که او هم اینچُنین رِیشِ دراز داشت *

۴۷ روزي اميري بر ميخ تير مي انداخت تيراندازانِ بسِيار آنجا حاضر بُودند * تيرِ كسي برميخ نميرسيد * فقيري آنجا رفت و از اميرِ چيزي سُوال كرد * اميرِ تير و كمانِ خود در دستِ فقير داد و فرمود ـــ ميخرا بِزن * فقير تير بر ميخ پرتاب كرد ـــ اتّفاقاً بزد * اميرِ بسِيار خُوشنُود گرديد و صد رُوپِيه فقيررا بخشيد و رُخصت كرد * فقير اميررا گُفت ـــ سُوال كردم ـــ هيچ نيافتم * اميرِ رُوي درهم كشيد و گُفت صد رُوپِيه تُرا بخشيده‌ام ـــ ميكوني هيچ نيافتم؟ ـــ اين چِه سُخن است؟ فقير گُفت صد رُوپِيه ميخ زده گرفتم ـــ و از سُوال چِه يافتم؟ اميرِ خنديد و اِنعامِ ديگرِ هم بخشيد *

۴۸ درويشي بر دُكانِ بقّالي رفت ـــ و در خريدن شِتابي كرد * بقّال درويشرا دُشنام داد * درويش در خشم شُد و پاپوشي برسرِ بقّال زد * بقّال پيشِ كوتّوال رفت و نالِش نمُود * كوتّوال درويشرا طلبيد و پُرسيد كِه چِرا بقّالرا زدي؟ درويش گُفت كِه بقّال مرا دُشنام داد * كوتّوال گُفت ـــ اي درويش تقّصيرِ بزرگ كردي ـــ ليكن فقير هستي ـــ ازين سبب تُرا سِياست نِي كُنم * برو هشت آنه بقّال را بِده كِه سزاي تقّصيرِ تُو همين است * درويش يكرُوپِيه از جيبِ خُود بر آورد و در دستِ كوتّوال داد ـــ و يك پاپوش برسرِ كوتّوال زد و گُفت ـــ اگر چُنين اِنصاف است ـــ هشت آنه تُو بِگير ـــ و هشت آنه آنرا بِده *

۴۹ غُلامي از نزدِ صاحِبِ خُود گُرِيخت * بعدِ چند روز صاحبِ او در شهرِ دِيگر رفت * آنجا غُلامرا دِيد و اورا گِرفت و گُفت — چرا گُرِيختِي؟ غُلام دست در دامنِ خواجه زده گُفت — غُلامِ من هستِي نقدِ بِسيار از من دُزدِيدِي و گُرِيختِي — حالا كِه تُرا يافته ام — برِ تُو سِياست خواهم نمُود * الْقِصّه هردُو پيشِ قاضِي رفتنّد و انْصاف خواسْتنّد * قاضِي آن هردُورا نزدِ درِيچه اِستاده كرد و فرمُود كِه بِيكبار هردُو از درِيچه سرها بيرُون كُنيد * چُون سر بيرُون كردنّد قاضِي جلّادرا فرمُود كِه شمّشير بر سرِ غُلام بِزن * غُلام چُون اِين سُخن بشُنِيد در حال سرِ خُود اندرُون كشِيد — و صاحِبِ او اصْلاً نجُنبِيد * قاضِي غُلامرا سِياست كرد — و بصاحِبِ او سِپُرد *

۵۰ روزِي اِبراهيمِ اَدْهم بر درِ سرايِ خويش نِشِسته بُود و غُلامان نزدِ او صفّ زده * ناگاه درويشِي درآمد — با دلّقِي و انّبانِي و عصانِي * خواسْت كِه در سرايِ اِبراهيم رود * غُلامان گُفتنّد اَي پيرگُجا مِي روِي؟ پِير گُفت درين خان مِي روم * گُفتنّد اِين خانه پادْشاه بلْخست نه خان * اِبراهيم فرمُود تا اورا پيشِ آوردنّد — گُفت اَي درويش اِين سرايِ منست * پِير گُفت اَي اِبراهيم اِين خانه اوّل ازآنِ كِه بوده است؟ گُفت ازآنِ جدّم * گُفت چُون او در گُذشّت ازانِ كِه شُد؟ گُفت ازانِ پدرم * گُفت چُون پدرت بمُرد ازانِ كِه شُد؟ گُفت ازانِ من * گفت چُون تُو بِمِيرِي كِرا باشد؟ گُفت بِسرِ مرا * گُفت اَي

اِبراهیم جائی کِه یکی درمی رَوَد و یکی بیرُون می آید خانی باشد نه سرائی *

۵۱ بخیلی دوستی را گفت یك هزار روپیه نزدِ من است می خواهم که این روپیه‌ها را بیرون از شهر دفن کنم — و سِوای تو با کسی این راز نگویم. * القصّه هر دو کسان بیرونِ شهر رفته زیرِ درختی نقدِ مذکور را دفن کردند * بعدِ چند روز بخیل تنها زیرِ آن درخت رفت — از نقد هیچ نشان نیافت * با خود گفت که سِوای آن دوست کسی دیگر نبود — لیکِن اگر از او بپرسم هرگز اقرار نخواهد کرد * پس بحانهٔ او رفت و گفت — بسیار نقد بدستِ من آمده است — می خواهم که هم‌انجا نهیم لیکِن اگر فردا بیائی با هم برویم * دوستِ مذکور بطمعِ نقدِ بسیار آن نقدرا آنجا باز نهاد * بخیل روزِ دیگر آنجا تنها رفت — نقدِ خود یافت — حکمتِ خودرا پسندید و باز بر دوستیِء دوستان اعتماد نکرد *

۵۲ زنی پیشِ قاضی رفت و گفت که فلان مرد با من بزورِ زنا کرد * قاضی آن مردرا طلبید و پرسید که چرا آبرویِ این زن ریختی؟ مرد انکار کرد * قاضی فرمود که ده روپیه جُرمانه باین زن بده * مرد ناچار بموجبِ حکمِ قاضی زر بزن داد * چون زن بیرون رفت قاضی مردرا فرمود — برَو و نقدِ خود از زن باز گیر * مرد چون این حکم یافت دوید — و هرچند خواست که روپیه از زن بزور بگیرد نتوانست * زن پیش قاضی باز آمد و عرض کرد که آن مرد روپیه از من بزور میگیرد هنوز نداده ام — اگر مرضیِء حضرت است بدهم * قاضی گفت

مرد که نقدرا بزور از تو گرفتن نتوانست ــ بي رضاي تو چگونه با تو زنا کرد؟ تو دروغ گوئي ــ برو و نقد باو بسپار و باز اينچنين اِفتِرا مکن *

۳ دو کس مالِ خود پیرِ زني‌را سپردند و گفتند ــ که هرگاه ما هردو خواهیم آمد خواهیم گرفت * بعدِ چند روز شخصي از آنها نزدِ زن آمد و گفت ــ شریکِ من مُرد ــ حالاً مال مرا بده * پیرِ زن ناچار شد و داد * پسِ چند روز شخصِ دیگو آمد و مال خواست * زن گفت که شریکِ تو آمده بُود و ترا مُرده ظاهر ساخت ــ هر چند مبالغه کردم لیکن سخنِ من نشنید ــ همه مال‌را بُرد * شخصِ مذکور زن‌را پیشِ قاضي بُرد و انصاف خواست * قاضي بعد از تأمل دریافت که زن بي تقصیر است ــ فرمود که تو اوّل شرط کرده بودي که هرگاه ما هردو شریک خواهیم آمد مال خواهیم گرفت * تو شریکِ خودرا بیار و مال بگیرید ــ تنها چگونه بیاِبي؟ مرد لا جواب شده راهِ خود پیش گرفت *

۴ در شهري انبارِ پُنبه بدُزدِي رفت * پنبه‌فروشان شِکایت به پادشاه بردند * پادشاه هرچند که تجسّس فرمود دزدي‌را نیافت * امیري عرض کرد که اگر فرمان باشد دزدان‌را بگیرم * پادشاه حکم داد * امیر بهانهء خود رفت و خورد و بزرگِ شهررا بیبهانهء ضیافت طلبید * چون همه مردمان جمع شدند و نشستند امیر در آن مجلس رفت و بر روي همه مردمان نظر کرد و گفت ــ چه حرامزاده و بیحیا و احمق مردمان اند که پُنبه دزدیده اند؟ و ریزهاي پُنبه در ریشهاي ایشان

جا کرده است ــ و در مجلس من آمده اتد * چند کس همان وقت ریشهاي خودرا از دست پاك کردند ـــ و معلوم شد که آنها دزدان اند *

۵۵ سوداگران پیشِ پادشاهي رفتند و اسپانرا بر او عرض نمودند * پادشاه بسیار پسندید و خرید و دولك روپیه زیاده ازقیمت بسوداگران داد و فرمود ـــ که از مُلکِ خود باز اسپانرا بیارید * سوداگران رخصت شدند * روزي پادشاه در حالتِ خوشي و مستي وزیررا گفت که اسامي جمیعِ احمقان بنویس * وزیر عرض کرد که پیش ازین نوشته ام و اوّلِ نامها نامِ حضرتست * پرسید چرا؟ گفت سوداگرانرا دو لك روپیه که براي آوردنِ اسپان بي ضامني و اِطّلاعِ مساکنِ انها عنایت شد ـــ علامت حماقت است * پادشاه گفت اگر سوداگران اسپانرا بیارند پس چه باید کرد؟ گفت اگر بیارند نامِ حضرت از دفترِ احمقان مَحُو خواهم کرد و نامِ سوداگران آنجا خواهم نوشت *

۵۶ پادشاهي آهنگريرا فرمود که جوشنِ خوب براي من تیّار کن * آهنگر تیّار کرده پیشِ پادشاه برد * پادشاه بقصدِ آزمودن جوشنرا بر زمین نهاد و شمشیر بر آن زد ـــ دو نیم شد * آهنگررا فرمود که اگر باز چنین جوشن خواهي ساخت سرِ تو دو نیم خواهم کرد * آهنگر بخانه خود رفت * دختري داشت ـــ با او این احوال گفت * دختر اورا مصلحت داد که باز جوشن بساز * این بار من پیشِ پادشاه خواهم برد * القصّه آهنگر جوشنرا ساخت * دخترِ او آن جوشنرا پوشید و شمسیري در دست گرفت و پیشِ پادشاه رفت و عرض کرد که حالاً جوشنرا بیازمائید * پادشاه گفت چرا اینرا پوشیده * گفت اي خداوند

ـــ دستور آن است که جوشن بر اندام آزموده میشود ازاین سبب پوشیده‌ام * پادشاه این سخن پسندید و اورا انعام بخشید *

۵۷ جماعتي نزدِ قاضي قرضدارِ خود را آوردند و گفتند که این مرد از ما هزار دینار قرض گرفته است و نمیدهد * قاضي باو گفت که چه میکوئي * گفت ایشان راست میگویند و دعوای ایشان حقّ است * غایتش اینکه این مقدارِ فرصت ازایشان میخواهم که گلهٴ شترهاي خود را بفروشم و باغها را گِرو کنم و حقِّ ایشان را ادا سازم * آن جماعت گفتند واللّٰه سراپا دروغ میگوید مالكِ یك دینار نیست و یك وجبِ زمین در ملكِ خود ندارد مالكِ یك گوسفند نیست چه جاي گلهٴ شتران * قرضدار جواب داد که اي عدالت‌پنـاه اکنون اقرارِ ایشان بمفلسي و بیچیزيٴ من استمع نمودي پس چگونه ازمفلس چیزي طلب مي نمایند * قاضي رو به ایشان کرد و گفت اَلْمُفْلِسُ فِي أَمَانِ اللّٰهِ و اورا از دستِ آنها خلاص کرد *

۵۸ شخصي پیش پادشاهي رفت و عرض کرد که مردي همیشه در خانهٴ من مي آید و با زنِ من دوستي دارد لیکن گاهي اورا نمي بینم و نمیدانم که کیست میخواهم که گرفتارش کنم که از حضرت آمیز، وارا اِنصاف ام * پادشاه شیشهٴ عِطْر باو داد و فرمود که بزنِ خود سِپار و بگو که کسي را مدِه * آن شخص همچنان کرد * پادشاه جاسوسي چندرا بر گماشت که گِردِ خانهٴ او بنشینند و از پارچهٴ هر کسي که بوي عِطْر آید اورا گرفته بیارند * القصّه حریف قابو یافته نزدِ زن رفت * زن عِطْررا در پارچهٴ او مالید و گفت که شوهرِ من اگرچه مرا فرمود که کسي را

این عطر مدِه لیکن تو که جان و دلِ مي اگر بکارت نیاید بچِه کار آید *
چون حریف از آن جا بر آمد جاسو سان ببوي عطر سر راهش
گرفتند و اسیر کرده پیشِ پادشاه بُردند * پادشاه آن شخص را طلبید و
گفت حریفِ زرِ نو حاضر است اورا ببر و بکُش یا بِخش *

۵۹ زني با زنِ همسایهٔ خود دشمني داشت* شبي مَي بسیار خورد
و مست شد و طفلِ خودرا کُشت و در خانهٔ زنِ همسایه انداخت و
صباح برو تهمت نهاد که طفلِ مرا کشته است و اورا پیش قاضي
برد * قاضي اوّل زنِ همسایه را در خلوت طلبید و بسیار ترسانید و
گفت راست بگو و گرنه ترا خواهم کُشت * زن قسم خورد و انکار کرد *
قاضي گفت که اگر روبروي من برهنه شوي سخنِ تو راست پندارم *
زن از حیا سر فرو کرد و گفت مرا کشته شدن قبول است لیکن زنهار
برهنه نخواهم شد * قاضي اورا رخصت کرد و زنِ فریادي را در خلوت
طلبید و گفت اگر پیشِ من برهنه شوي سخنِ تو باور کنم * آن زن
خواست که خودرا برهنه کند * قاضي اورا منع کرد و گفت که پسررا
خود کشتي * چون چند تازیانه اورا زد اقرار کرد که خود تقصیر کردم و
تهمت برو نهادم * القصّه قاضي اورا بر دار کشید *

۶۰ شخصي گرسنه مِیرفت اعرابي را دید که بر کنارهٔ بِرکه طعام
میخورد * نزدِ او رفت و گفت از طرفِ خانهٔ تو مي آیم * اعرابي پرسید
که زن و فرزند و شترِ من همه بخَیریَت اند * گفت بلي * اعرابي را
خاطر جمع شد و باز بران شخص نظر نکرد * آن شخص آغاز کرد که
اي اعرابي این سگ که حالاً بحضورِ تو نشسته است اگر سگِ تو زنده

میماند چنین میشد * اعرابي سر بالا کرد و گفت سگِ من از چه

سبب مُرد * گفت گوشتِ شترِ تو بسیار خورد * پرسید شتر چگونه مُرد *

گفت زنِ تو مُرد از این سبب کسي اورا کاه و دانه و آب نداد *

پرسید زن چگونه مُرد گفت درغمِ پسرِ تو بسیار گریست و سنگ بر سر

و سینه زد * پرسید پسر چگونه مُرد گفت خانه برو اُفتاد * اعرابي چون این

احوالِ خانه خرابي شنید خاك برسر انداخت و طعام را همانجا گذاشت

و طرفِ خانهٔ خود روانه شد * آن شخس بدین حکمت طعام یافت *

۶۱ بخیلي خریطهٔ صد دینار گم کرد * چندانکه طلب نمود کم

یافت * گفت هر که یافته باشد بیارد که ازان ده دینار ازانِ اوست *

اتفاقاً بدستِ صالحي افتاد و بخیل را بداد و ایفاي وعده خواست *

لئیم که حبهٔ سیم را بصد جان عزیز میداشت گفت که درین خریطه

یکصد و ده دینار بود حقِّ خود گرفتهٔ دیگر چه میخواهي * مردِ نیکسرشت

پیشِ قاضي رفت * قاضي مدعا علَیه را طلبید و پرسید که وفاي وعده

چرا نمیکني و حقِّ این بیچاره نمیدهي ؟ گفت حقِّ خود گرفته است

دیگر چه میخواهد * قاضي خریطهاش طلبید دید که همچنان سر بمهر

است * گفت که تو میگوئي در خریطهٔ مفقود یکصد و ده دینار بود

و درین خریطه یکصد دینار است این خریطهٔ تو نیست از جاي

دیگر طلب کن و این کیسه حوالهٔ این مرد نما که ازانِ دیگر است

و مالِك این دیگر بوده باشد * و آن مرد را گفت که تو این کیسه را

امانت نزدِ خود دار تا که مالِك آن پیدا شود *

۶۲ روزي پادشاهي با وزیر براي سیر رفت بکشتزاري رسید

درختانِ گندم دید از قدِّ آدم درازتر * پادشاه متعجّب شد و گفت چنین دراز درختانِ گندم گاهي نديدم * وزير عرض كرد كه اي خداوند در وطنِ من درختانِ گندم همچو قدِ فيل بلند ميشوند * پادشاه تبسّم نمود * وزير با خود گفت كه پادشاه سخنِ من دروغ پنداشت ازاين سبب تبسّم كرد * چون از سَير باز آمد خطّ بمردمانِ وطنِ خود براي چند درختانِ گندم فرستاد * تا كه خطّ آنجا رسيد فصلِ گندم گذشته بود * القصّه بعدِ يكسال درختانِ گندم از آنجا رسيدند * وزير پيشِ پادشاه بُرد * پادشاه پرسيد چرا آوردي * عرض كرد كه در سالِ گذشته روزي عرض كرده بودم كه درختانِ گندم همچو قدِ فيل بلند مي شوند تبسّم كرديد * با خود گفتم كه سخنِ من دروغ پنداشتيد * براي تصديقِ سخنِ خود آوردم * پادشاه گفت حالاً باور كردم ليكن زنهار پيشِ كسي چنين سخن مگو كه بعدِ سالي باور كند *

۶۳ روزي پادشاهي بر بامِ قصرِ خود نشسته بود * شخصي‌را زيرِ ديوار استاده ديد كه مرغي در دست گرفته مي نمود * پادشاه اورا طلبيد و پرسيد چرا مرغ بمن مي نمائي * گفت اي خداوند با شخصي از طرفِ حضرت شرط كردم و اين مرغ در بازي يافتم براي خداوند آورده ام * پادشاه خوشنود گرديد و مرغ‌را در مطبخ فرستاد * بعد از دو سه روز باز آن شخص پيشِ پادشاه آمد و گوسپندي آورد و گفت اين هم از نام آنحضرت در بازي يافته ام * پادشاه آنرا نيز قبول كرد * سيوم بار پيشِ پادشاه رفت و شخصي ديگررا با خود برد * چون پادشاه اورا تهيدست ديد پرسيد براي من هيچ نه آورده‌ء * عرض كرد

که از طرفِ حضرت با این شخص دو هزار روپیه را شرط نمودم و بازي
نیافتم حالاً این شخص براي زرِ پیشِ حضرت آمده است * پادشاه
تبسّم کرد و زر اورا بخشید و فرمود گاهي از طرفِ من با کسي قِمار
مباز * دیگر هیچ از تو نخواهم گرفت و نه ترا چیزي خواهم داد *

۶۴ آورده اند که سلطان محمود ایّاز را بسیار دوست داشتي ازین
سبب همه ارکانِ دَولت برو حسد بردند وپادشاه را گفتند که ایّاز هر
روز تنها به جَوَاهرخانه میرود ومعلوم میشود که چیزي مي دُزدد وگرنه در
جَوَاهر خانه اورا چه کار است * پادشاه گفت هر گاه بچشمِ خود خواهم
دید باور خواهم کرد * روزِ دیگر پادشاه را خبر دادند که ایّاز تنها در
جواهرخانه رفته است پادشاه از غرفه درونِ جواهرخانه نظر کرد چه مي
بیند که ایّاز صندوقي را کشاده پارچهٴ کهنه وغلیظ پوشیده است *
پادشاه درون تشریف برد پرسید چرا چنین پارچه پوشیده٬ه * عرض
کرد که اي خداوند چون در بندگيٴ حضرت نبودم چنین پارچه داشتم
حالاً که بدولتِ خداوند پارچه‌هاي پاکیزهٴ دارم جامهٴ کهنهٴ خود هر
روز مي بینم و مي پوشم تا حالتِ قدیمِ خود را فراموش نکنم وقدرِ
نعمتِ خداوندي شناسم * پادشاه چون این جواب شنید پسندید
و اورا در کنار کشید ومرتبهٴ او بزرگ کرد *

۶۵ شخصي مالِ بسیار صرّافي را سپرد و بسفر رفت * چون باز آمد
تقاضا نمود * صرّاف انکار کرد و قسم خورد که مرا نه سپرده٬ه * آن
شخص پیشِ قاضي رفت و احوالِ خود گفت * قاضي تأمّل کرد و فرمود
کسرا مگو که فلان صرّاف مالِ نمیدهد تدبیري براي مالِ تو خواهم

کرد * روزِ دیگر قاضي آن صرّاف‌را طلبید و گفت کارهاي بسیار بمن
پیش آمده است تنها کردن نمیتوانم ترا نائبِ خود کردن میخواهم زیرا
که مُتَدَیّن هستي * صرّاف قبول کرد و بسیار خوش گردید چون بهانه
رفت قاضي آن شخص‌را طلبید و گفت حالاً مالِ خود از صرّاف بجواب
البتّه خواهد داد * شخصِ مذکور پیشِ صرّاف رفت وصرّاف چون
روي او دید گفت بیا بیا خوش‌آمدي مالِ تو فراموش کرده بودم
دي شب مرا یاد آمد * القصّه مال باو داد و از طمعِ نیابت پیشِ
قاضي رفت * قاضي گفت امروز پیشِ پادشاه رفته بودم شنیدم که
کاري بزرگ ترا سپردن میخواهد خدارا شکر کن مرتبهٔ بزرگ خواهي
یافت حالاً نائبِ دیگر براي خود تلاش خواهم کرد * القصّه قاضي اورا
بدین حیله رخصت کرد *

۶۶ سواري در شهري رفت شنید که اینجا دزدان بسیار اند * وقتِ
شب سائس‌را گفت که تو بِخُسپ من بیدار خواهم ماند زیرا که مرا بر
تو اعتماد نیست * سائس گفت اي خداوند این چه سخن است؟
نمي پسندم که من در خواب باشم و صاحب بیدار زنهار اینچنین
نخواهم کرد * القصّه صاحبِ او خفت و بعدِ یکپاس بیدار گردید
سائس‌را گفت چه میکني * گفت در فکرهستم که خدا زمین‌را برآب
چگونه گسترد * گفت میترسم که دزدان آیند و ترا خبر نشود * گفت اي
خداوند خاطر جمع دارید خبردار هستم * سوار باز خفت و نصف
شب بیدار شد و پرسید اي سائس چه میکني * گفت در فکرم که
خدا آسمانرا چگونه بي ستون استاده کرد * گفت در فکر تو میترسم

مبادا كه دزدان اسپرا برند * گفت اي خداوند بيدار هستم چگونه دزدان خواهند آمد * سوار گفت اگر خفتن ميخواهي بخسپ من بيدار خواهم ماند * گفت مرا خواب نمي آيد * سوار باز خفت و چون ساعتي شب باقي ماند بيدار شد سائس‌را پرسيد چه ميكني * گفت در فكر هستم كه اسپ‌را دزد برده است و فردا زين‌را من بر سر خواهم برداشت يا صاحب *

٦٧ شخصي پيش درويشي رفت و سه سوال كرد * اوّل آنكه چرا ميگوئي كه خدا همه جا حاضر است هيچ جا نمي بينم بنما كجاست * دوم آنكه انسان‌را براي تقصيري چرا سياست ميكنند؟ هرچه ميكند خدا ميكند انسان‌را هيچ قدرت نيست و بي ارادت خدا هيچ نمي تواند كرد و اگر انسان‌را قدرت بودي همه كارها براي خود بهتر كردي * سيوم آنكه خدا شَيطان‌را در آتش دوزخ چگونه عقوبت تواند كرد زيرا كه سرشت او از آتش است وآتش در آتش چه اثر خواهد كرد؟ درويش كلُوخي بزرگ بر سر او زد * آن شخص گريان پيش قاضي رفت و گفت از فلان درويش سه سوال كردم بر سر من چنان كلُوخي زد كه سر من درد ميكند و هيچ جواب نداد * قاضي درويش‌را طلبيد و گفت چرا كلوخ بر سر او زدي و جواب سوال او ندادي؟ درويش گفت كه آن كلوخ جواب سخن اوست * ميگويد كه درد در سر دارد بنمايد كجا است تا من خدا‌را باو بنمايم * و چرا پيش حضرت نالش من نمود؟ هرچه كردم خدا كرد بي ارادت خدا اورا نزدم مرا چه قدرت است؟

وسرشتِ او از خاك است از خاك چگونه اورا رنج رسید؟ آن شخص شرمنده گردید قاضي جوابِ درویش بسیار پسندید ٭

٦٩ شخصي پیشِ پادشاه رفت و گفت دي شب مردي از فوج پادشاهي بزور درخانهٴ من آمد و با كنیزِ من زنا كرد ٭ پادشاه فرمود كه اگر آن مرد باز در خانهٴ تو بیاید همان‌دم مرا خبر كن ٭ شبِ دوم آن مرد باز آمد و در خانهٴ او رفت ٭ صاحبِ خانه پادشاه‌را خبر داد ٭ پادشاه شمشیري در دست گرفت و با او روان شد ٭ چون بخانهٴ او رسید اوّل چراغ را كُشت و بعدِ آن آن مرد‌را بقتل رسانید و باز چراغ را طلبید و روي آن مرد دید و خدا‌را شكر كرد وصاحبِ خانه‌را گفت هر طعام كه این وقت درخانهٴ تو موجود باشد بیار ٭ صاحبِ خانه طعام آورد پادشاه بسیار بخوشي خورد ٭ صاحبِ خانه پرسید كه اي خداوند بچه سبب اوّل چراغ‌را كشتید بعد از آن آنمرد‌را بقتل رسانید و چون روي آن مرد دیدید خدا‌را شكر كردید و طعام بي‌وقت خوردید؟ پادشاه فرمود كه پنداشته بودم كه سواي پسرِ من كسي‌را چنین قدرت نیست از این سبب اول چراغ‌را كشتم كه اگر روي پسر خواهم دید از شفقت اورا كشتن نخواهم توانست ٭ چون كشته شد چراغ طلبیدم و روي او دیدم و خدا‌را شكر كردم كه پسرِ من نیست ٭ و آن وقت كه از‌من انصاف خواستي باخود گفتم كه تا آنمرد‌را نكشم هیچ نخورم ٭ از آن وقت هیچ نخورده بودم از این سبب سخت گرسنه بودم و طعام بي وقت خوردم ٭

۷۰ دانشمندي هزار رویپه عطّاري را سپرد و بسفر رفت ٭ بعدِ

مدّت از سفر باز آمد و روپیه از عطّار خواست * عطّار گفت دروغ
میگویُی مرا نه سپرده‌ٔ * دانشمند باوی دراویخت * مردمان جمع شدند
و دانشمندرا تکذیب کردند و گفتند این عطّار بسیار دیانت‌دار است
گاهی خیانت نکرد اگر با این مناقشه خواهی کرد سزا خواهی یافت *
دانشمند ناچار شد و احوال بر کاغذی نوشت و پادشاه‌را نمود * پادشاه
فرمود بِرَو نزدِ دوکانِ عطّار سه روز بنشین و اورا هیچ مگو چهارم روز آن
طرف خواهم رفت و ترا سلام خواهم کرد سوای جوابِ سلام هیچ
بامن نگویُی* چون از آنجا بروم نقدِ خود از عطّار بخواه * آنچه او بگوید مرا
خبر کن * دانشمند موافقِ حکمِ پادشاه بر دوکان عطّار نشست * روزِ
چهارم پادشاه با حشمتِ بسیار آن طرف رفت چون دانشمندرا دید
اسپ‌را استاده کرد و بر دانشمند سلام خواند * دانشمند جوابِ سلام
گفت * پادشاه فرمود ای برادر گاهی نزدِ من نمی آیی و هیچ احوالِ خود
با من نمیگویُی * دانشمند اندک سر جُنبانید و دیگر هیچ نگفت *
عطّار این همه میدید و می ترسید * چون پادشاه رفت عطّار دانشمندرا
گفت که هرگاه نقد مرا سپردی کجا بودم و کدام شخص نزدِ من حاضر
بود باز بگو شاید فراموش کرده باشم * دانشمند همه احوال باز گفت *
عطّار گفت راست می گویُی حالاً مرا یاد آمد القصّه هزار روپیه
دانشمندرا داد و عُذرِ بسیار نمود *

۷۱ جوانی پیرمردی‌را صد دینار سپرد و بسفر رفت * چون باز آمد
دینارِ خود خواست * پیرمرد انکار کرد که مرا نداده‌ٔ * جوان همه احوال
پیشِ قاضی ظاهر نمود * قاضی پیرمردرا طلبید و پرسید که این جوان

زر بتو سپرد؟ گفت نه * قاضي جوانرا فرمود کسي گواه داري؟ گفت
نه * قاضي پيرمردرا گفت سوگند بخور * جوان گريان شد و گفت اورا از
سوگند هيچ باك نيست بارها سوگندِ دروغ خورده است * قاضي جوانرا
گفت آنوقت كه زر باو سپردي كجا نشسته بودي * گفت زيرِ درختي *
گفت چرا گفتي كه گواه ندارم؟ آن درخت گواهِ تُست نزدِ آن درخت
بِرَو و بگو كه قاضي ترا مي طلبد * پير مرد تبسّم كرد * جوان گفت
اي قاضي مي ترسم كه درخت از حكمِ تو نخواهد آمد * قاضي گفت
مُهرِ من ببر و بگو كه اين مُهرِ قاضي است البتّه خواهد آمد * جوان
مُهرِ قاضي گرفت و رفت * قاضي بعدِ ساعتي از پيرمرد پرسيد كه آن
جوان نزدِ درخت رسيده باشد * گفت نه * چون جوان نزدِ درخت
رفت و مُهرِ قاضي نمود و گفت قاضي ترا مي طلبد از درخت هيچ نشنيد *
غمگين باز آمد و گفت مُهرِ تو درختِرا نمودم هيچ جواب نداد *
قاضي گفت درخت آمد و گواهي داده باز رفت * پير مرد گفت اي
قاضي اين چه سخن است هيچ درخت اينجا نه آمد * قاضي گفت
راست ميگوئي نه آمد ليكن آنوقت كه از تو پرسيدم كه جوان نزدِ
درخت رسيد جواب دادي كه نرسيد * اگر تو زيرِ آن درخت نقد
نگرفتي چرا نگفتي كه كدام درخت است آنرا نميدانم * ازين معلوم
ميشود كه جوان راست ميگويد * پير مرد الزام يافت و زر بجوان داد *

۷۲ دو برادرِ مفلس بسفر رفتند و در راه كيسهٔ پُر از زر و دو پارهٔ
لعل يافتند * برادرِ خورد گفت كه غرضِ من حاصل شد حالاً بخانه
خواهم رفت * برادرِ بزرگ گفت سَيرِ جهان خواهم كرد * آن زررا

قِسمت کردند * برادرِ کلان حِصّهٔ خودرا به برادرِ خورد سپرد و گفت
بزنِ من بِده * چون او بهانه رسید حِصّهٔ برادررا بزنِ او داد مگر لعل
نداد * بعدِ سه سال برادرِ کلان از سفر بهانه آمد پارهٔ لعل پیشِ زنِ
خود ندید * از برادر پرسید که لعل چه شد * گفت بزنِ تو دادم *
گفت او میگوید که نیافتم * گفت دروغ میگوید * آن مرد زنِ خودرا
تنبیه آغاز کرد * زن گُریخت و پیشِ قاضی رفت و احوالِ خود باز نمود *
قاضی شوهرِ اورا با برادرِ او طلبید و از برادرِ او پرسید که چون لعل
باین زن سپردی کسی آن وقت حاضر بود؟ گفت دو کس * قاضی
فرمود بطلب * او آنهارا اندکی نقد داد و گفت با من بیائید و پیشِ
قاضی بدروغ گواهی دِهید * القصّه آن هردو گواهی دادند * قاضی شوهرِ
آن زنرا فرمود که بِرَو و از زنِ خود پارهٔ لعل بگیر * زن گریان پیشِ
سلطان رفت و احوالِ خود عرض کرد * سلطان فرمود چرا پیشِ قاضی
نمیرَوی؟ گفت رفته بودم لیکن بخوبی انصاف نکرد * سلطان آن
هردو برادر و گواهانرا طلبید و هریکرا جُدا کرد و موم داد که بصورتِ
آن لعل بسازید * آن هردو برادر یکسان ساختند و آن هردو گواهان
بصورتِ مُختلف * سلطان زنرا فرمود که تو هم بساز * عرض کرد که
لعل گاهی ندیدم چگونه سازم * سلطان گواهانرا سیاست فرمود که اگر
راست بگوئید خواهم گذاشت و گرنه خواهم کُشت * ناچار عرض
کردند بدروغ گواهی دادیم * سلطان برادرِ خوردرا چند تازیانه زد اقرار
کرد که تقصیر کردم * پادشاه بر قاضی عِتاب فرمود که چرا بخوبی انصاف
نکردی و لعلرا بآن زن دِهانیدید *

۷۳ شخصي دو هزار روپيه در كيسهٔ سربمُهر به قاضي سپرد و خود بسفر رفت * چون باز آمد كيسهٔ خود همچنان سر بمهر از قاضي گرفت و كشاد فلوس ديد * با قاضي مواخذه نمود قاضي گفت برَو دروغ ميگوئي مرا روپيه‌ها نموده نسپرده بودي كيسهٔ سر بمهر چنان كه سپردي باز گرفتي * مردمانِ قاضي اورا راندند * آن شخص پيشِ پادشاه رفت و احوالِ خود عرض كرد * سلطان اندك تامل نموده فرمود كه حالاً برَو و كيسه‌را نزدِ من بدار انصافِ تو خواهم داد * روزِ ديگر پادشاه مسندِ نوَ كه بر تخت بود اندك پاره نمود و بشكار رفت * فرّاشي كه آن روز نوبتِ خدمتِ او بود چون مسندرا پاره ديد ترسيد و لرزه بر اندامِ او افتاد و فرّاشِ ديگررا نمود و گفت اگر پادشاه خواهد ديد مرا خواهد كُشت * پرسيد كه ديگري اين سخن شنيده است يا مسندرا ديده؟ گفت نه * گفت خاطر جمع دار دريـن شهر رفوگري است كامل مسند پيشِ او بِبر او المجنان رفو خواهد كرد كه كسي نخواهد دريافت * فرّاش بدوكانِ او رفت و مسند برفوگر داد و گفت هر چه بخواهي ترا بدهم ليكن بخوبي رفو كُن رفوگر نيم دينار خواست * فرّاش يك دينار اورا بخشيد * رفوگر در يكشب مسندرا رفو كرده داد * فرّاش روزِ ديگر آنرا بر تخت گسترد * پادشاه چون مسند درست ديد از فرّاش پرسيد كه اين مسند كه رفو كرد؟ فرّاش تجاهُل نمود * پادشاه فرمود كه هيچ مترس براي مصلحتي اين را پاره كرده بودم ـــ فرّاش نِشان داد * پادشاه آن رفوگررا طلبيد و پرسيد كه مثلِ اين كيسه رفو كرده‌؟ گفت بلي * گفت اگر آن كيسه‌را ببيني شناسي؟ گفت آري * پادشاه كيسه‌را نمود *

رفوگر کیسه‌را شناخت و گفت قاضيِ این شهر مرا براي رفو داده بود * پادشاه قاضي‌را طلبید و گفت بر دیانتِ تو اعتمادِ تمام داشتم * بنابر این منصبِ قضا بتو دادم * نمیدانستم که دُزدي * مالِ این شخص چرا دُزدیدي * گفت اَي خداوند که میگوید؟ گفت من میگویم * پس کیسه‌را نمود و رفورا نشان داد * قاضي شرمنده شد * پادشاه قاضي‌را در زندان فرستاد و مالكِ کیسه‌را فرمود که نقدِ خود از قاضي بگیر * قاضي ناچار نقد اورا داد *

۷۴ آورده اند که در زمانِ پیشین خطیبي بزرگ بتفرّجِ بلدان بیرون رفت * هر شام در شهري و هر بامداد بر رهگذري میگذرانید * شبي در سرايِ رسید و بساطِ راحت چید ــ بعدِ فراغِ طعام بالاي بام برآمد و هر سو نظري افگند * از دور آوازِي موهوم بگوشش رسید * یکي را بدریافتِ آن رَوان کرد * خادم دیده و شنیده عرض نمود * خطیب نمودِ او بسمع قبول نفرمود ــ خود بر اثرش روان شد * چون بدانجا رسید دید که مجرّدي مجذوب است و از عقل بالكُلّ مسلوب * بعدِ اداي تعظیم گفت که در چه‌کار مشغوالي که از نعم دنیا ملولي ؟ گفت با حریفِ خود بازي میکنم * خطیب گفت حریفِ تو کیست و بازيِ تو چیست؟ گفت حریفِ من خداوندِ گله است و بازيِ من شطرنج * خطیب گفت چرا بازي میکني و خود را در تكِ پیلِ حرمان مي انگي؟ مجذوب گفت تا از دست‌بردِ زمان رهائي یابم و کُشتنش مخورم * خطیب گفت از حریفِ خود بازي مییابي یا رخ مي تابي ؟ مجذوب پیاده‌وار سراسیمه و کج مج بر زبان آورده گفت گاهي

شه مات میکنم و گاهي مات ميشوم * خطيب گفت مات بچه طَور ميشوي و وقتي كه مات میكني چەكار میكني؟ مجذوب گفت هنگامي كه مات ميشوم نقدش بمسكينان نفقه ميدهم و گاهي كه بازي میكنم خداوند عزّوجلّ از بندگانِ خويش مرا ميدهاند * اكنون بازِم از دست رفت و پنجاه دینار خسارت پذیرفت * این بگفت و خریطهٔ از جیب بر آورد و پنجاه دینار ازان بخطیب داد و سر در راهِ خود نهاد * خطیب ازین ماجراي عجیب سخت درماند و ندانست كه این زر را چه توان كرد * كام ناكام روان شد و نقد را بفُقَرا داد وازین سانحهٔ غریب همسایگان را مُطّلع كرد * چون شب درآمد باز همان حالتِ دوشينه معاينه ديد ــ و آرزومندِ ديدارِ او گرديد * هرگاه نزدِ او رسيد بادب سلام نمود * مجذوب جوابِ سلام گفته پردهٔ راز بكشود و گفت از نفع و زیان چارہ نیست * این بار من شاه را مات نمودم و نقدي گِران يافتم * خطيب گفت چه قدر يافتي؟ گفت پانصد دينار بدستِ من آمد * لحال حاملِ كيسهٔ نقد توئي كه خداي تعالي براي دادنِ آن نزدِ من ترا فرستاده است * و آن روز خطيب نقدِ گِران يافتهبود ــ بر غيب دانئهٔ او حيران بماند و جبراً و قهراً پانصد دينار حوالهٔ او نمود * و يقين دانست كه اين مردِ حيلهسازِ شطرنج باز رهزن است * ترسان و لرزان سراسيمه بگریخت و بر ناداني و حماقتِ خود آگاہ گرديد و كسي را ازین واردات اِطّلاع نكرد كه حمل بر حُمق خواهند نمود *

مُنتخباتِ منظومه

۱ ــ حِکایت از بوستانِ شیخ سعدیِ شیرازی

شنیدم که یک هفته ابنُ السبیل   نیامد بهمان سرای خلیل

ز فرخنده خویی نخوردی پگاه   مگر بینوائی در آید ز راه

برون رفت و هر جانبی بنگرید   در اطرافِ وادی نگه کرد و دید

به تنها یکی در بیابان چو بید   سرو مویش از برفِ پیری سپید

بدلداریش مرحبائی بگفت   برسم کریمان صلائی بگفت

که ای چشمهای مرا مردُمک   یکی مردُمی کن بنان و نمک

نعم گفت و برجست و برداشت کام   که دانست خلقش علیهِ السلام

رفیقان مهمان سرای خلیل   بعزّت نشاندند پیرِ ذلیل

بفرمود ترتیب کردند خوان   نشستند بر هر طرف همگنان

چو بسم اللّه آغاز کردند جمع   ز پیرش نیامد حدیثی بسمع

چنین گفت کای پیرِ دیرینه روز   چو پیران نیبینمت صدق و سوز

نه شرطست وقتی که روزی خوری   که نامِ خداوندِ روزی بری

بگفتا نگیرم طریقی بدست   که نشنیدم از پیرِ آذرپرست

بدانست پیغمبرِ نیک فال   که گبرست پیرِ تبه کرده حال

براندش چو بیگانه دید   که منکر بُوَد پیشِ پاکان پلید

سروش آمد از کردگارِ جلیل   بهیبت ملامت کنان کای خلیل

منش داده صد سال روزی و جان   ترا نفرت آمد ازو یک زمان

گر او مي برد پيش آتش سجود — تو واپس چرا مي بري دست جود

برو پير ديرينه‌را باز خوان — تو از من سلامي مراو رسان

همي نالد و گريه بر من كند — سر و روي را خاك بر تن كند

روان شد بسويش نبي‌ء زمان — بخواندش از آن باديه دلكشان

چو نزديك آمد بگفت اين سخن — كه صد آفرين باد برسر و تن

خدايت بكرد استجاب دعا — بسويت فرستاد مارا خدا

چو بشنيد اين پير ديرينه سال — بقول شهادت بر آورده قال

بحمد الله آن كس مسلمان شده — اگرچه گدا بود سلطان شده

٢ ــ حكايت از حديقهء حكيم سنائي

چون تبه شذ خلافت مأمون — ريخت مر جلق را بناحق خون

كرد بر آل برمك آن بي داد — كه كسي زان صفت ندارد ياد

يحيي‌ء بي گناه را چون كشت — گشت بروي زمانه تند و درشت

مادري داشت يحيي‌ء مظلوم — پير و عاجز ز كام دل محروم

جفت اندوه گشته اندر دهر — عيش شيرين برو شذه چون زهر

باز گفتند حال مأمون را — عرضه كردند حال محزون را

كه دعاي بذت همي گويذ — مملكت را زوال ميجويذ

دل او خوش كن و ز حقد بكاه — بازخواه از عجوزه عذر گناه

رفت مامون شبي ز خلق نهان — بر كشاده بعذر جرم زبان

در و گوهر بذو بسي بخشيذ — راه و سامان كار خون آن ديذ

گفتش اي مادر آن قضائي بود — چون قضا رفت زاري تو چه سود

بعد ازین کارهای بهوش کن   وز دعای بدم فراموش کن

گرچه پیی نماند و یافت گزند   مرترا من کنون بوم فرزند

من بجای ویم تو دل خوش دار   کین و حقد و دعای بذ بگذار

مادر پیر داد کار بداذ   درزمان پیش وی زبان کشاذ

گفت ای میر بازده خبرم   من بشخصی چگونه غم خورم

کی ورا چون تو شه عوض باشذ   راست چون جوهر و عرض باشذ

با بزرگی که آمدت حاصل   هم نباشی بجای وی در دل

چون وئی را بگوی بتوان کرد   که بوذ مادرش ز اندوه فرد

چون توئی با هزار حشمت و جاه   نیست مارا بجای آن دلخواه

اینچنین لفظ چون در شهوار   یادگارست از ان زن بیزار

گشت ازان یک سخن خجل مأمون   بعد ازان خوذ نریخت از کس خون

٣ — غزل از دیوان خاقانی

لاله رخا سمن برا روح روان کیستی   سنگدلا ستمگرا آفت جان کیستی

در چمنی که رسته دیده گل ببسته   قدر شکر شکسته غنچه دهان کیستی

سرو قد تو دیده ام آه الف کشیده ام   نرگس دیده دیده ام سرو روان کیستی

دام نهاده میروی مست ز باده میروی   شست کشاده میروی سخت کمان کیستی

ابروی تو چو ماه نو برده ز ماه نو گرو   ناله و آه من شنو فتنه جان کیستی

خاقانی غلام تو مست شده ز جام تو

جان بدهد بنام تو روح روان کیستی

۳ ــ غزل از دیوانِ حافظِ شیرازی

اگر آن تُرکِ شیرازی بدست آرد دلِ مارا
بخالِ هِندوش بخشم سمرقند و بُخارا را

بده ساقی مَیِ باقی که در جنّت نخواهی یافت
کنارِ آبِ رُکنآباد و گُلگشتِ مُصلّا را

فغان کین لولیانِ شوخ و شیرینکارِ شهرآشوب
چُنان بُردند صبر از دل که تُرکان خوانِ یغما را

زِ عشقِ ناتمامِ ما جمالِ یار مستغنیست
بآب و رنگ و خال و خط چه حاجت رُوی زیبا را

حدیث از مُطرِب و مَی گو و رازِ دهر کمتر جو
که کس نکشود و نکشاید بحکمت این مُعمّا را

من از آن حُسن روزافزُون که یُوسُف داشت دانستم
که عِشق از پردهٔ عِصمت برُون آرد زُلیخا را

نصیحت گوش کن جانا که از جان دوستتر دارند
جوانانِ سعادتمند پندِ پیرِ دانا را

بدم گفتی و خرسندم عفاکَ الله نِکو گفتی
جوابِ تلخ میزیبد لبِ لعلِ شکرخا را

غزل گفتی و دُر سُفتی بیا و خوش بخوان حافظ
که بر نظمِ تو افشاند فلک عِقدِ ثُریّا را

۵—غزل از دیوانِ حافظِ شِیرازی

ساقیا مایهٔ شراب بِیار   یکدو ساغرِ شراب ناب بِیار

داروی دردِ عِشق یعنی مَی   کوست درمانِ شَیخ و شاب بِیار

آفتابست و ماه باده و جام   در میانِ مه آفتاب بِیار

بزن اِین آتش مرا آبی   یعنی آن آتش چو آب بِیار

گل اگر رفت گو بشادی رَو   بادهٔ ناب چون گُلاب بِیار

غلغلِ قُمری ار نماند رَواست   قلقلِ شیشهٔ شراب بِیار

میکند عقل سرکشیٔ تمام   گردنش را زِ مَی طناب بِیار

یا صوابست یا خطا خوردن   گر خطا هست و گر صواب بِیار

غمِ دَوران مخور که رفت برفت   نغمهٔ بربط و رباب بِیار

وصل او جز بخواب نتوان دید   داروی کوست اصلِ خواب بِیار

کرچه مستم بِده دو جامِ دِگر   تا بکُلّی شَوَم خراب بِیار

یکدو رطلِ گِران بحافِظ دِه   گر عذابست و گر ثواب بِیار

۶ — غزل از دیوانِ مَولانا جلالُ الدّین رُومِي

من آن روز بودم که اَسما نبود   نشان از وجودِ مُسمّا نبود

نشان کشت مظهر سرِ زلفِ یار   بجز مظهرِ حقِ تعالی نبود

مُسمّا و اَسما ز ما شد پدید   در آن دم که آنجا من و ما نبود

من آن دم بکردم خدارا سجود   که در بطنِ مریم مسیحا نبود

چلیپا و نصرانیان سر بسر   به پیمودم اندر چلیپا نبود
به بتخانه رفتم بدیرِ کهن   درو هیچ رنگِ هویدا نبود
بکعبه کشیدم عنانِ طلب   در آن مقصدِ پیر و برنا نبود
بکوی هرا رفتم و قندهار   بجستم در آن زیر و بالا نبود
بعمداً شدم بر سرِ کوهِ قاف   وآنجا نشائی ز عنقا نبود
بهفتم زمین و بهفتم سما   در آن بارگاهِ معلّا نبود
ز لوح و قلم باز پرسیدمش   کزو هر دو شان هیچ گویا نبود
بچشمِ خدابینِ خود دیده ام   صفاتی که ذاتِ خدا را نبود
نظر کردم اندر دلِ خویشتن   درین جاش دیدم دگر جا نبود
حقیقت چنان مست و حیران شدم   که از هستیم ذرّه پیدا نبود

که چون شمسِ تبریزِ پاکیزه رو

کسی مست و مدهوش و شیدا نبود

٧ ــ ترجیع بند از دیوانِ حافظِ شیرازی

آی سرو سمنبرِ گل اندام   از عارضِ تو خجل مهِ شام
باز آی که هجرِ جانگدازت   برد از دلِ من قرار و آرام
از دانهٔ خال و دامِ زلفت   مرغِ دلِ من فتاده در دام
چون کام نشد ز وصل حاصل   قانع شده ام به هجرِ ناکام
مائیم و غمِ فراق و حالی   تا خود بکجا رسد سرانجام
جز محنت و درد گویا نیست   دور از تو نصیب ما ز ایام
مقصود و جود حافظا چیست   جز صحبتِ یار و باده و جام
حالی چو نمیشود مهیّا   کام دلم از تو ای دلارام

آن بِه که ز صبرِ رُخ نتابم
باشـــد که مُرادِ دِل بِیابم

در سَختيِ عِشـــق گر بِمیرم / من دِل ز غمِ تُو بر نگیرم
پیوستـه کمانِ ابروانـت / از غمزه همي زنـد به تِیرم
نتْوان بقلم نوِشـت شوقم / گر پیرِ فلـك شوَد دبیرم
پیر غم عشقـم ار چه طفلم / طفل رهِ عِشقـم ار چه پیرم
چون کرد زمانــهٔ ستمگار / دور از تو به بندِ غمِ اسِیرم

آن بِه که ز صبرِ رُخ نتابم.
باشـــد که مُرادِ دِل بِیابم

۸ ي‌ قصیدهٔ رُودکي

یادِ جُوي مُولیان آیـــد همي / یادِ یارِ مِهْربان آیـــد همي
ریگِ آمُو با دُرشْتِیهاي او / زیرِ پایم پرنیان آیـــد همي
آبِ جَیحُون از نِشاطِ رُوـــوست / خِنگ ‌مارا تا مِیان آیـد همي
اَي بُخارا شاد باش و دیر زِي / مِیرِ ثَروت شادمان آید همي
میر سَرْو است و بُخارا بوستان / سَرْو سُوي بوستان آیـــد همي
میر ماه است و بُخارا آسمان / ماه سُوي آسمان آیـــد همي

تمّت بِاَلخَیَر